# IN THE HUG OF HILLS

## Kelowna, British Columbia

# IN THE HUG OF HILLS

## Kelowna, British Columbia

Text & photographs by Cathryn Wellner

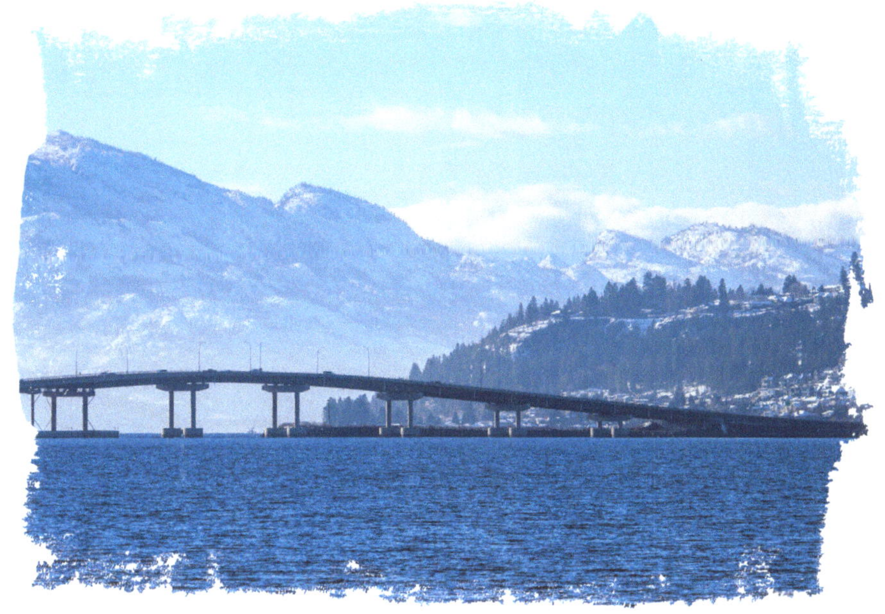

Espoir Press
British Columbia
2016

Espoir Press
1002 - 1128 Sunset Drive
Kelowna, B.C. V1Y 9W7
778-478-2760



Library and Archives Canada Cataloguing in Publication

Wellner, Cathryn, 1946-, author, photographer
    In the hug of hills : Kelowna, British Columbia / text & photographs by Cathryn Wellner.

Issued in print and electronic formats.
ISBN 978-0-9951653-3-5 (hardcover).--978-0-9951653-5-9 (softcover).--ISBN 978-0-9951653-4-2 (pdf)

    1. Kelowna (B.C.)--Description and travel.  2. Kelowna (B.C.)--Pictorial works.  I. Title.

FC3849.K36M55 2016          971.1'5          C2016-907190-1
                                             C2016-907191-X

For Robin Jarman, who invited me to share views like these.

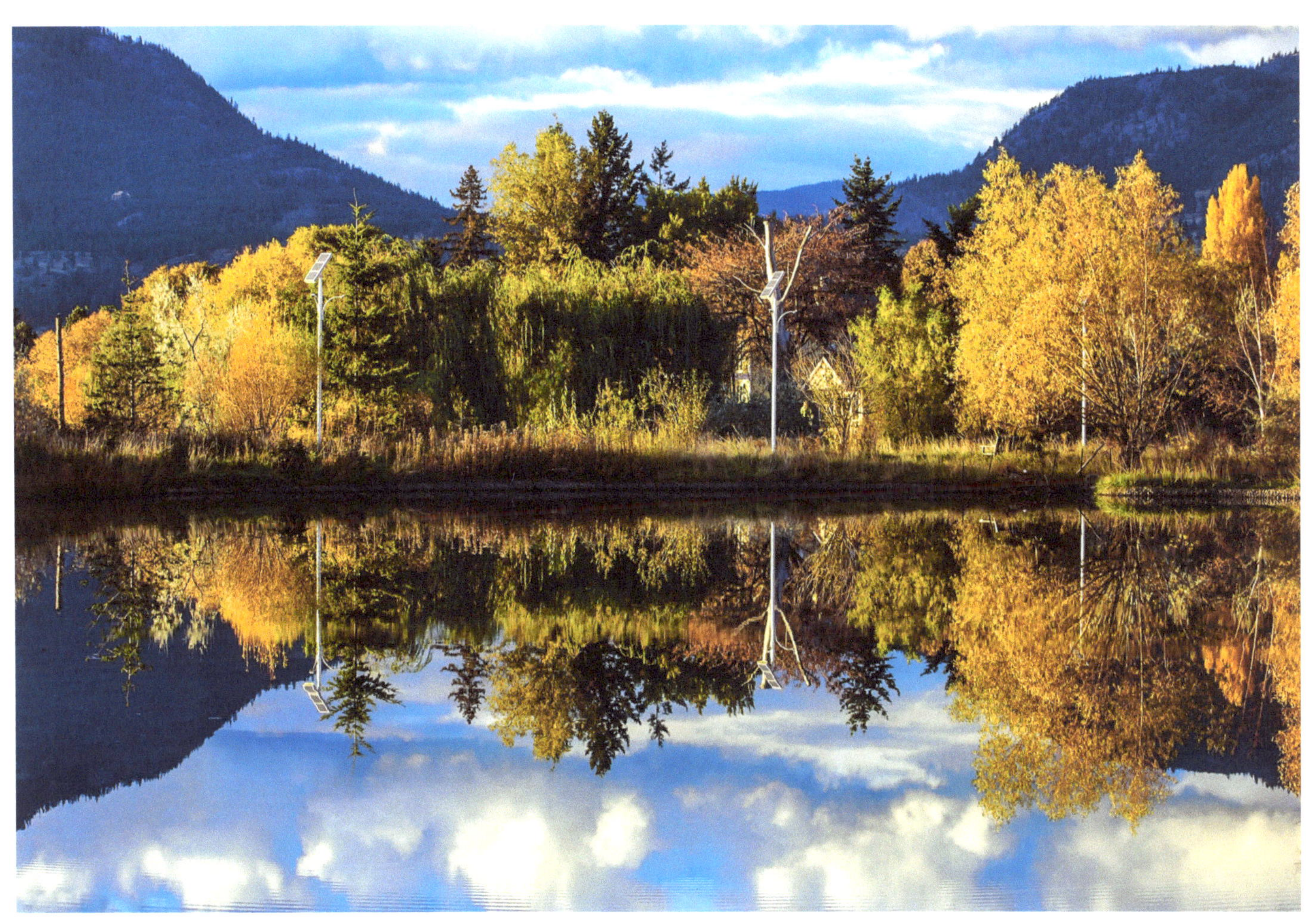

# Acknowledgements

Two kinds of friends keep me wanting to take more and better photographs. The first are pals from the Friday coffee group, the fitness classes and those not part of either group but a joyful part of my life.

The second are friends on Facebook and Instagram. Some of you overlap with those above, but most of you I have never had the chance to meet in person. We connect online around shared interests and encourage each other's creative efforts.

You not only bear with me when I post so many photographs. You give me frequent pats on the back. Your encouragement keeps me wanting to learn more about photography both as a way of preserving moments in time and as an art form I continue to explore.

## You are champions, & I am grateful.

# Introduction

We met online and felt a connection that made it seem normal to invite Brenda McIntyre to visit my partner and me when she came to Kelowna. We sat at the table in our small condominium and talked easily. At one point she said of our beautiful Okanagan Valley, "You live in the hug of hills."

The phrase stayed with me. When I began putting together this book, I knew it was the right title.

Some of the spots I photographed for *Kelowna's Waterfront: From City Park to Knox Mountain* have changed since 2011. When it came time to update the book, I decided to take a different, more personal approach and to expand the scope a bit. So, as it turns out, this book is not a second edition, which was my first intent. It is, rather, an entirely new book, exploring some of my favourite spots in and around the city that has wrapped itself around my heart.

The first book is available in print through Blurb.com and in digital format through iTunes and Gumroad.com. (Links can be found at cathrynwellner.com.) This new book is a love letter to one of the most beautiful spots on the planet.

Choosing only a handful of photos from thousands of possibilities is difficult. I take my camera for a walk nearly every day. I share some of the shots on my Facebook page, which anyone is welcome to follow or friend. When a photo tells me a story, I turn it into a micro tale and post it on Instagram, Facebook and my storytelling Web site, Story Route (http://storyroute.com).

Only a few of the photographs in this book have appeared anywhere else. As I scrolled through my Lighroom catalogue, they leapt out, begging to be shared. The result is a labour of love and of gratitude for this place I call home.

Cathryn Wellner

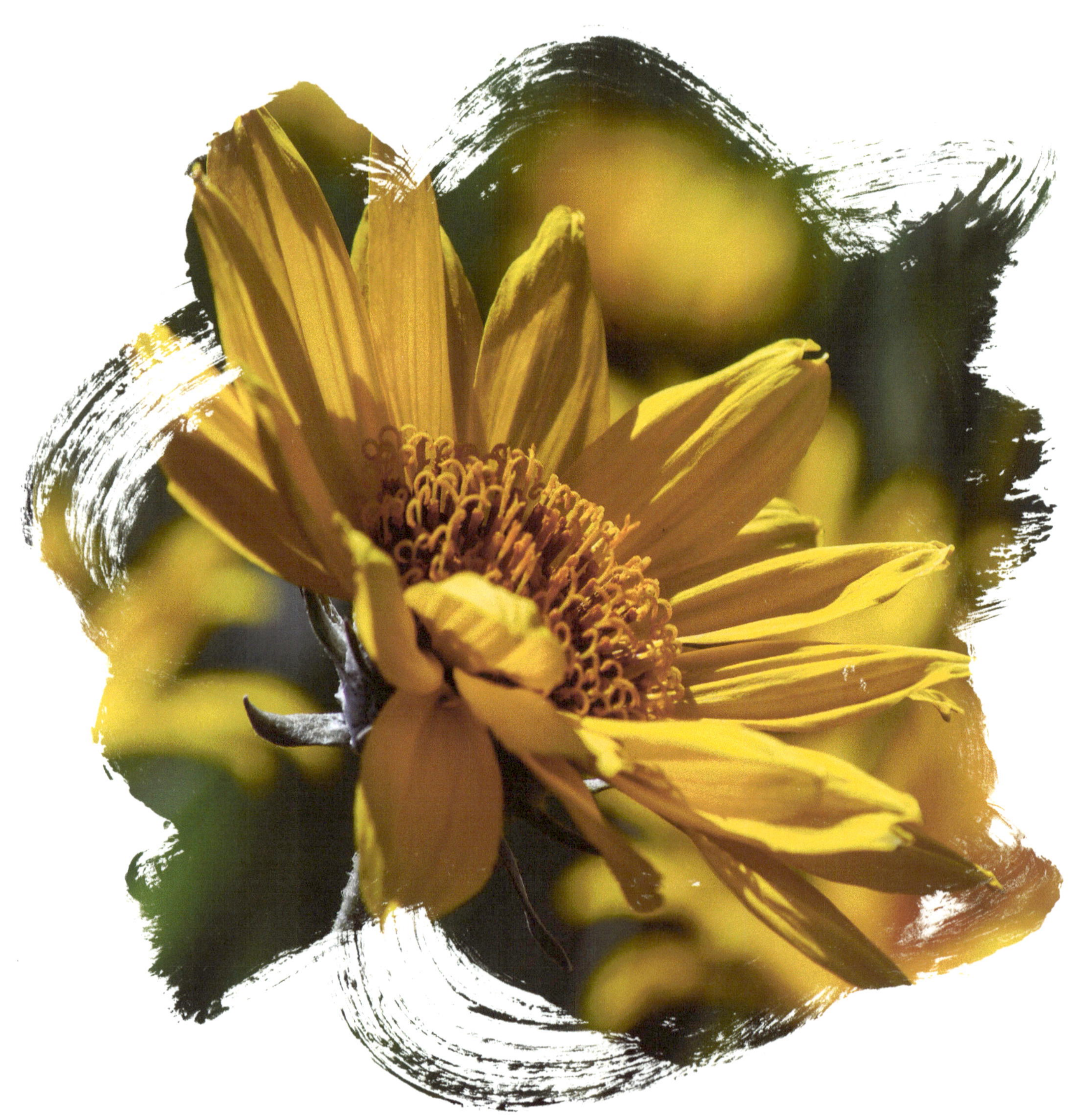

# THIS IS THE HUG OF HILLS

They are on all sides of us. They shelter us. They lift our hearts. They welcome our vibrant sunrises and sunsets. If you look closely, you will see a flock of geese flying toward their day's grazing. At day's end they will fly the other way, to wherever they spend the night.

You are welcome here. The land welcomes you. The people welcome you.


Downtown .......................2
Farmers' Market ...........25
Kasugai Garden............29
Waterfront ....................42
Rotary Marsh.................60
Brandt's Creek...............74
Knox Mountain..............80
On the City's Edges.......92
Sunsets & Sunrises.......100

# come, walk with me

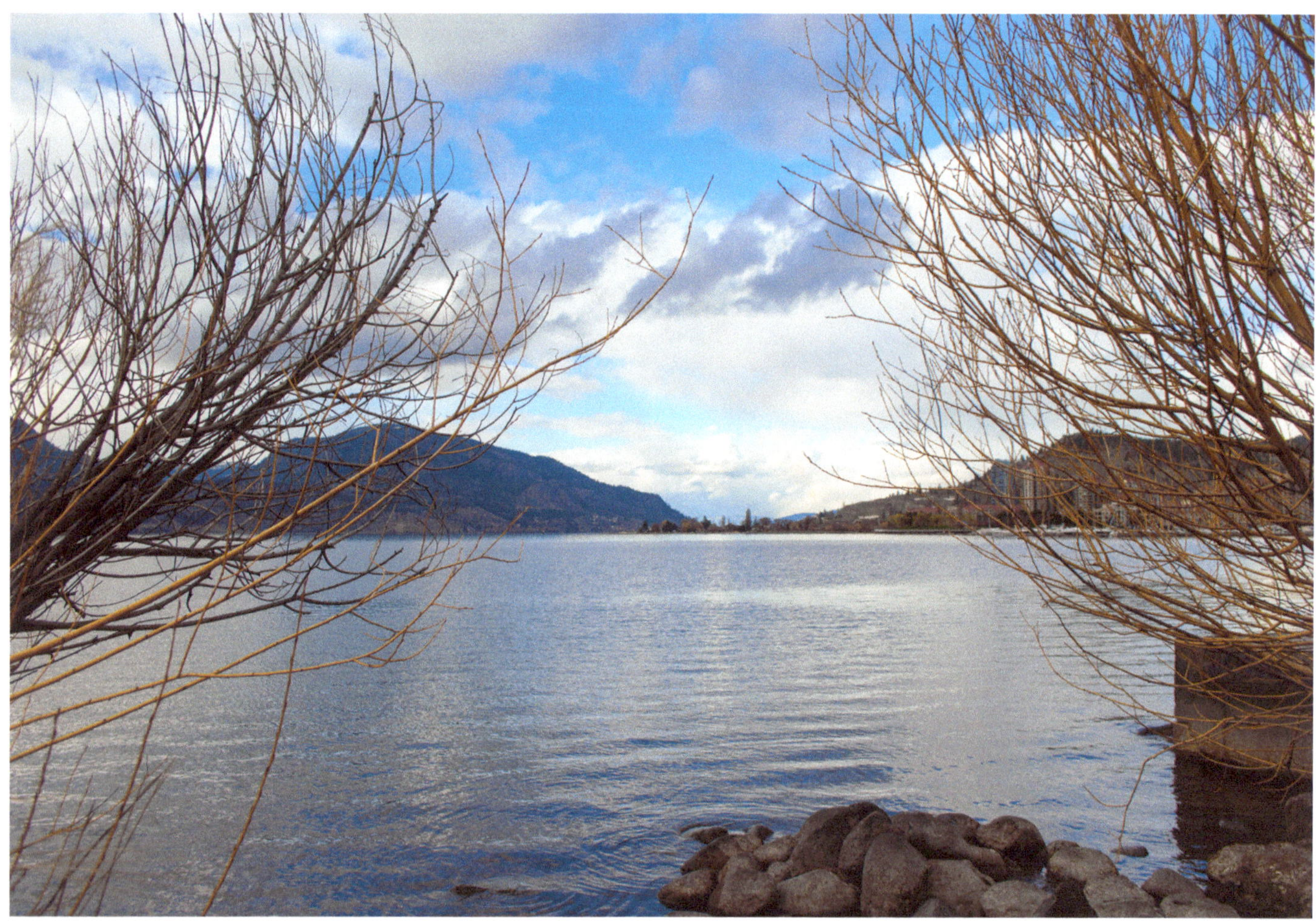

We'll start in City Park, then wander along Bernard Avenue, Kelowna's main downtown street. We'll saunter along the waterfront, then detour to a couple of community gardens. After a side trip to the Farmers' Market, we'll come back downtown for a breather in peaceful Kasugai Garden. We'll see more of the waterfront and Waterfront Park before heading to Rotary Marsh and Brandt's Creek. From there we'll hike Knox Mountain. Then we'll visit Sutherland Park and drive to Bertram Park and Myra Canyon. We'll wander through seasons and end the journey with views of Kelowna's spectacular sunrises and sunsets.

# A fragrant tribute

Though Kelowna and Veendam are no longer sister cities,
the rose garden still commemorates their association.

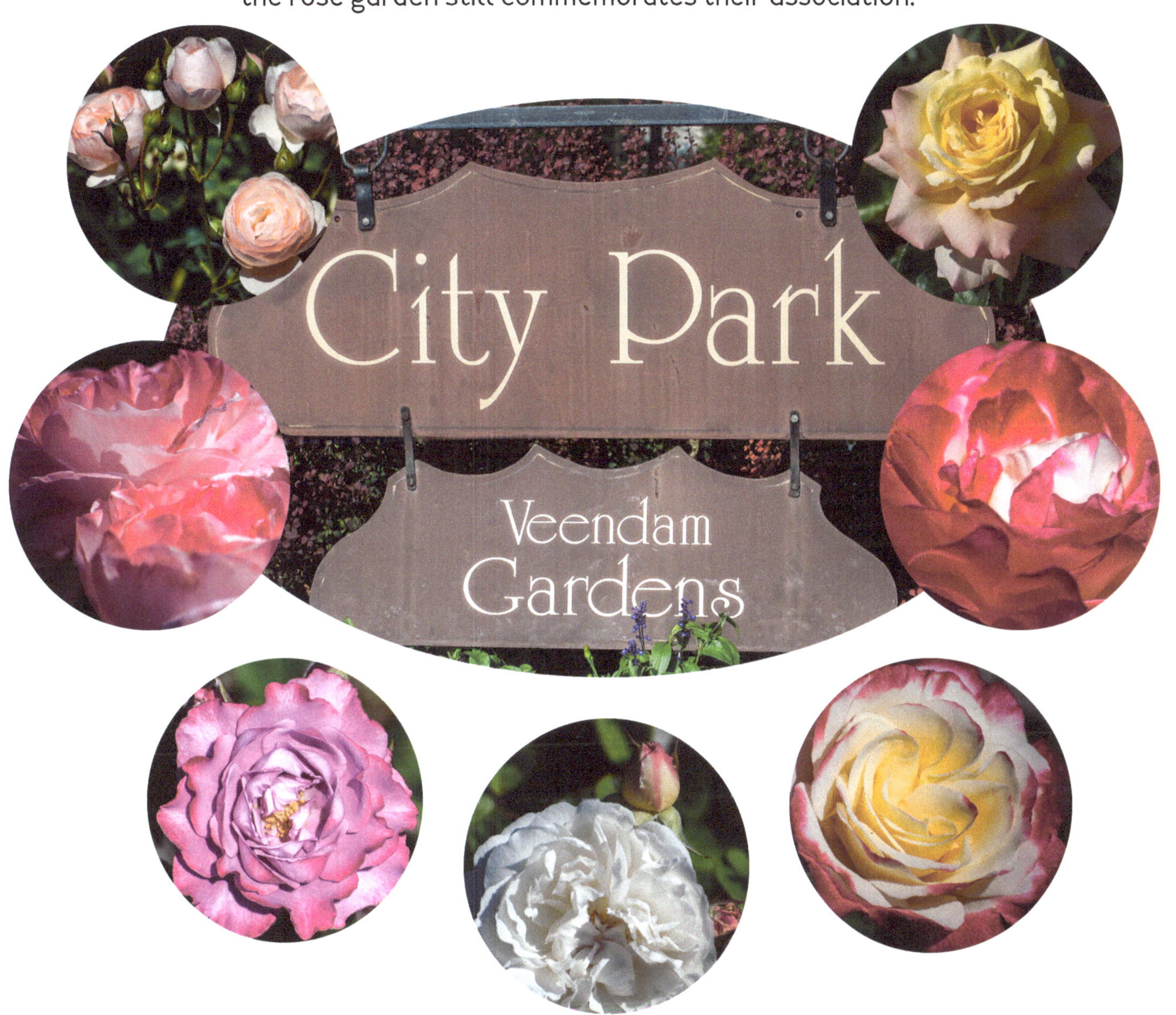

# The Water Park Refreshes

On hot summer days, children flock to it. Sprinklers spin. Buckets spill. Little legs dance. Laughter erupts. Adults mostly watch with envy.

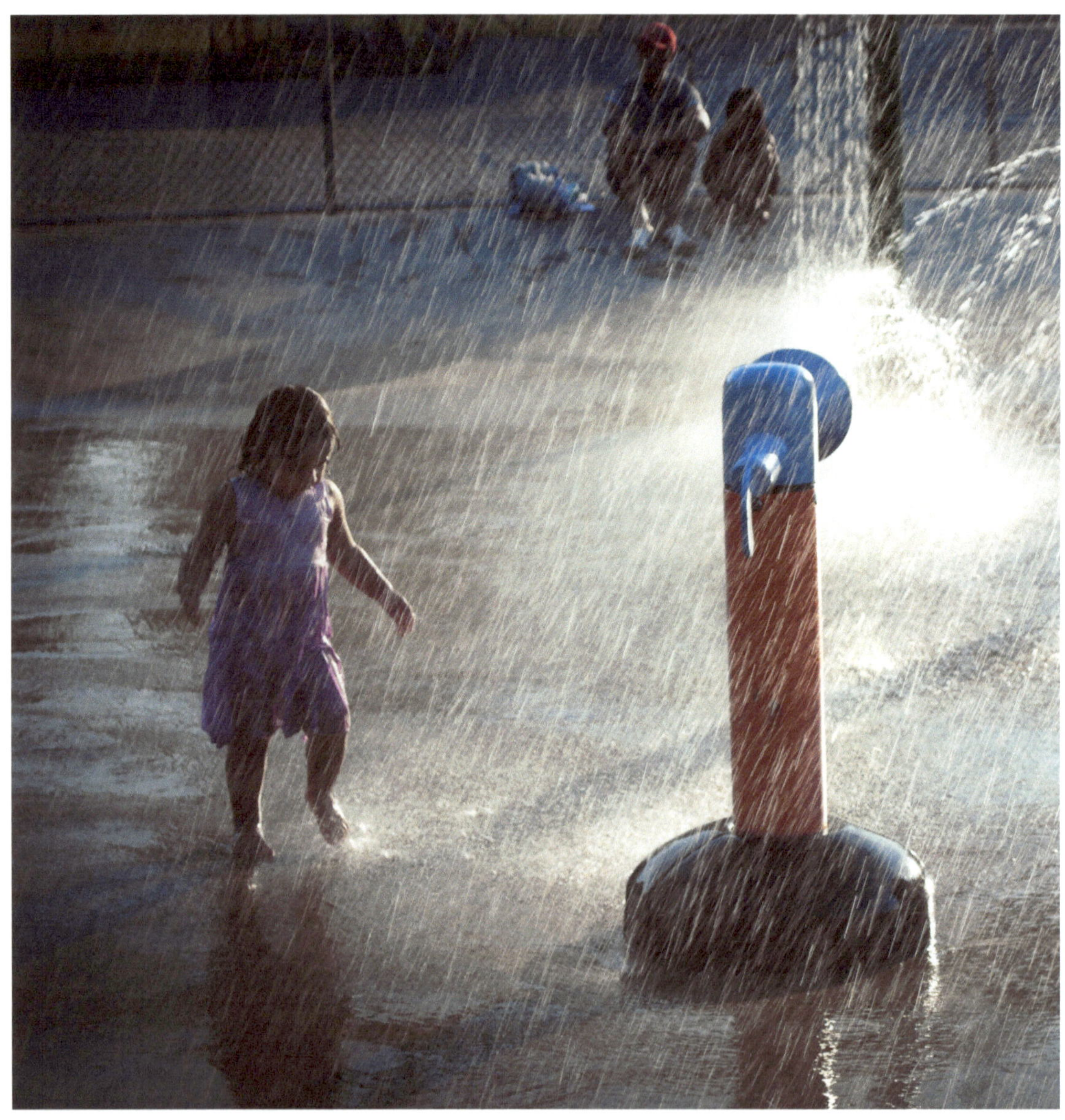

# When a Cottonwood Gets Too Tall

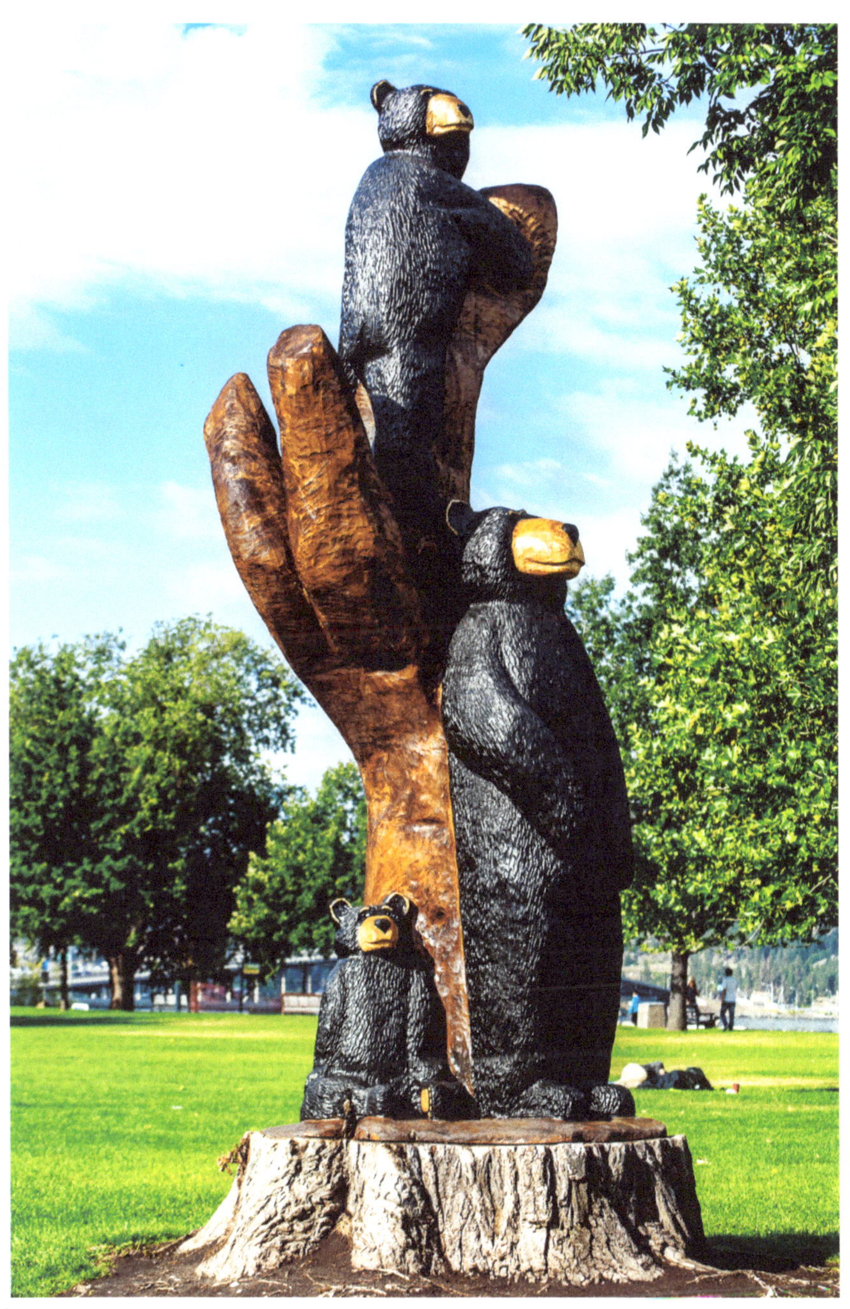

The city has to make a difficult decision. Limbs can fly off in a strong wind. So when this tree started losing limbs, a call for artist proposals went out. Randy Duff won the contract and turned the stump of the stately cottonwood into a family of bears. They will stay on the stump until it gradually dies and rots away. Then the parks staff will decide where the bears' permanent home will be.

# Bears are a popular Kelowna art subject

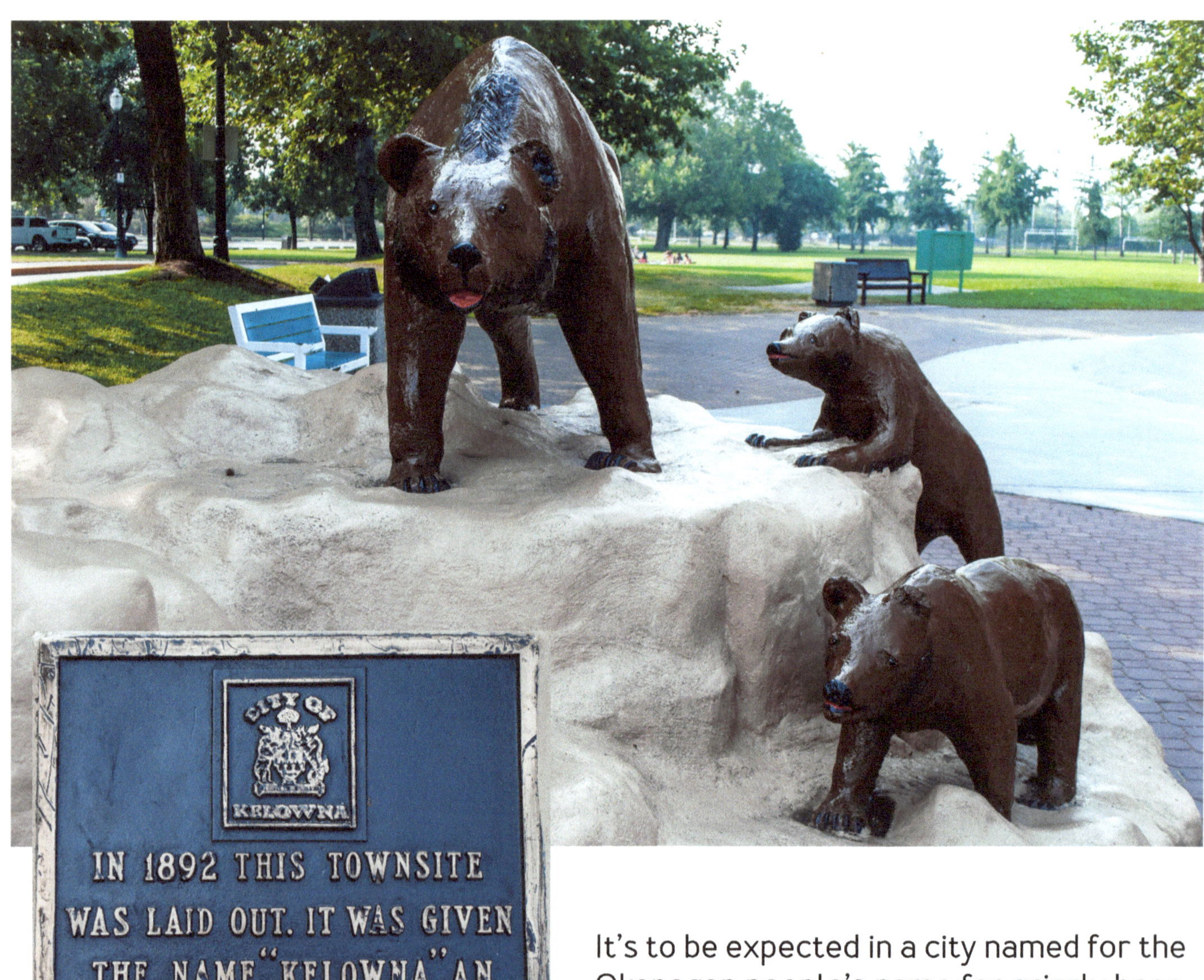



It's to be expected in a city named for the Okanagan people's name for grizzly bear. These bears aren't far from the cottonwood bears, but they can't get together for play dates.

# City park has some cheeky trees

This dancing woman is
one of them.
Somewhere inside her
strong trunk and
spreading limbs hides a
wild woman who moves
to her own music.

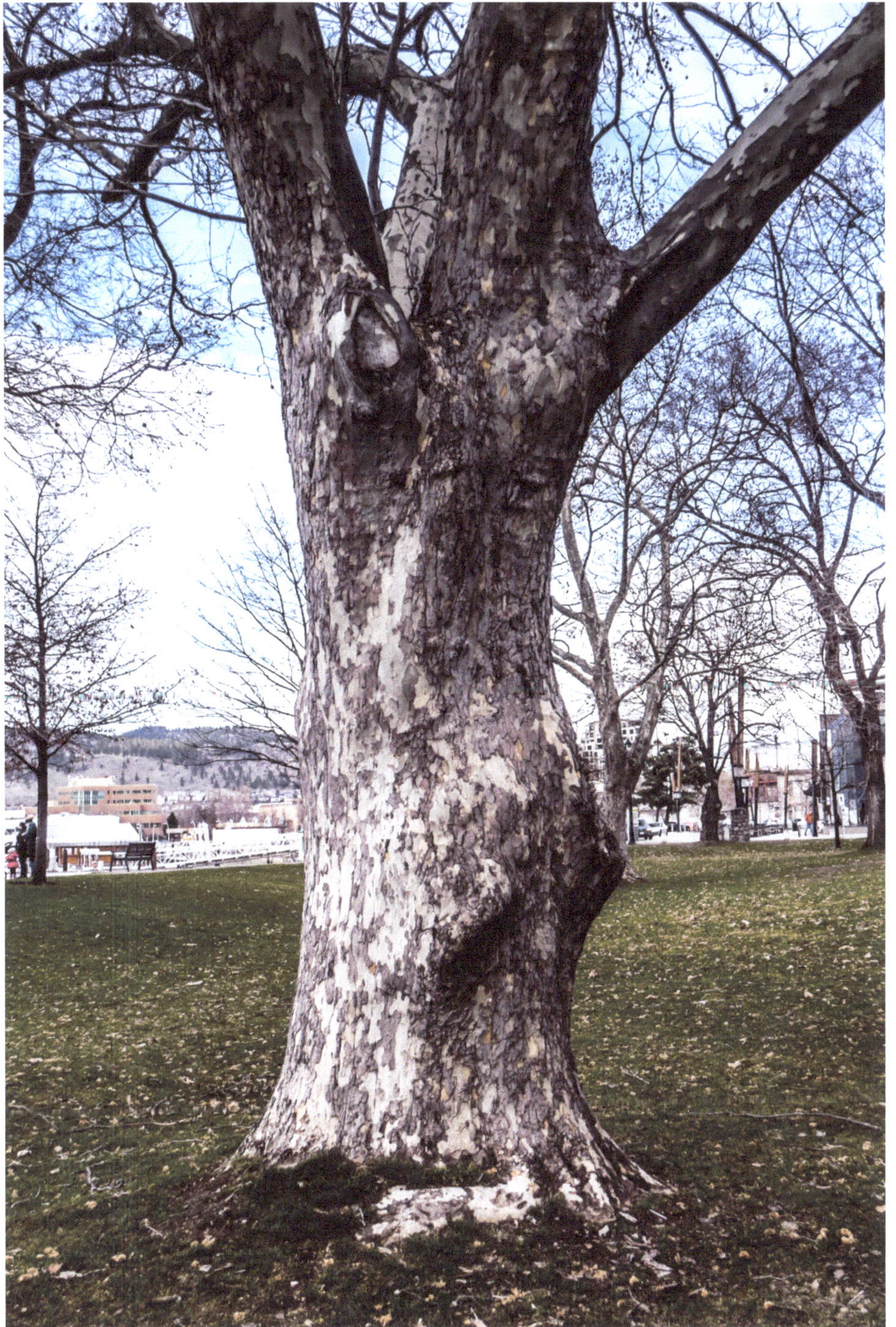

# spirit of sail puzzled me

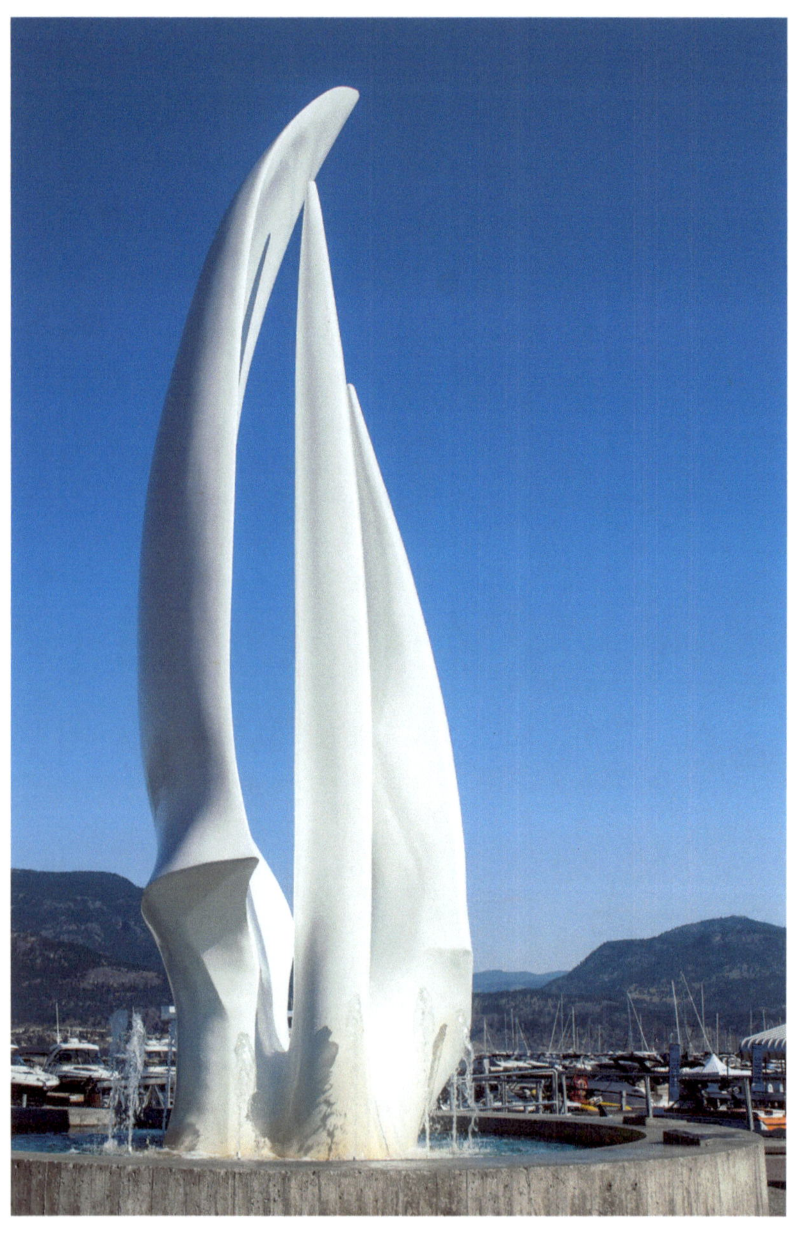

When I moved to Kelowna, I wondered how Robert Dow Reid's sculpted sails could be considered iconic for a land-locked city with limited sailing weather. Yet I soon found myself watching for their graceful curves along the waterfront and looking for wind-filled sails on the lake.

# Pianos in Parks

Musical twins, Robin and David Jarman, were two of many attracted by the pianos in Kelowna's downtown parks. Anyone could sit down at one of the colourfully painted pianos and belt out a tune or play quietly. Passersby appreciated pianists as talented as these two but also applauded the efforts of those just giving the pianos a try.

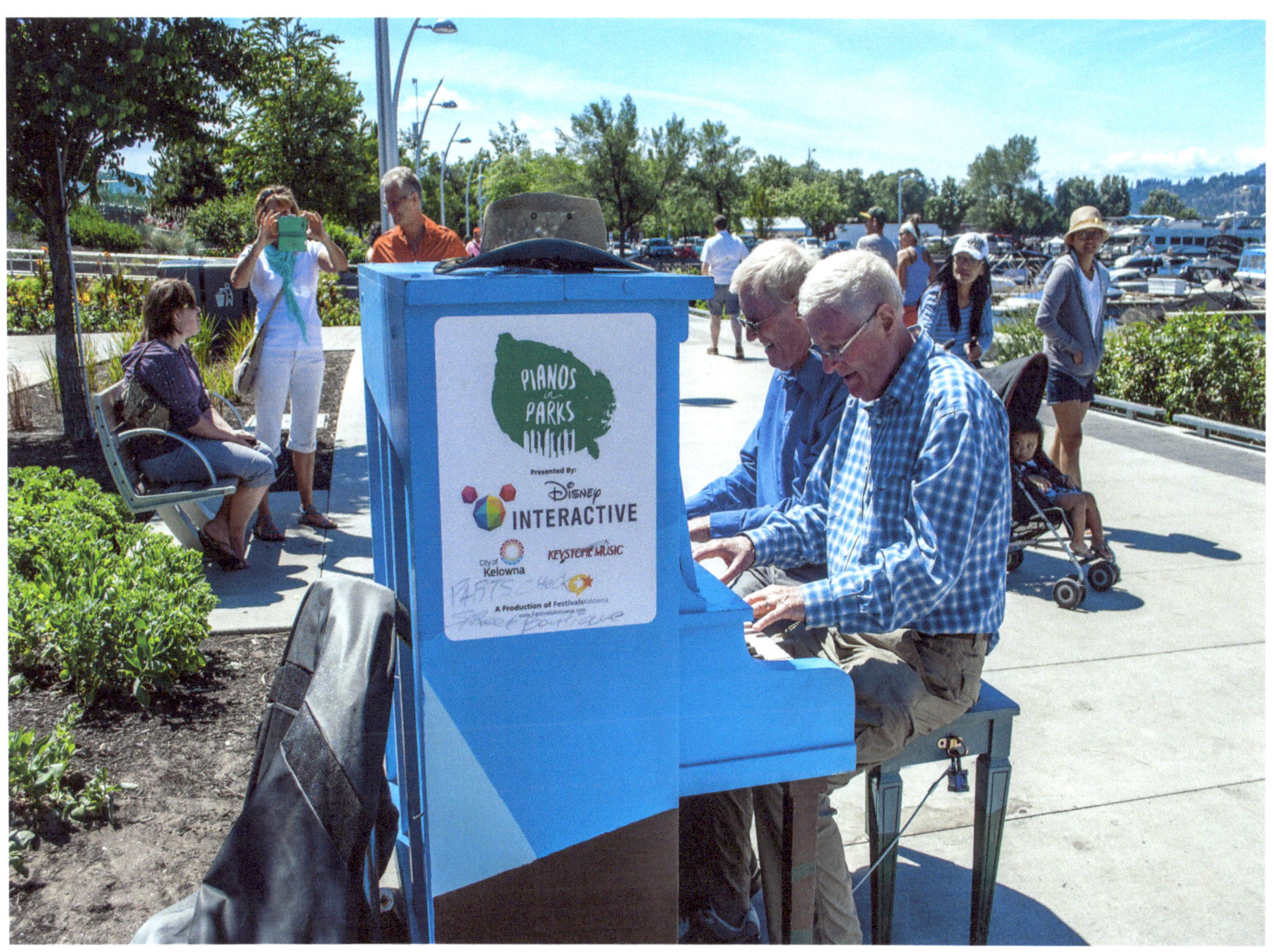

# How to Overcome "No Parking" Fears

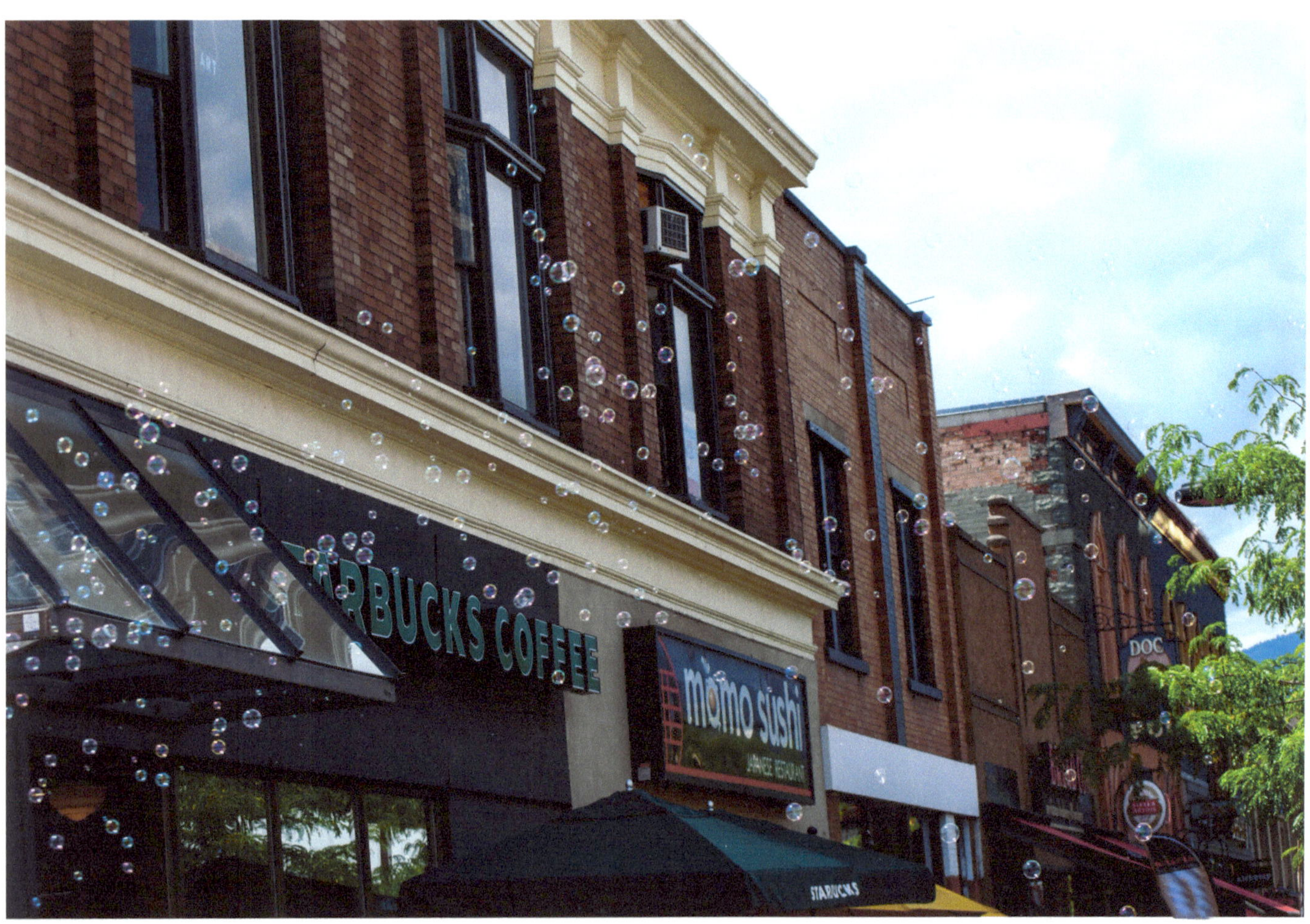

Throw a Block Party on Bernard Avenue. Bring on the musicians and food trucks. Send vendors into the street with all kinds of wares. Celebrations bring people downtown.

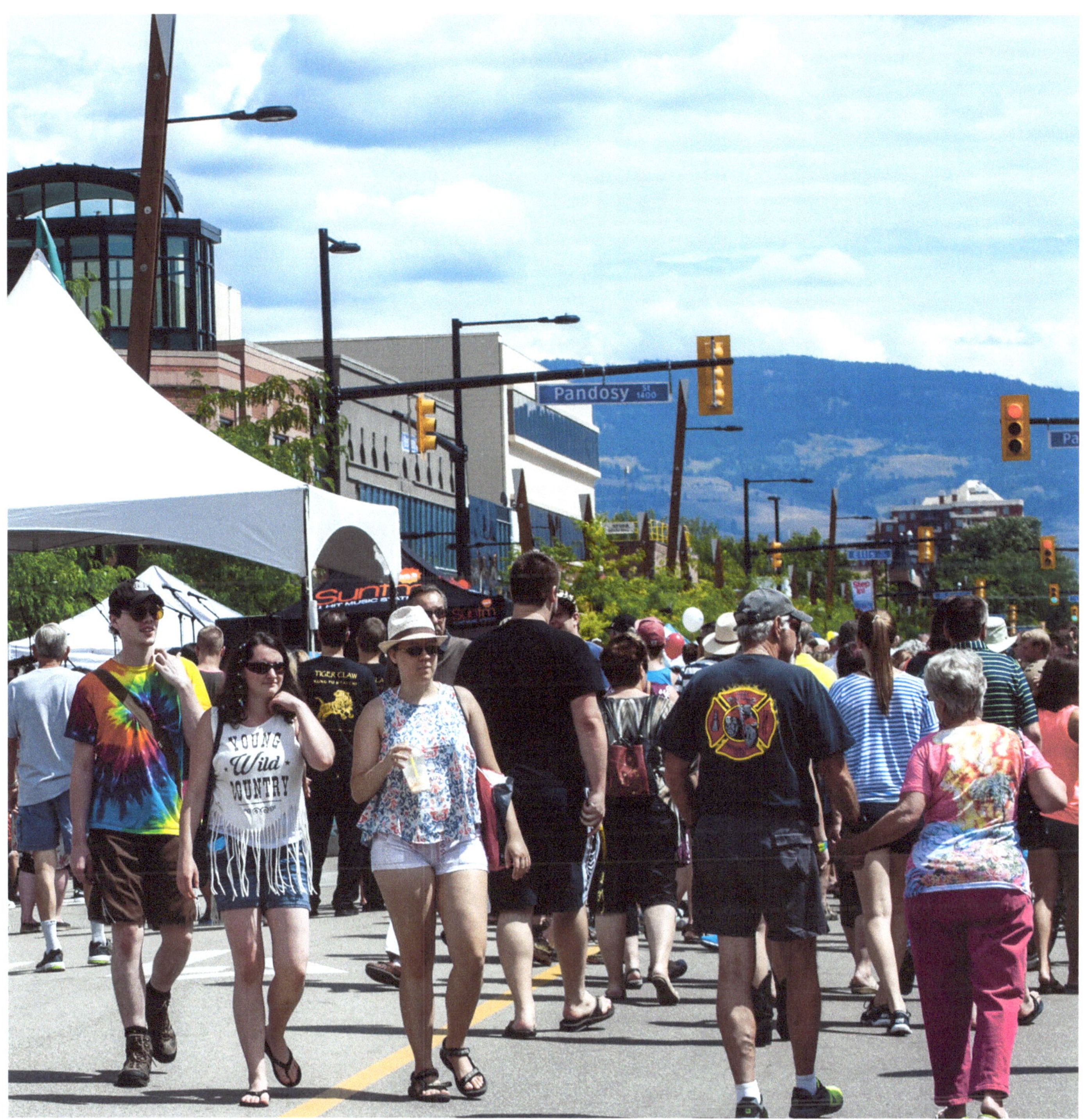

Pandosy St 1400
SUNFM
YOUNG Wild COUNTRY
TIGER CLAW

some find a space of quiet and

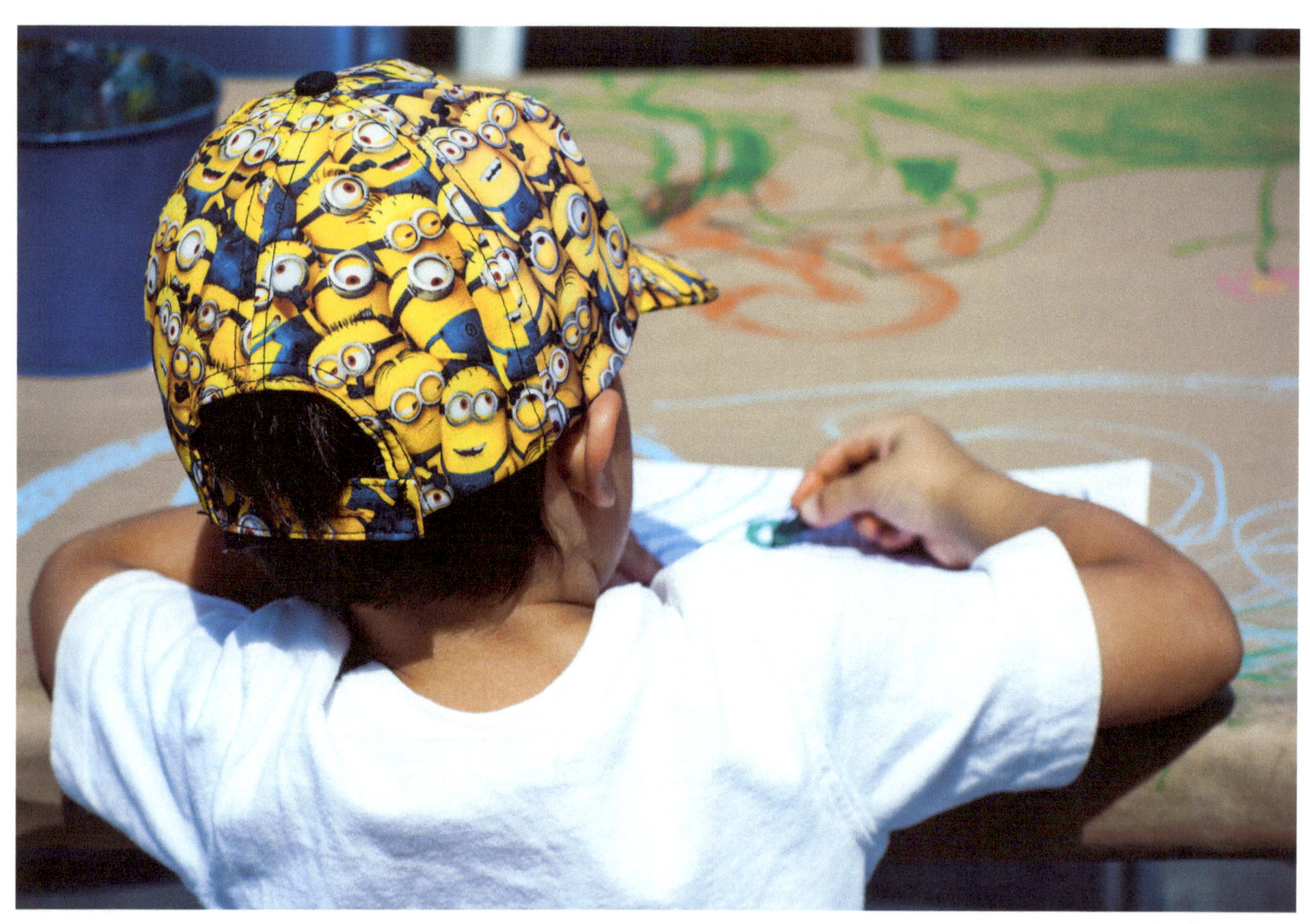

concentration in the middle of the hubbub

# The City plants
# a rainbow

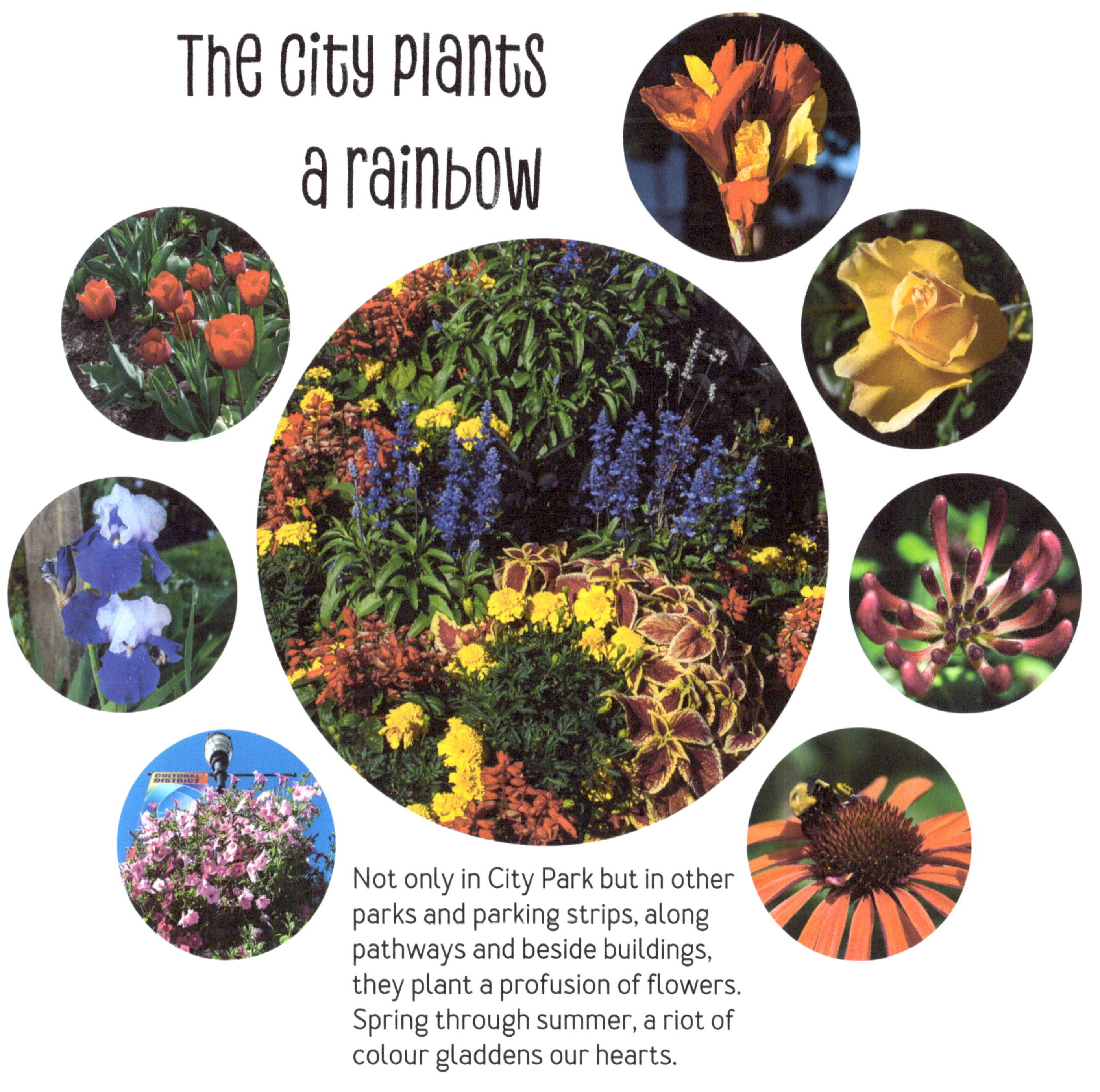

Not only in City Park but in other parks and parking strips, along pathways and beside buildings, they plant a profusion of flowers. Spring through summer, a riot of colour gladdens our hearts.

# Downtown Moves Through Changes

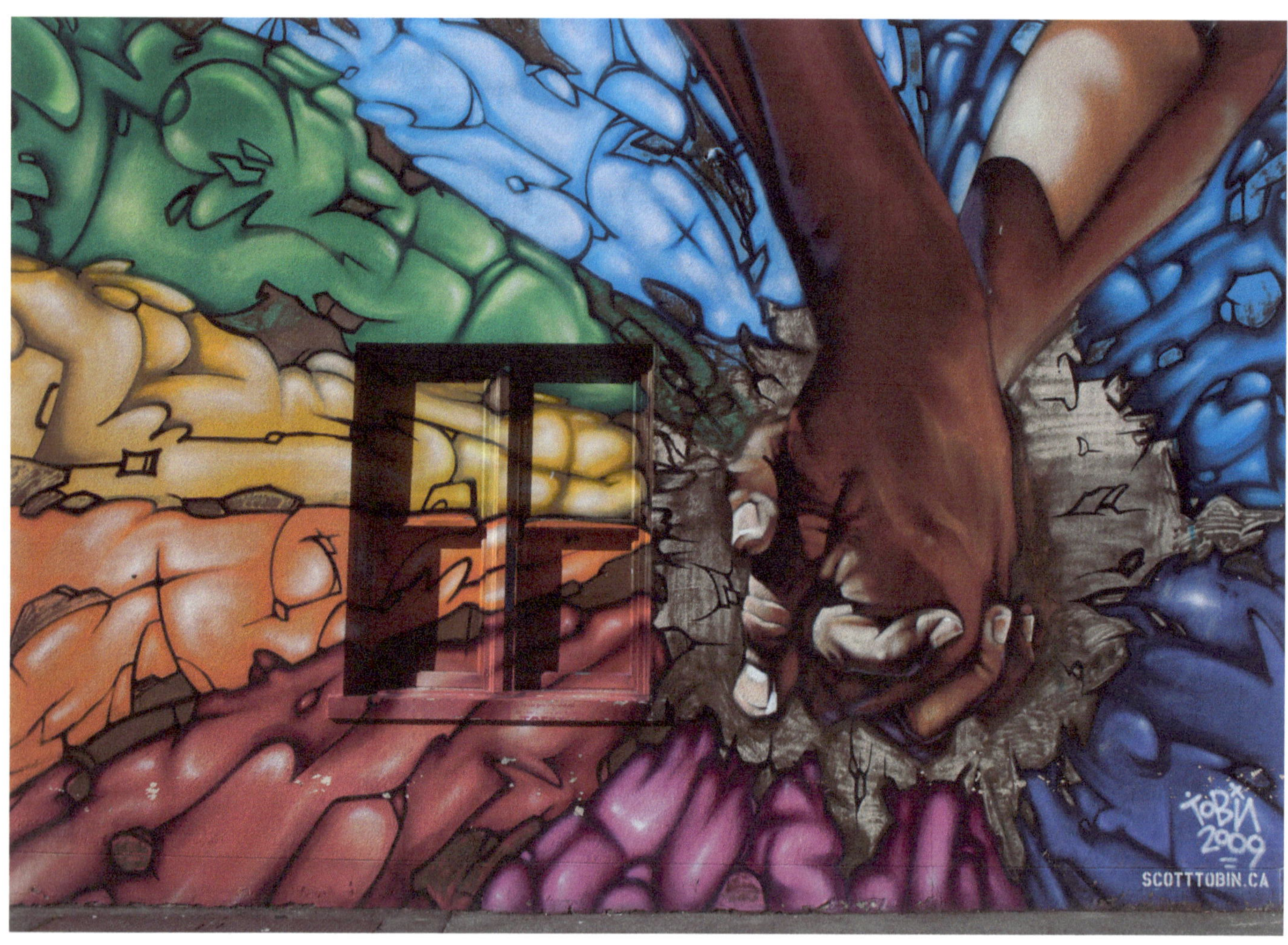



Some things are forever lost. This mural of rainbow connection was torn down to make space for a high-rise tower in the downtown core. In the six years before it crumbled into colourful shards, Scott Tobin's mural symbolized a positive shift away from old prejudices and stereotypes about Kelowna's LGBTQ residents.

# The building was slated for demolition

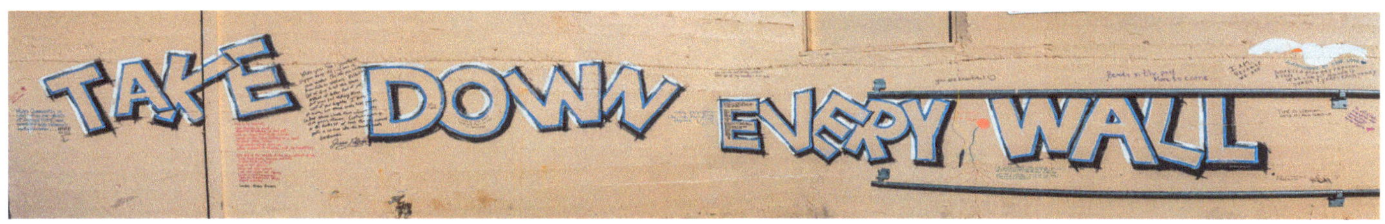


So poet Lesley-Anne Evans invited the community to write their hopes for the future on the wall facing the lake. Many of the hearts that stopped to spill their dreams beat in the breasts of some of the city's most disadvantaged neighbours, people struggling with poverty, addictions, and isolation who had found a refuge within the building's walls.

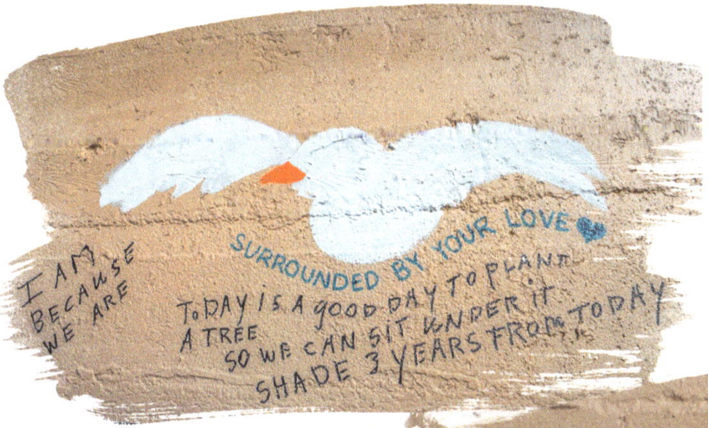

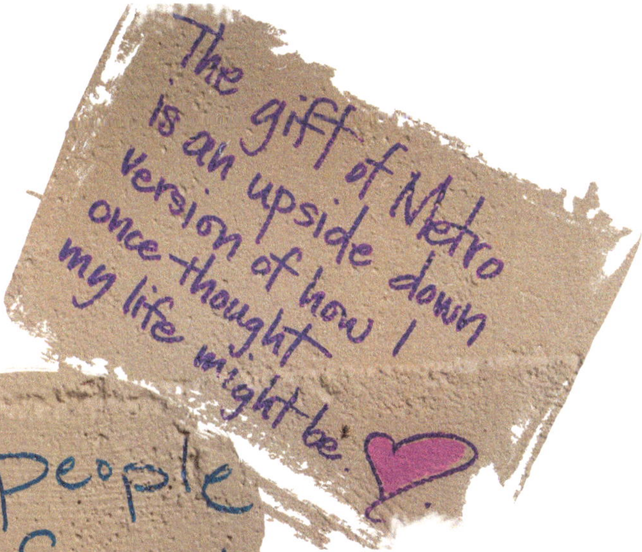

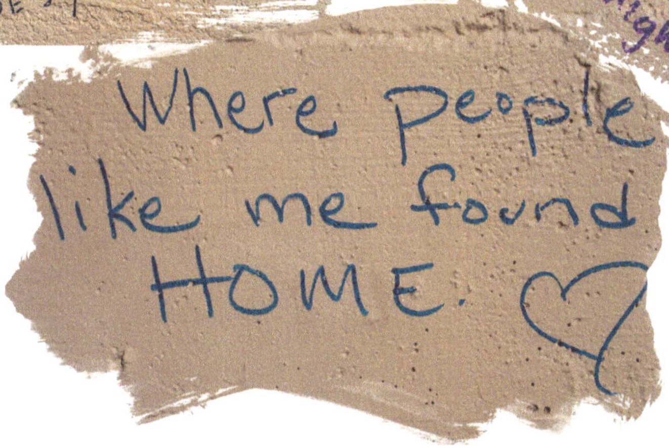

# sometimes the unexpected happens

One spring a pair of Great Horned Owls raised a family in a pine tree behind the Court House. They built a nest, hatched three eggs, and taught the owlets to fly and hunt, all within full view of the fascinated public.

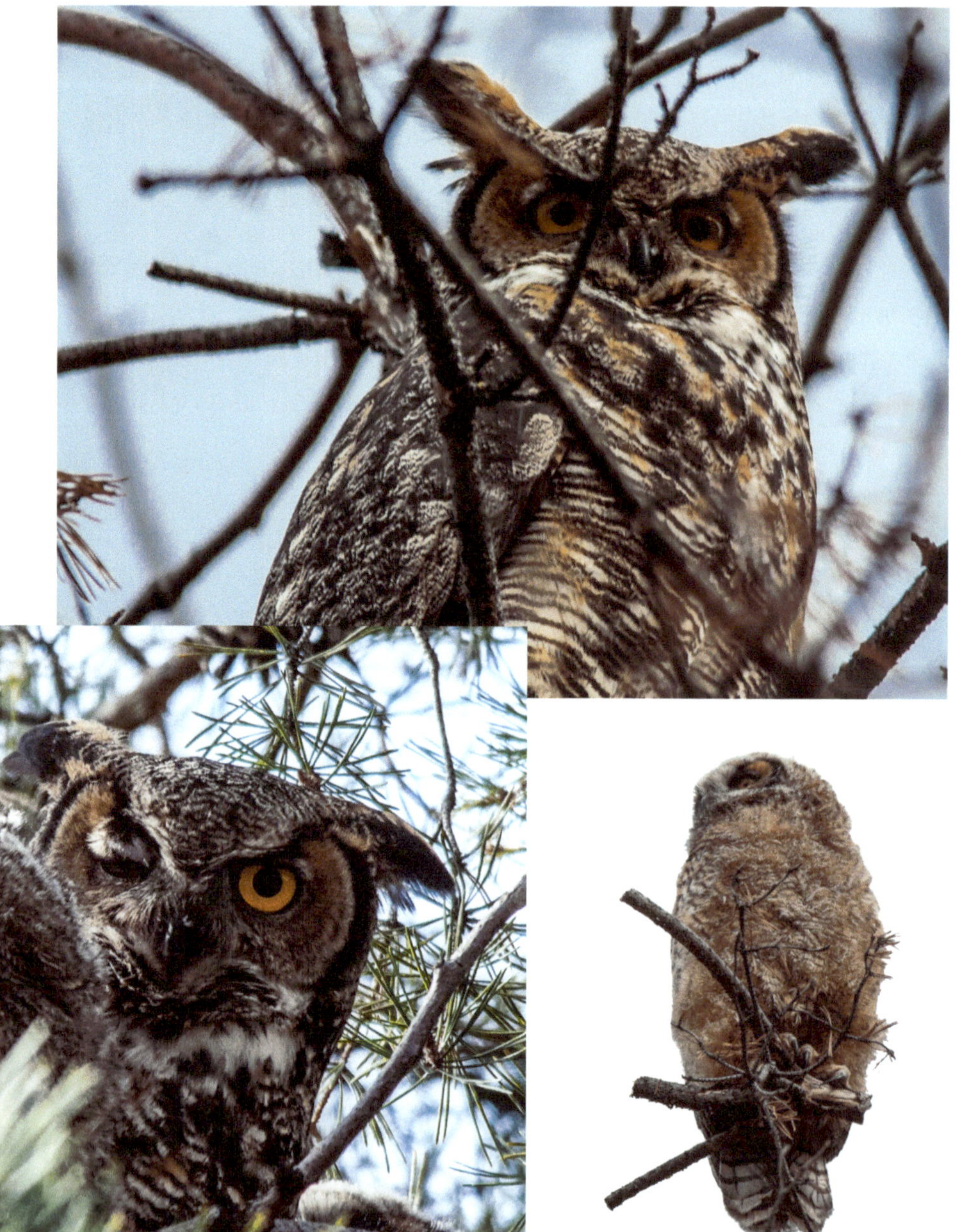

# Public Art Keeps Popping Up

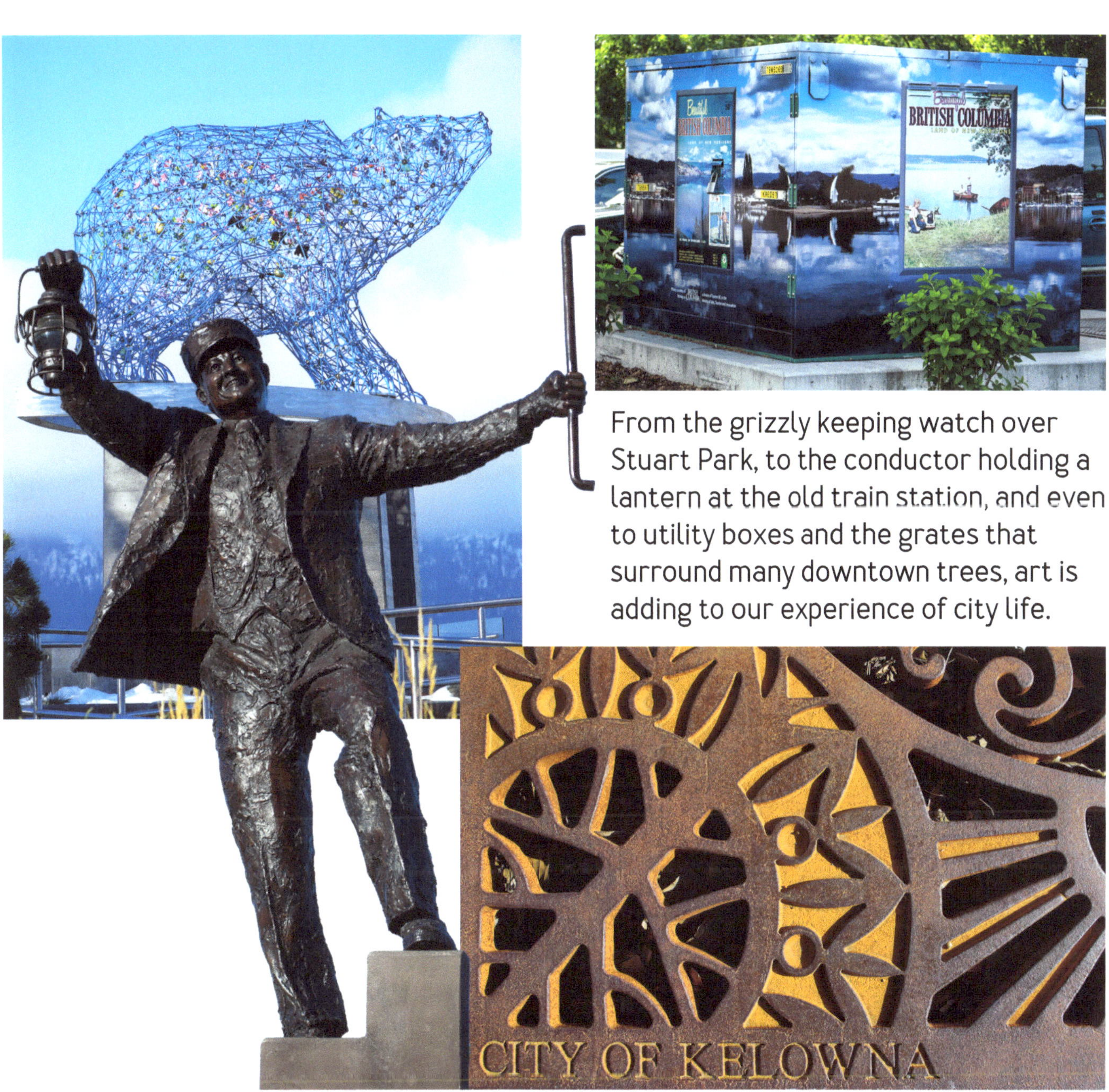

From the grizzly keeping watch over Stuart Park, to the conductor holding a lantern at the old train station, and even to utility boxes and the grates that surround many downtown trees, art is adding to our experience of city life.

# Natural Language

A two-part sculpture outside the library combines a spiral covered with examples of biological diversity and a mobius strip covered with letters and symbols. (Individual figures are enlarged.) It is a metaphor for the interweave of nature and culture found in a library. Artists Jennifer Macklem and Kip Jones created the sculptures.

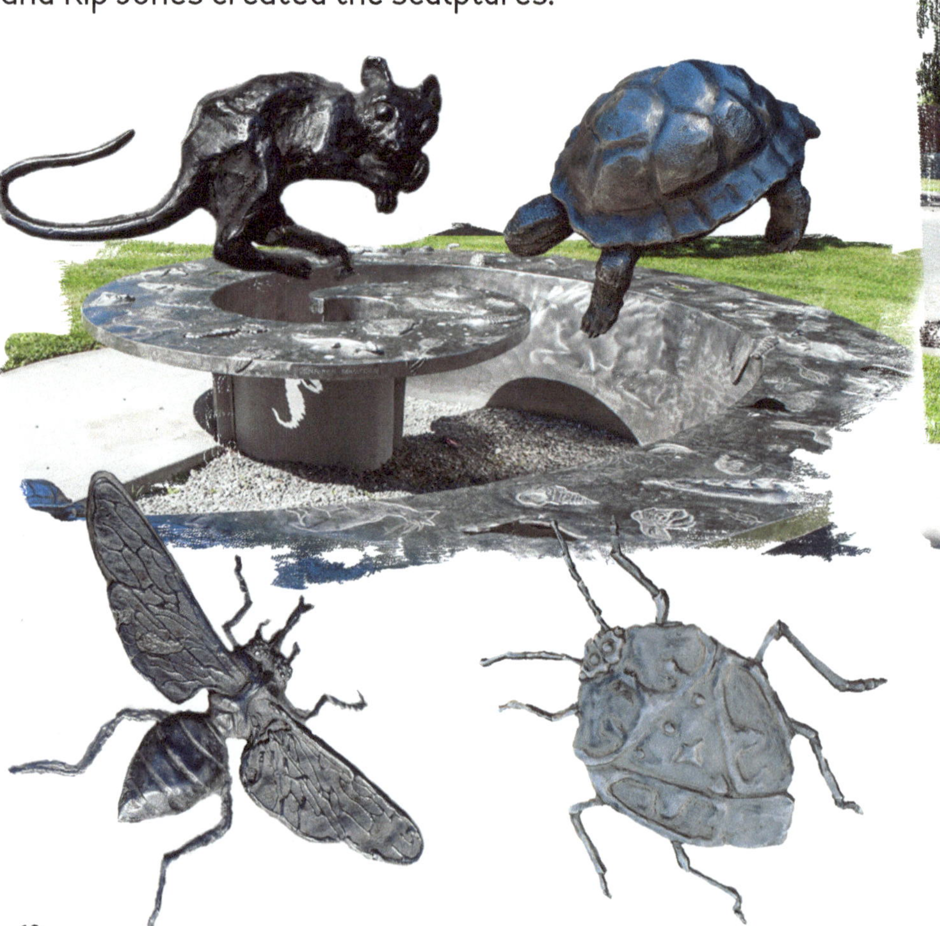

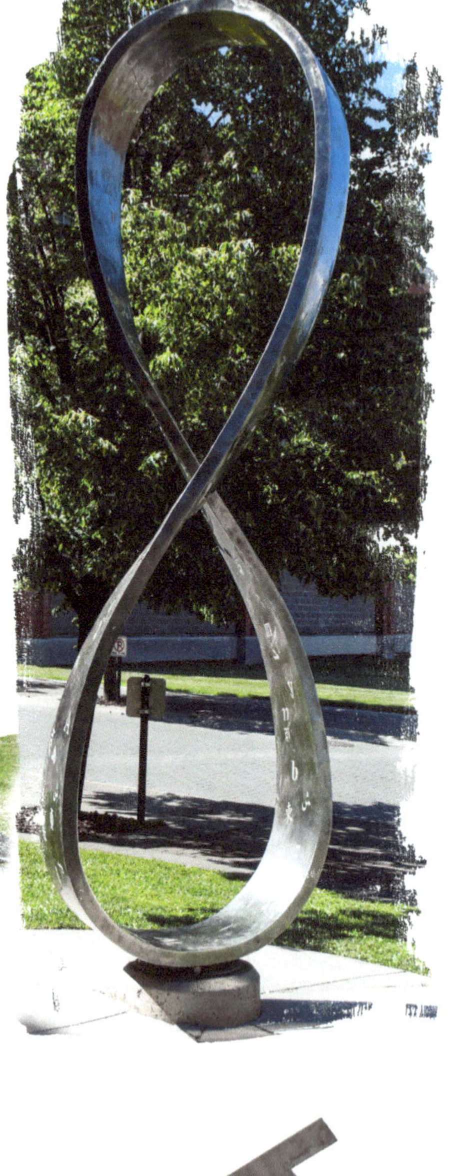

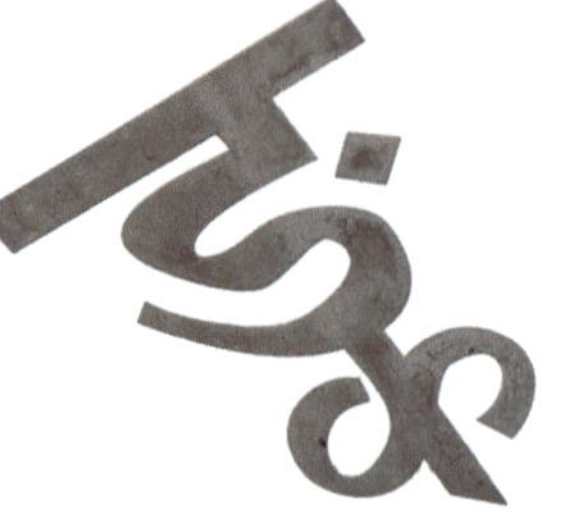

# Ogopogo Waits Patiently in Kerry Park

All summer long the lake serpent will be crawled on, photographed, leaned against and loved. Elsewhere in Kerry Park bands will play on the nearby stage. Excursion boats will sail out of the docks. Across the street, on Bernard Avenue, cafés and restaurants will keep their doors open well into the evening. Summer in Kelowna is shared with visitors from all over the world, who come to enjoy scenery, good food, wine and a friendly welcome.

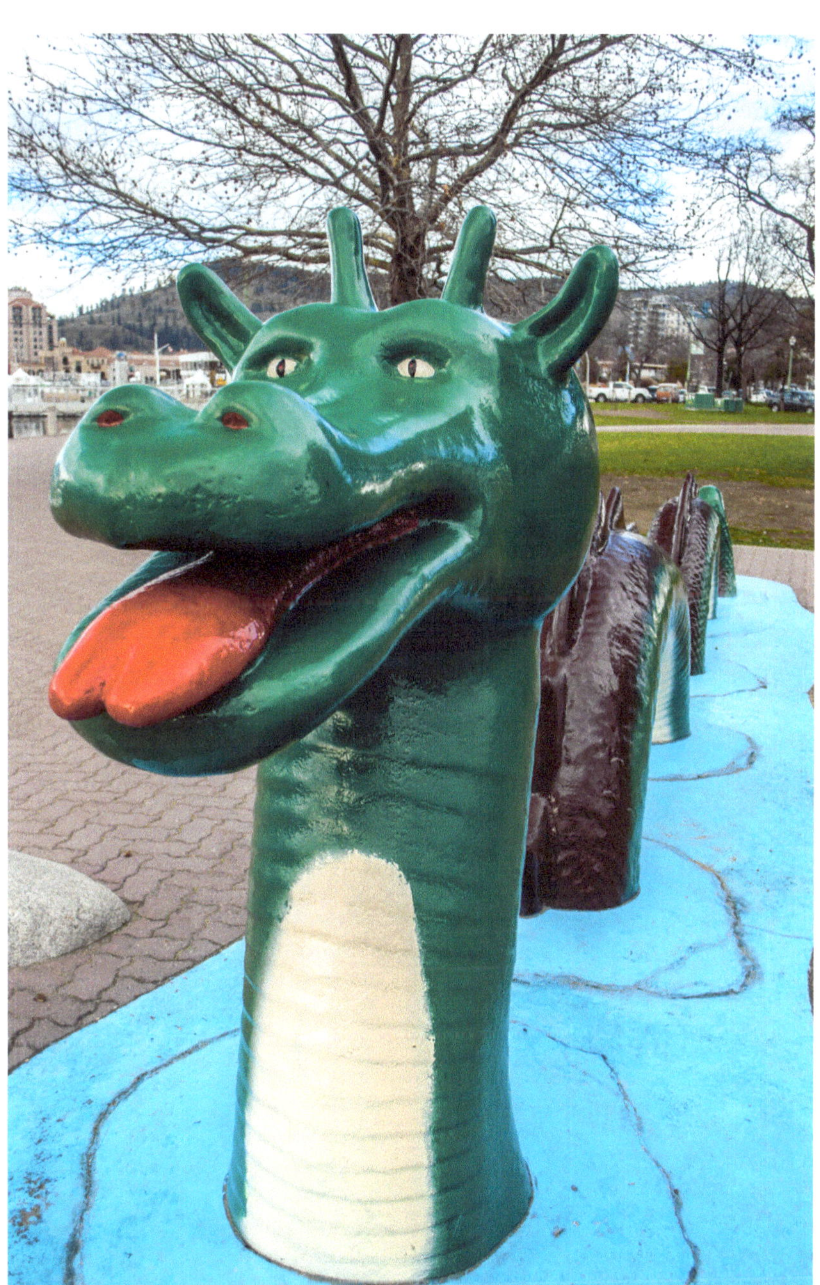

# future fossils

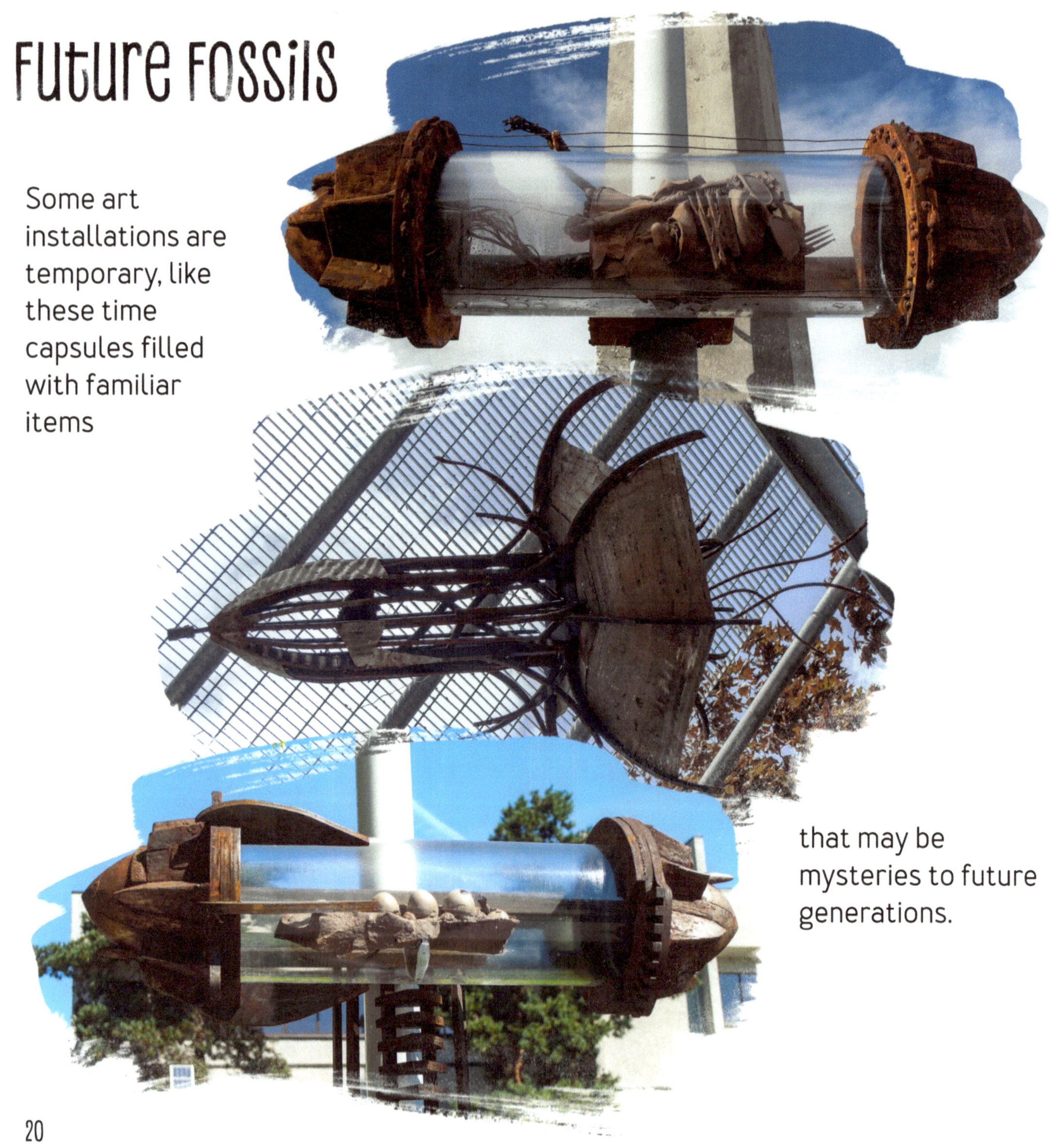

Some art installations are temporary, like these time capsules filled with familiar items

that may be mysteries to future generations.

# The Running Man hurries to work

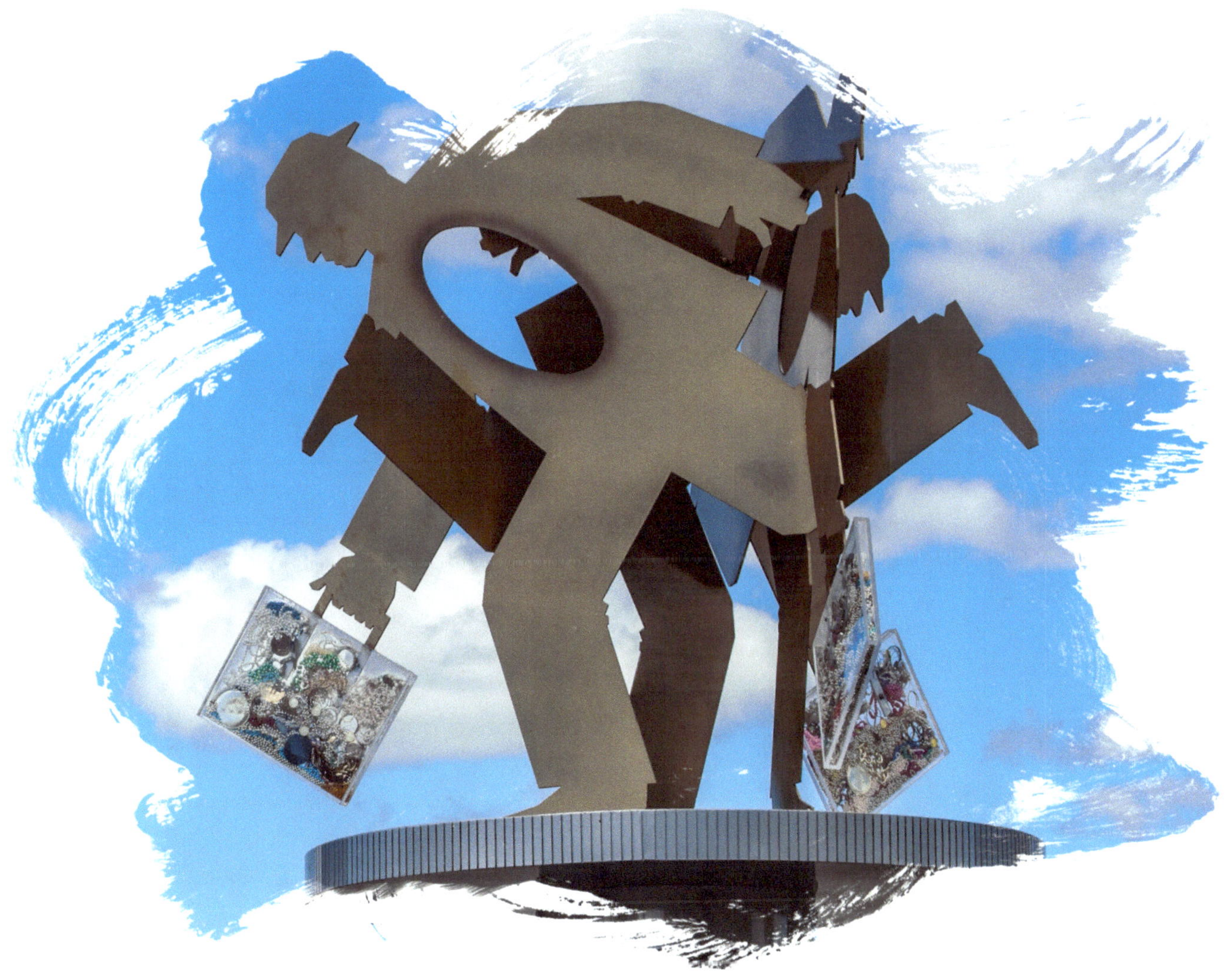

Atop his pedestal in the middle of the Queensway Roundabout, he rushes constantly, carrying a briefcase full of objects popular at the time he was designed. Marion Lea Jamieson created the piece, which has been on the run since 2002.

# Kelowna's community gardens are popular

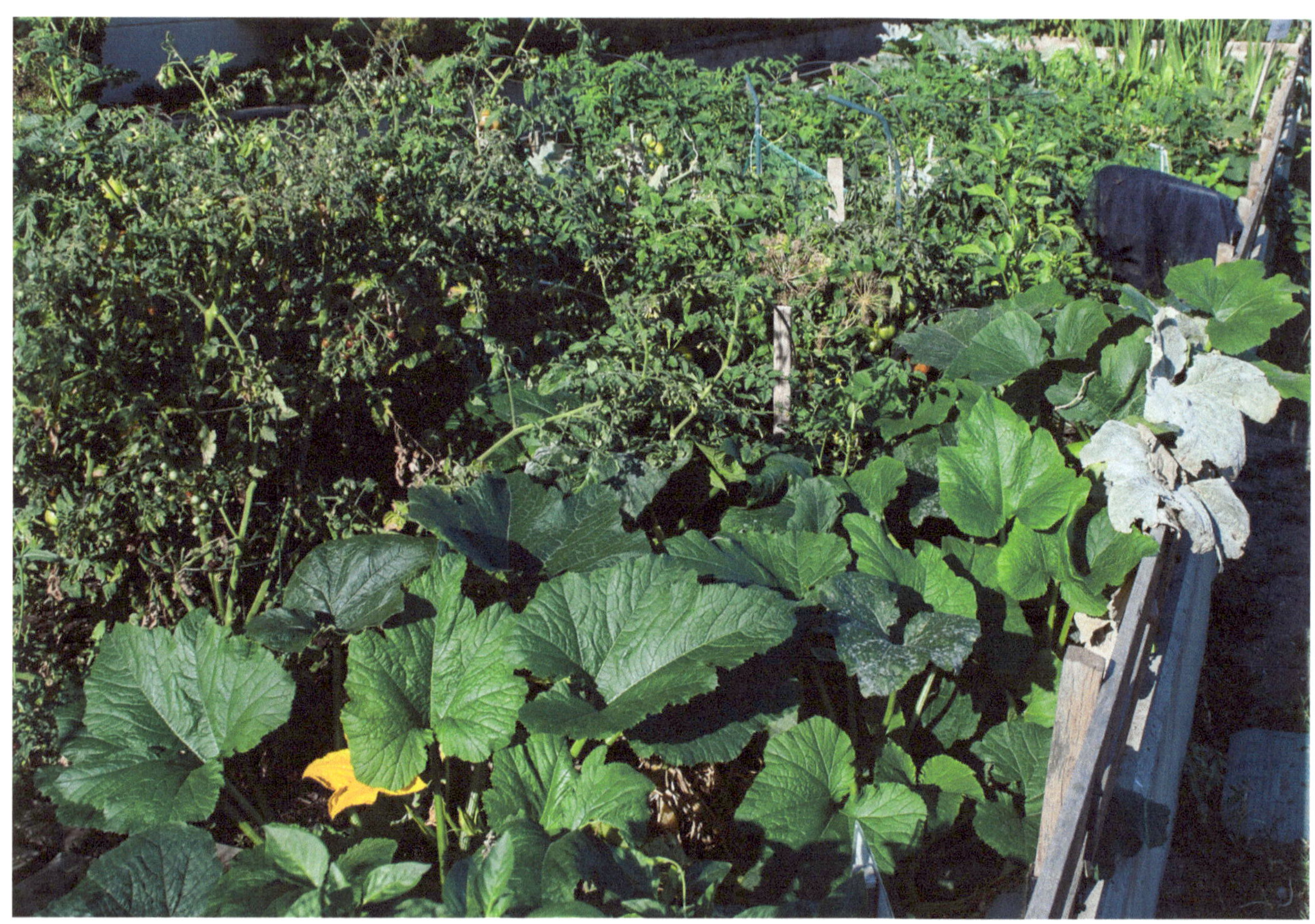

They always have waiting lists, including this one, along one edge of a parking lot at Cawston and St. Paul. Although vegetables and herbs are the most popular choices for the ample raised beds, some gardeners add colourful flowers, such as the cosmos on the next page. Urban dwellers grow more than produce in their plots. They also grow community, as they share tips and enthusiasm.

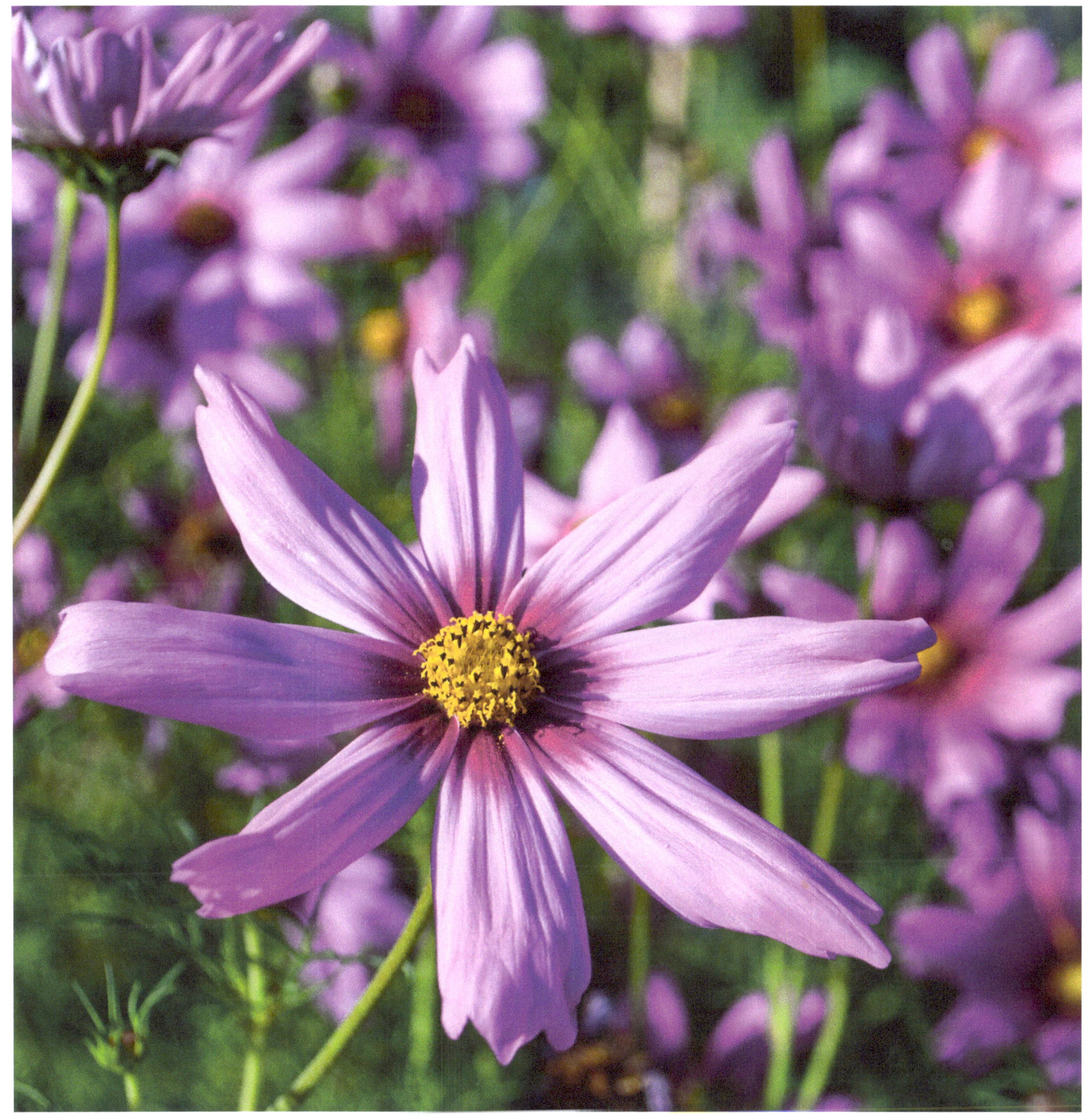

# Kelowna's 1st community garden flourishes

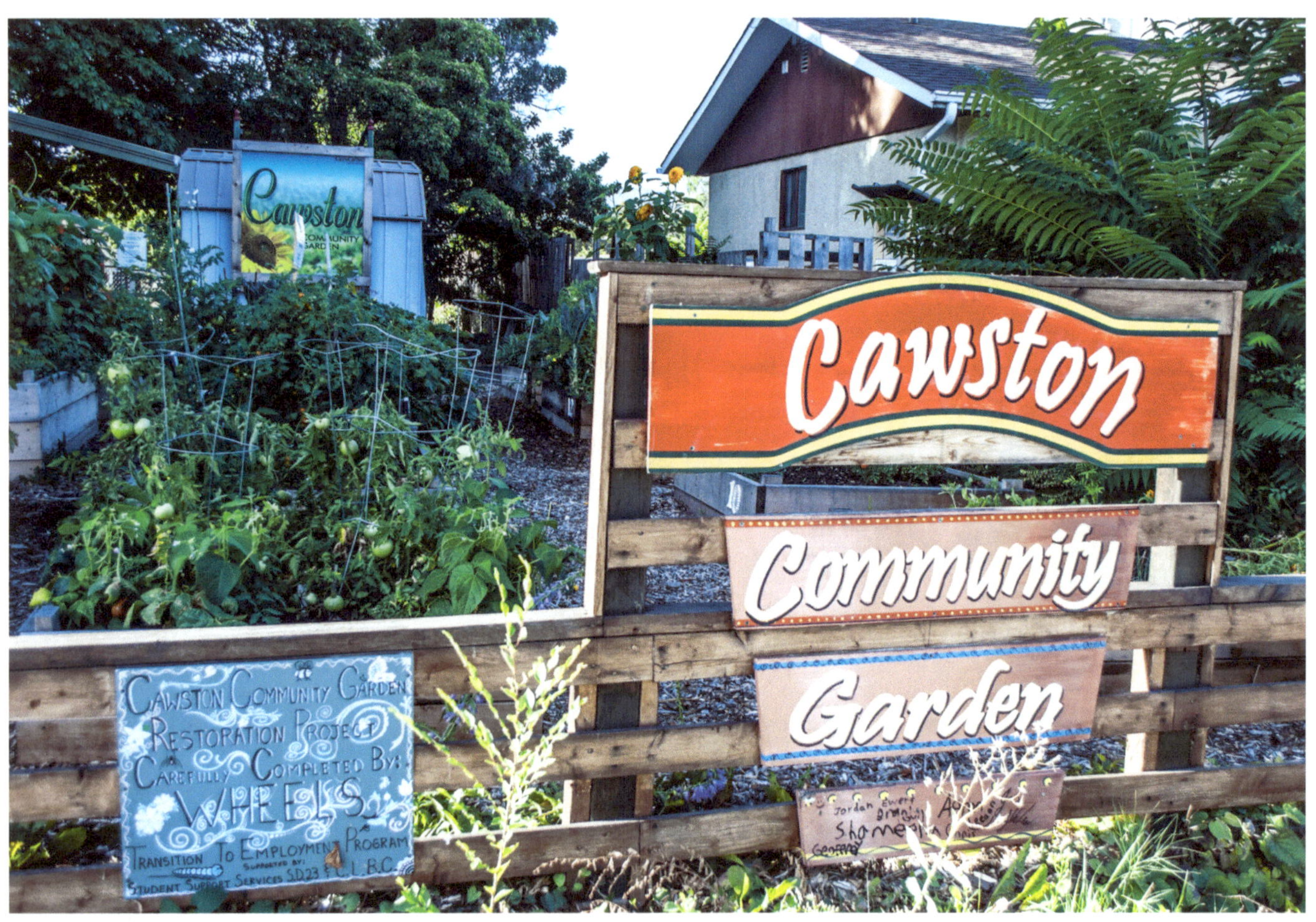


behind the unitarian fellowship

# A side trip to the farmers' market is next

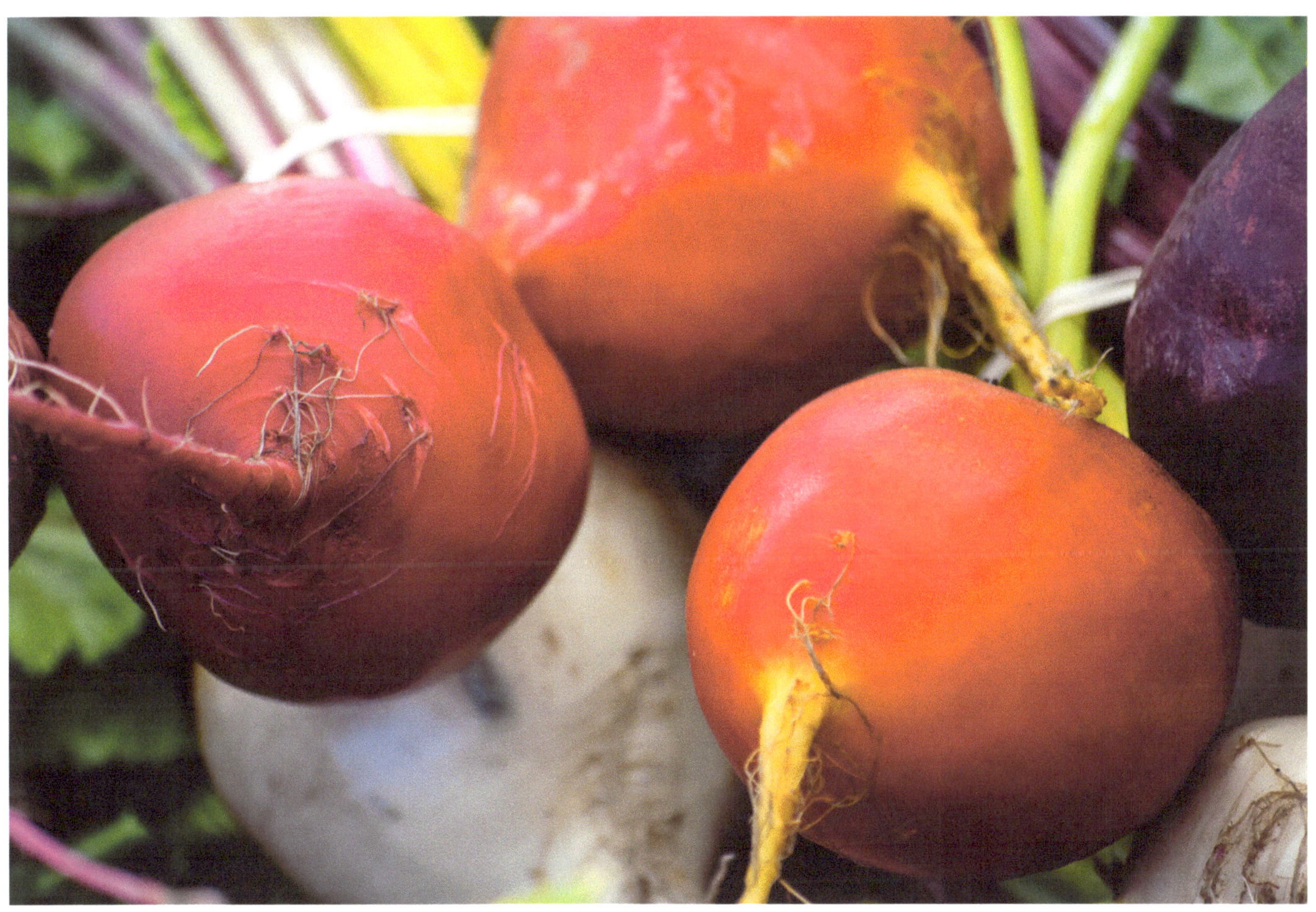

A food lover's delight, the Kelowna Farmers and Crafters Market is open
Wednesdays and Saturdays during growing season and Saturdays in late fall
through early spring. In addition to fruits and vegetables, expect to find the best
meats, cheeses, breads, flowers, preserves, sauces, pottery, clothing, jewelry, art,
soaps and so much more.

# every season has its stars

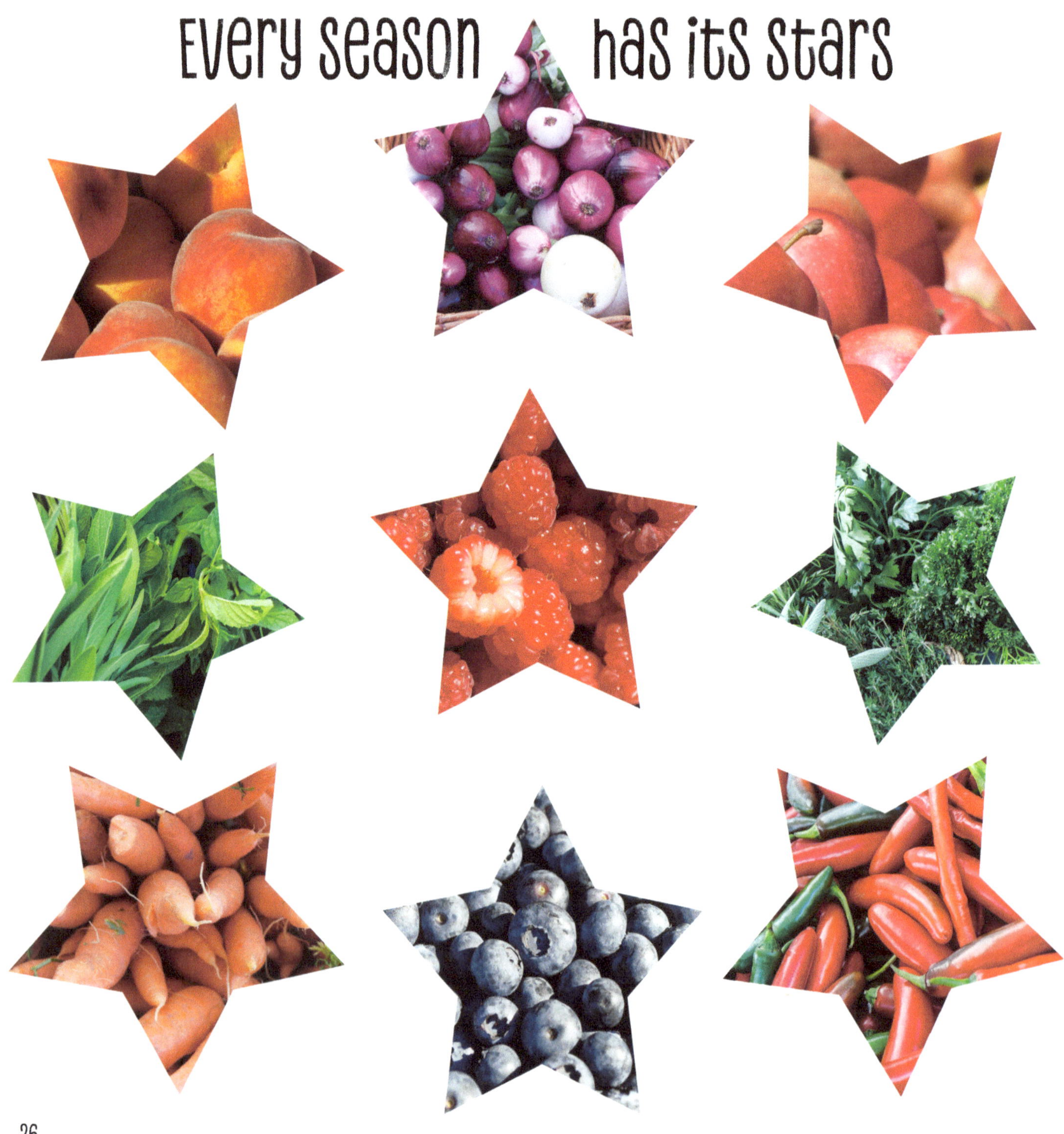

# The farmers' market has many heroes

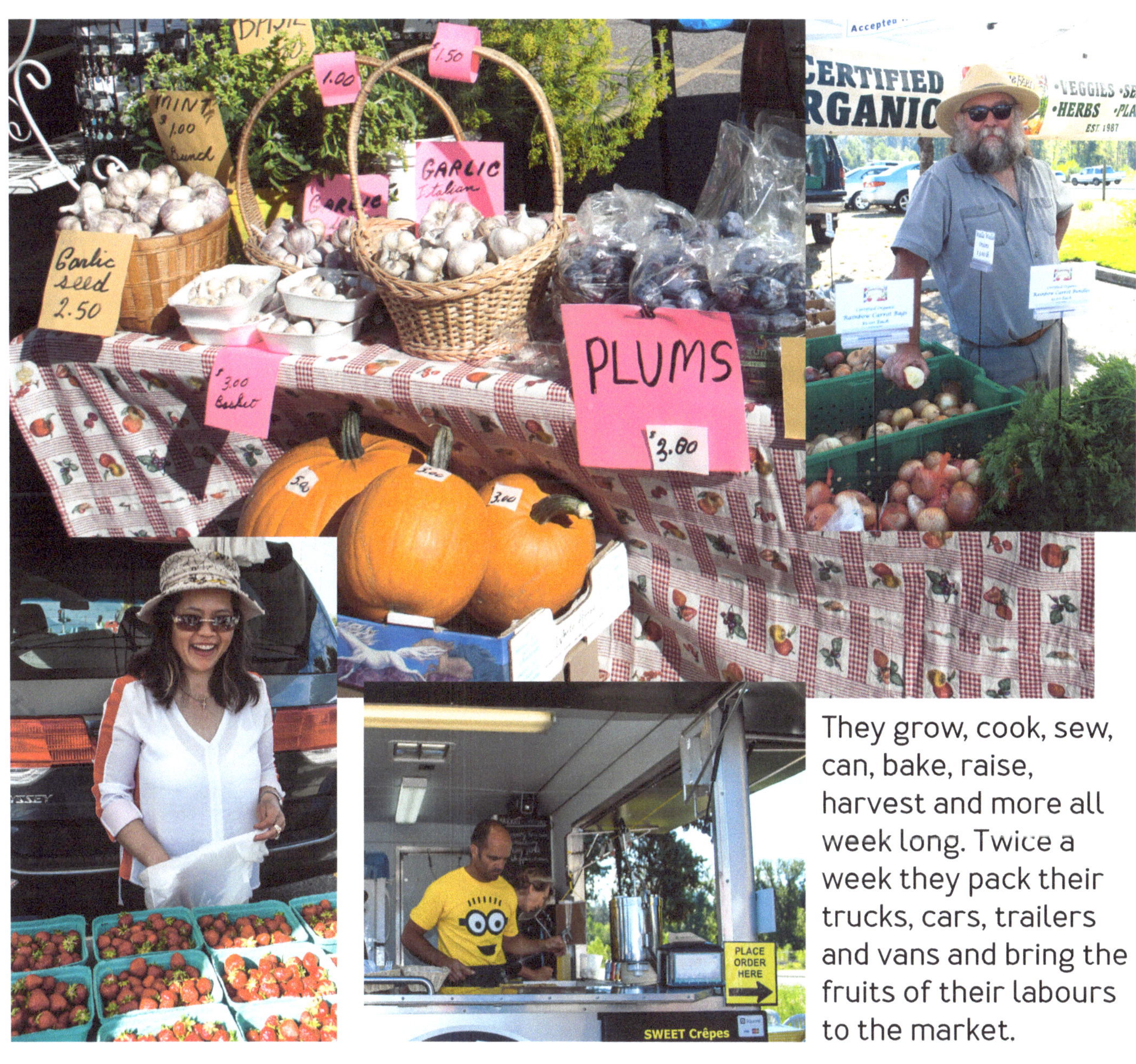



They grow, cook, sew, can, bake, raise, harvest and more all week long. Twice a week they pack their trucks, cars, trailers and vans and bring the fruits of their labours to the market.

# TO all the hard-working vendors

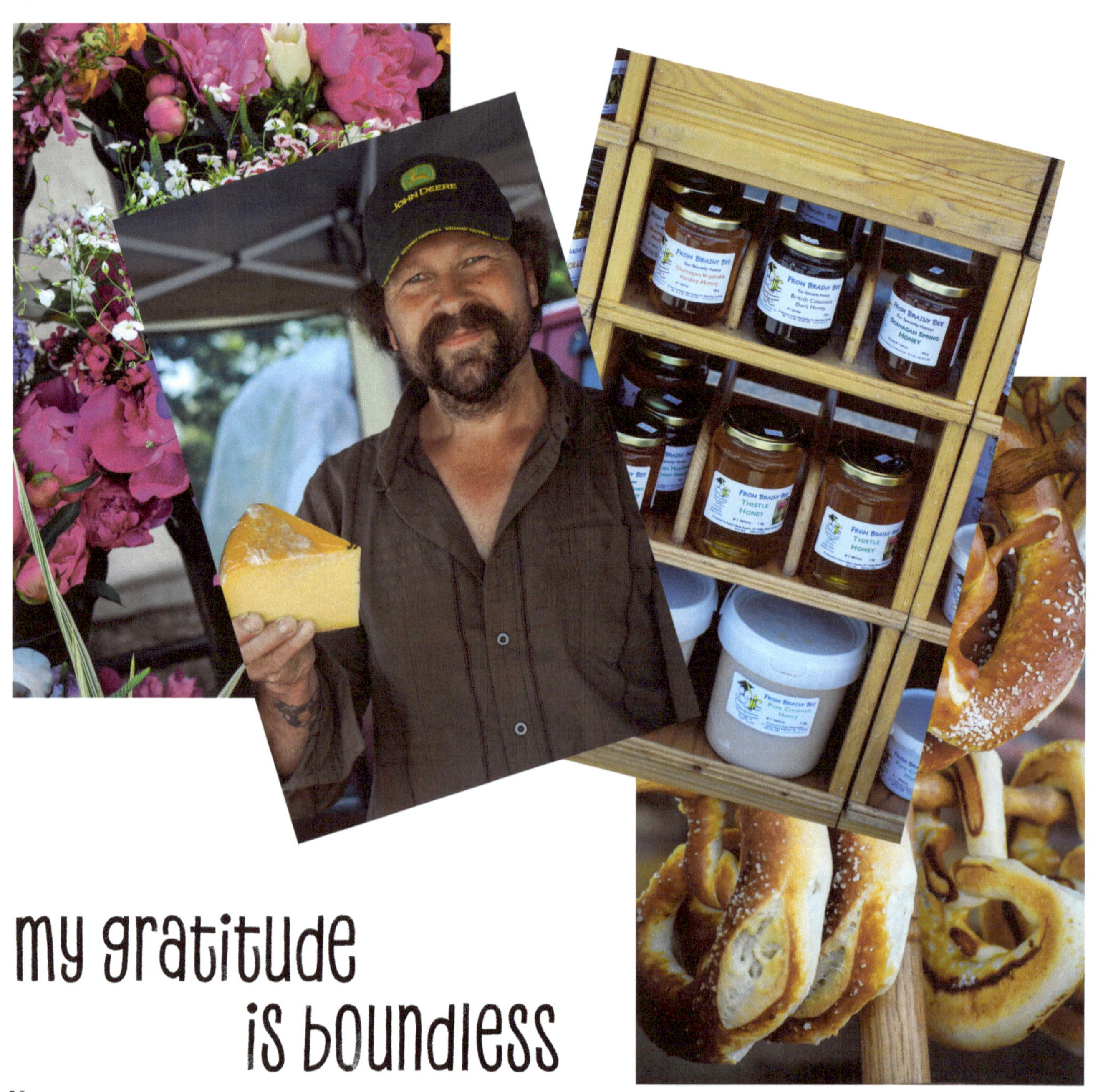

# my gratitude
## is boundless

# Kasugai, an oasis in downtown Kelowna

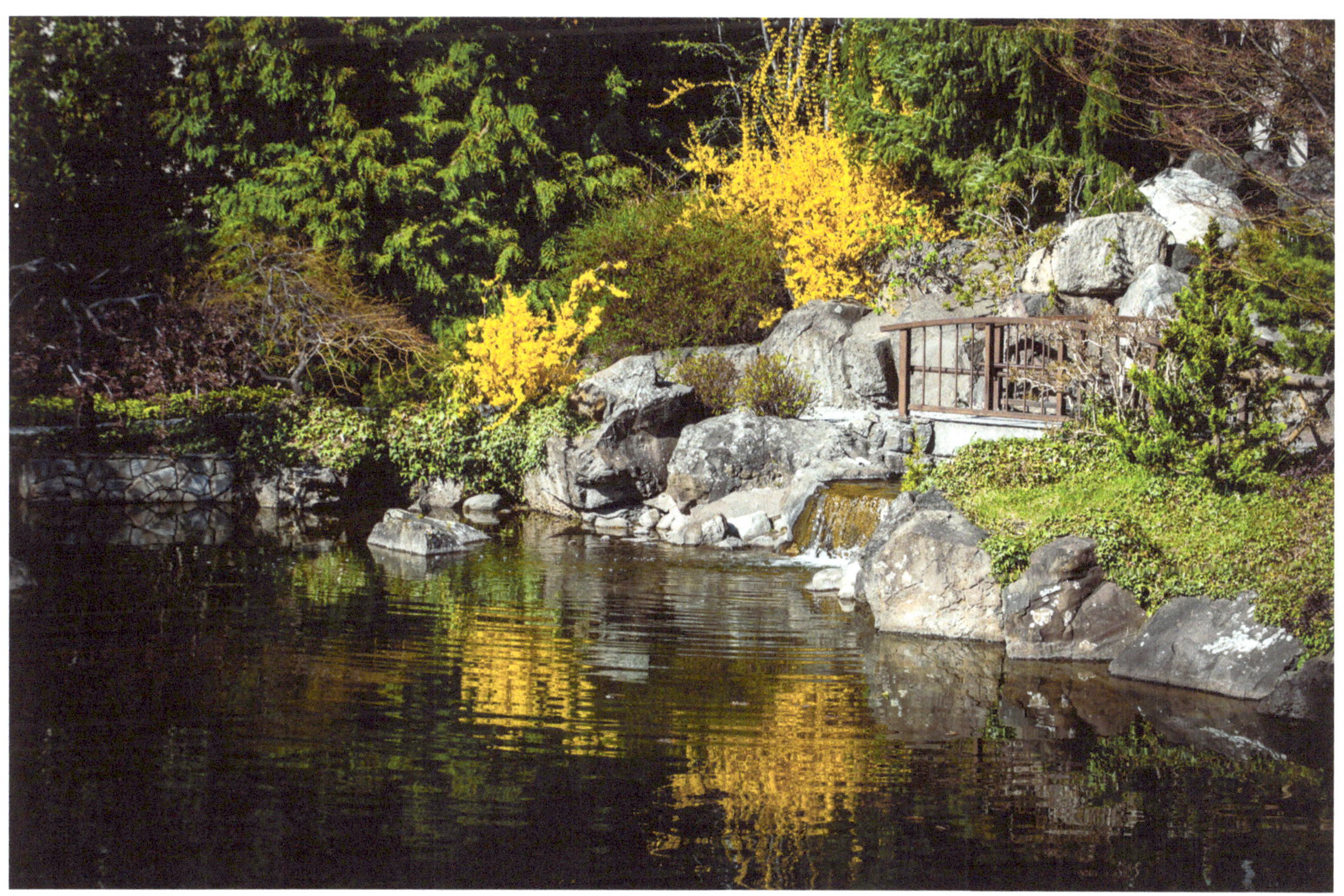

Named for Kelowna's sister city, this Japanese garden hides behind high walls.  Many visitors, and even locals, are unaware a secret garden exists right behind City Hall. It bursts into vibrant bloom in spring and ends its season when fall leaves carpet the ground. Then the resident turtles and bright koi retreat to the mud to sleep until spring brings them out again.

# The warmth

that wakes the forsythia also draws the western painted turtle out of his muddy winter nest. He climbs his rock to bask in the sun.

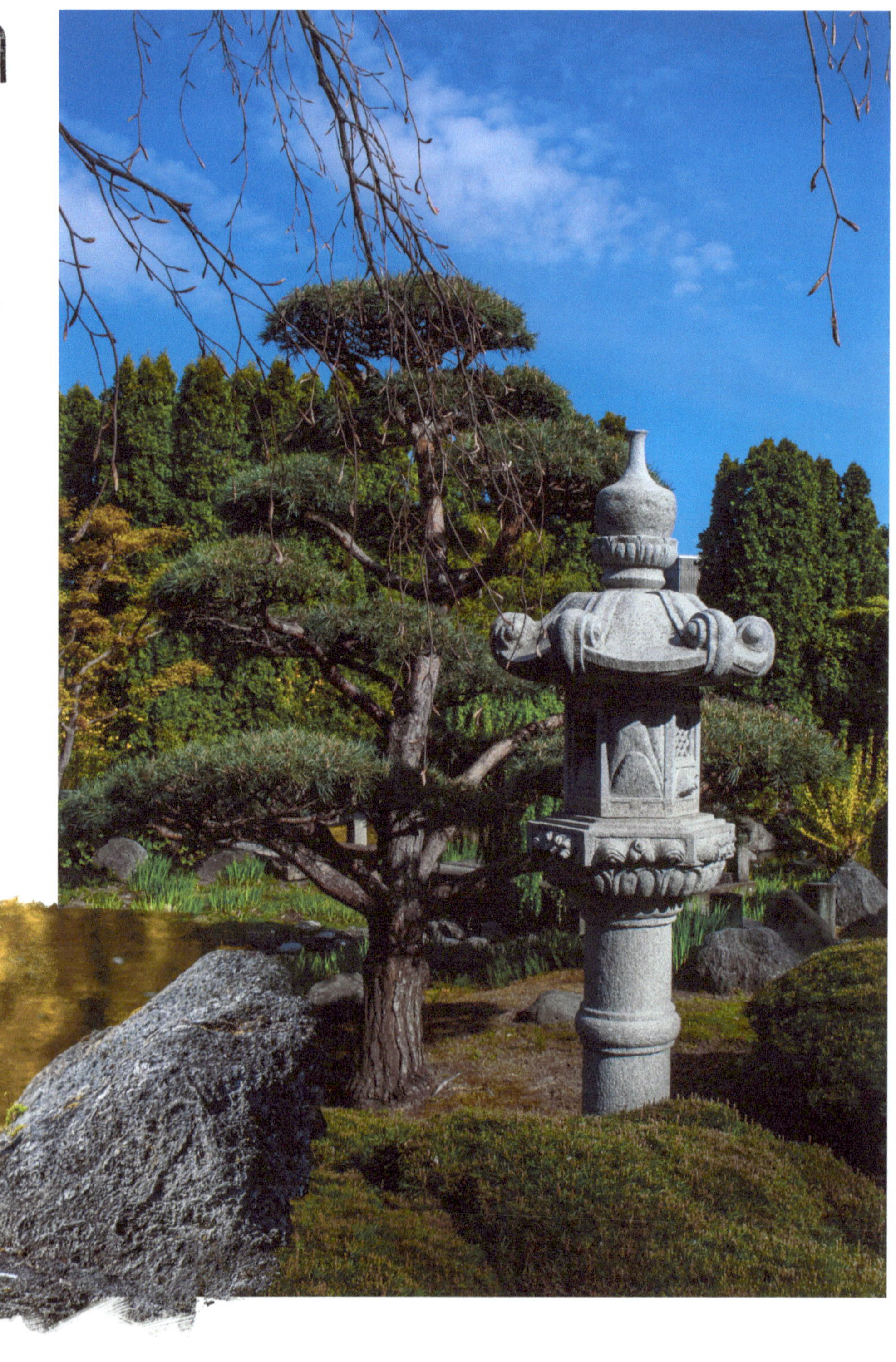

# Beauty abounds
# in simple juxtapositions

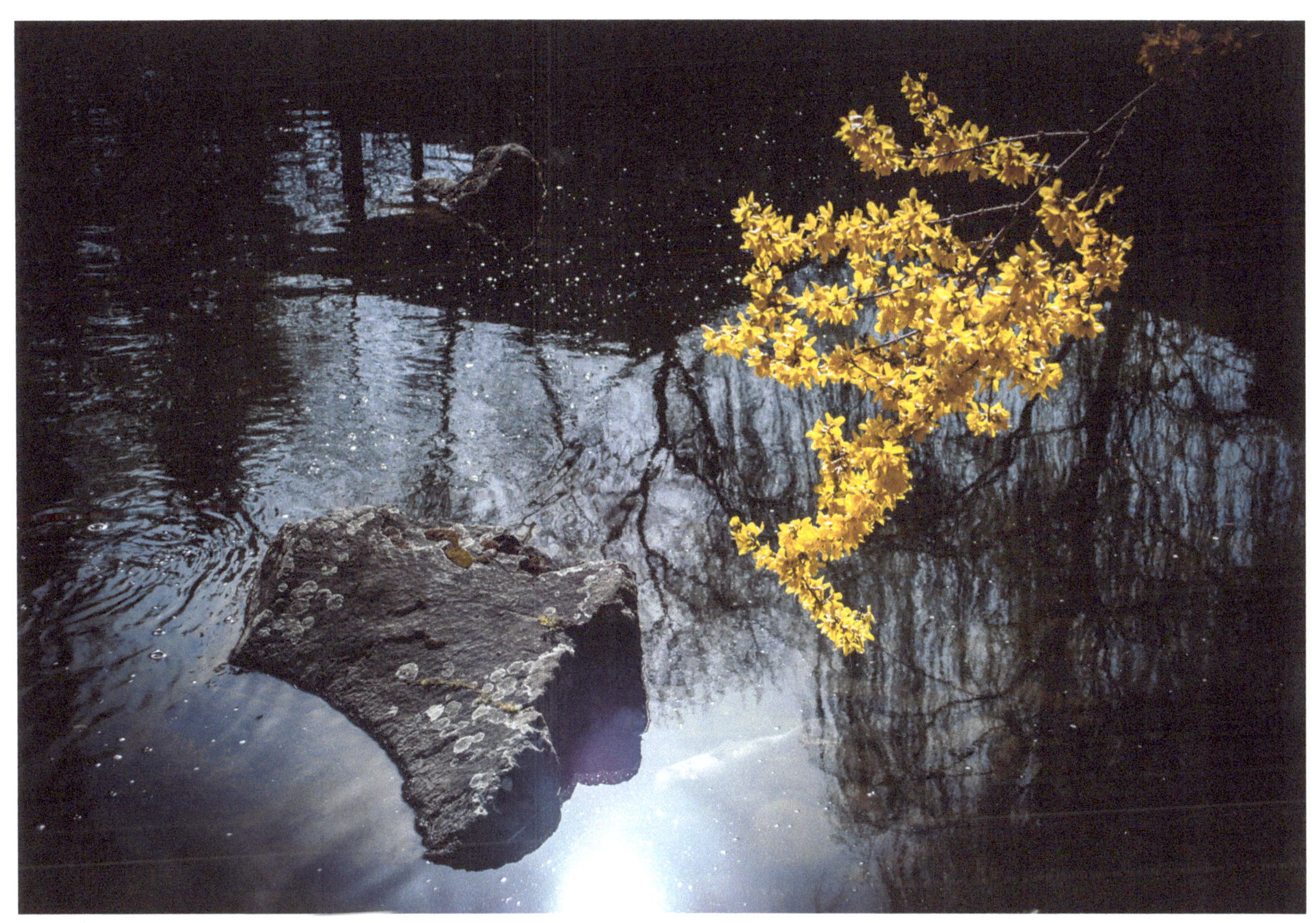

# Chiseled Limbs of a Japanese Maple

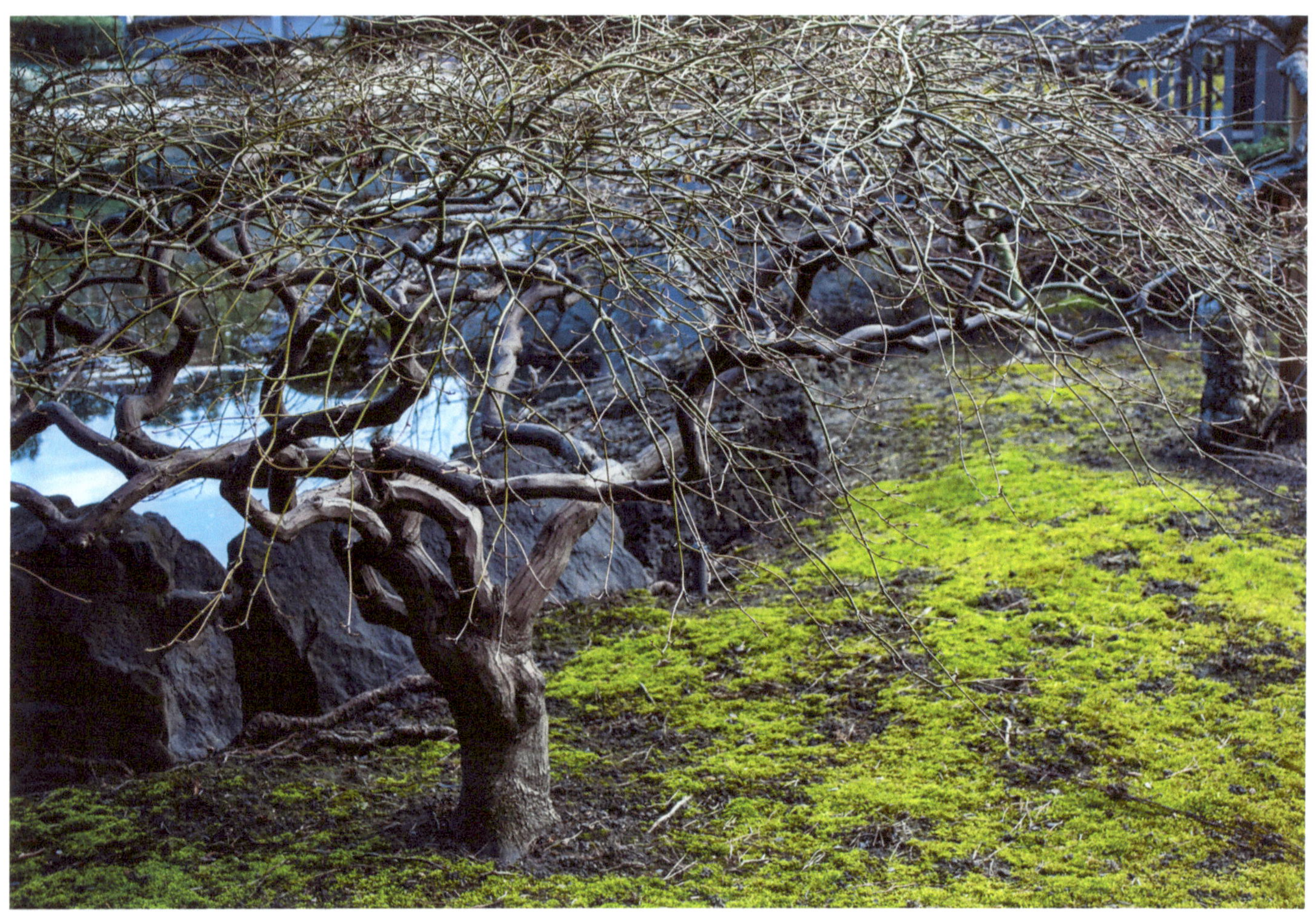

Before spring leaves cover the tree, the artistry of its limbs is striking. Moss gives colour to the pale landscape awaiting the first flowers of the year. The garden was carefully planned to reveal delights in every corner, in every season, whether trees stand bare or their leaves are backlit by the sun.

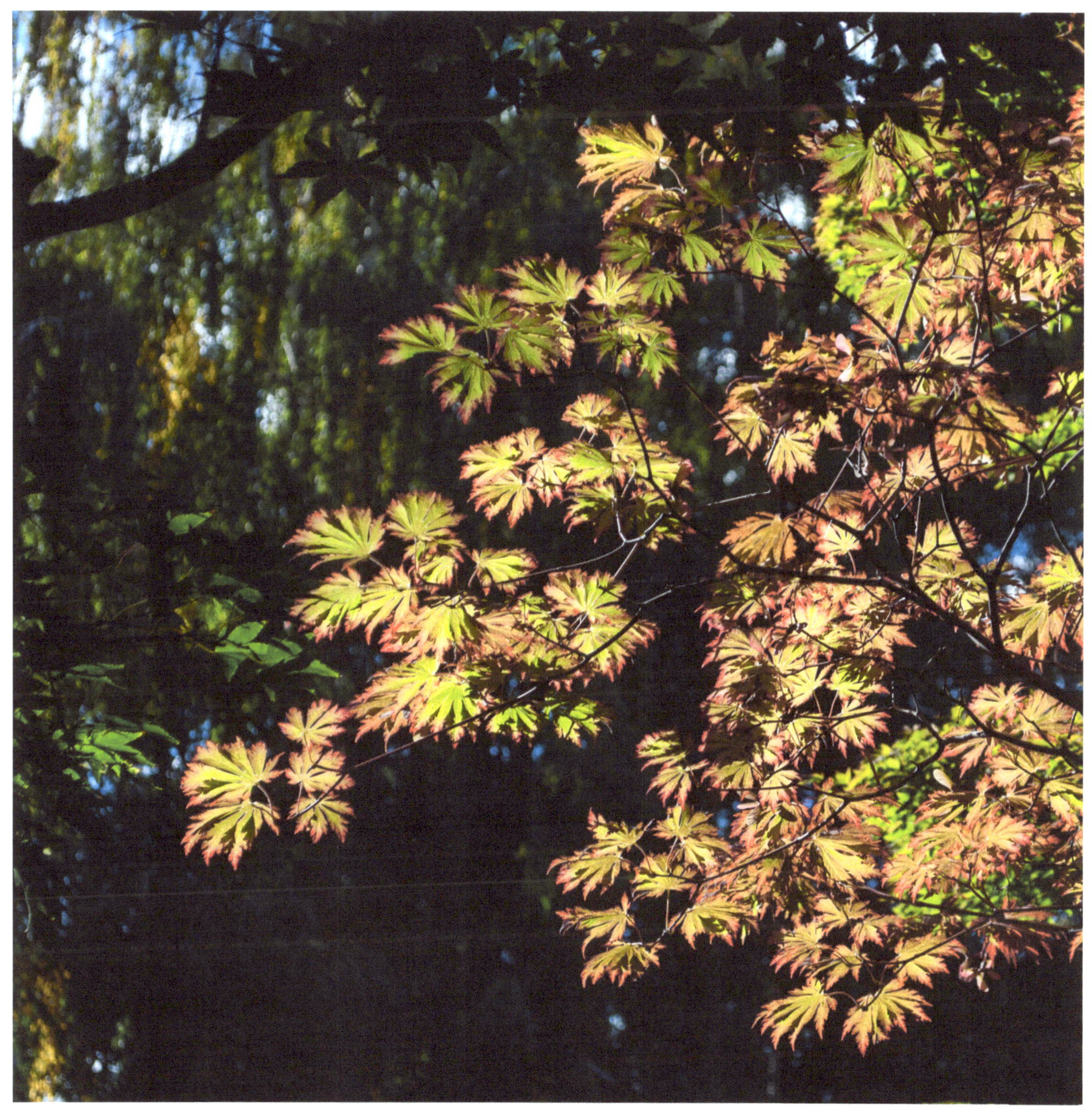

# Tranquility, elegance & grace

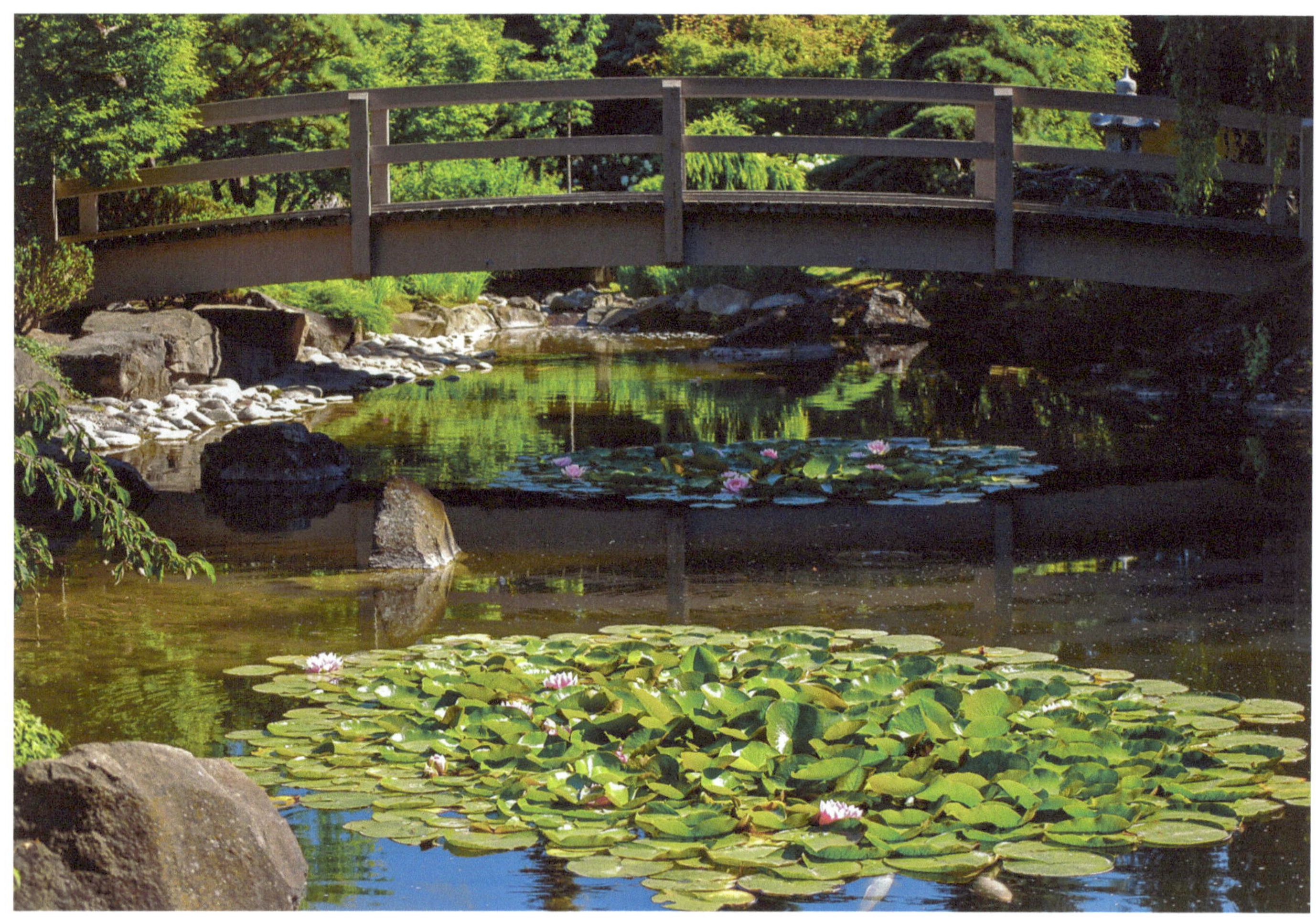

The three words characterize this jewel of a garden. Wedding parties come to be photographed on the bridge. Children shout with delight when they see turtles sunning on rocks. Workers take a quiet break from the pressures of the day.  All find peace here.

# pathways & bridges invite contemplation

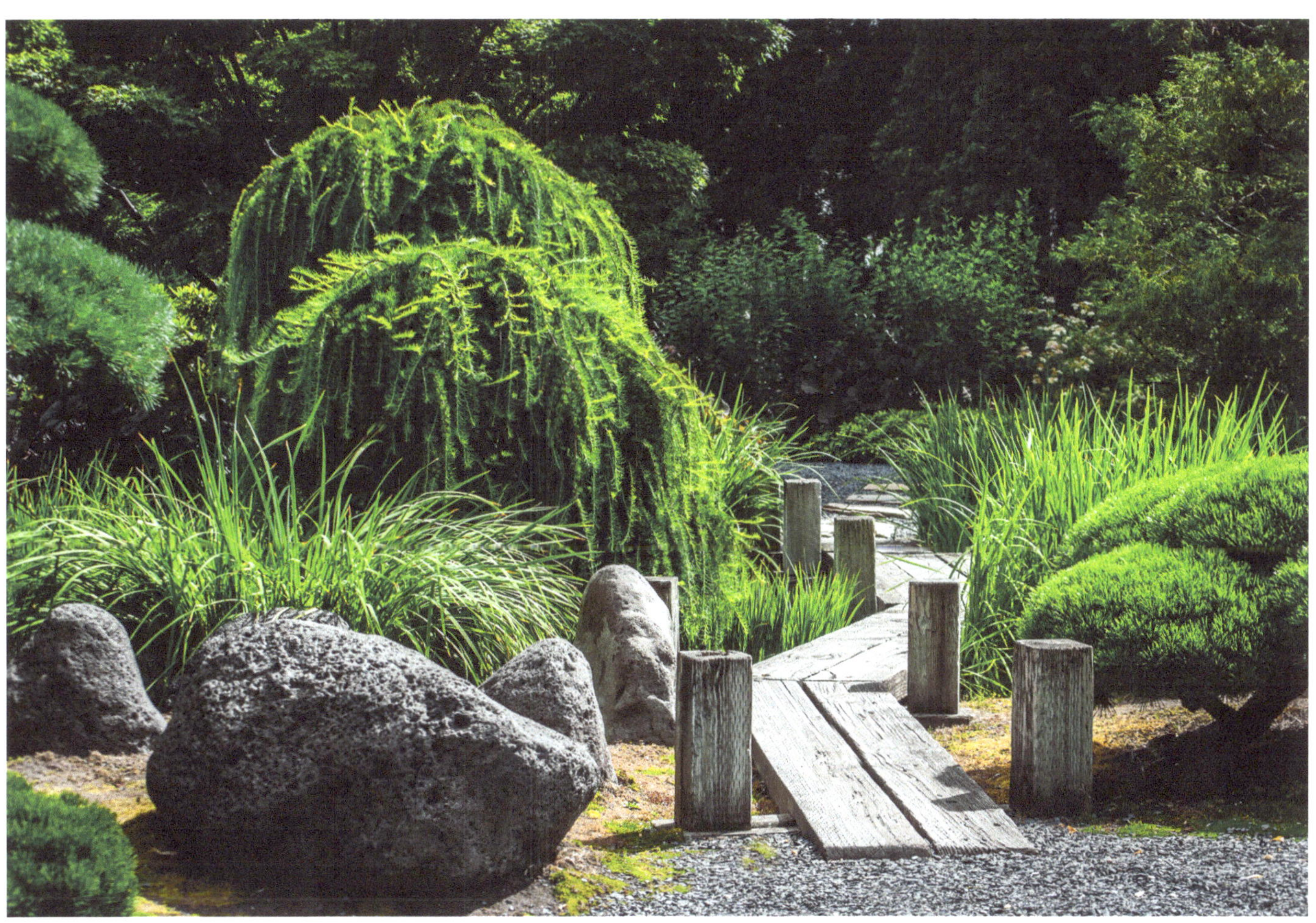

Built to encourage visitors to slow down, they wander among trees and bushes, across the stream, past the waterfall, and in and out of the two gates that punctuate the boundary walls of the garden.

# The same water

that quenches the thirst of visitors gives life to the flowers and animals flourishing within the walls of Kasugai Garden.

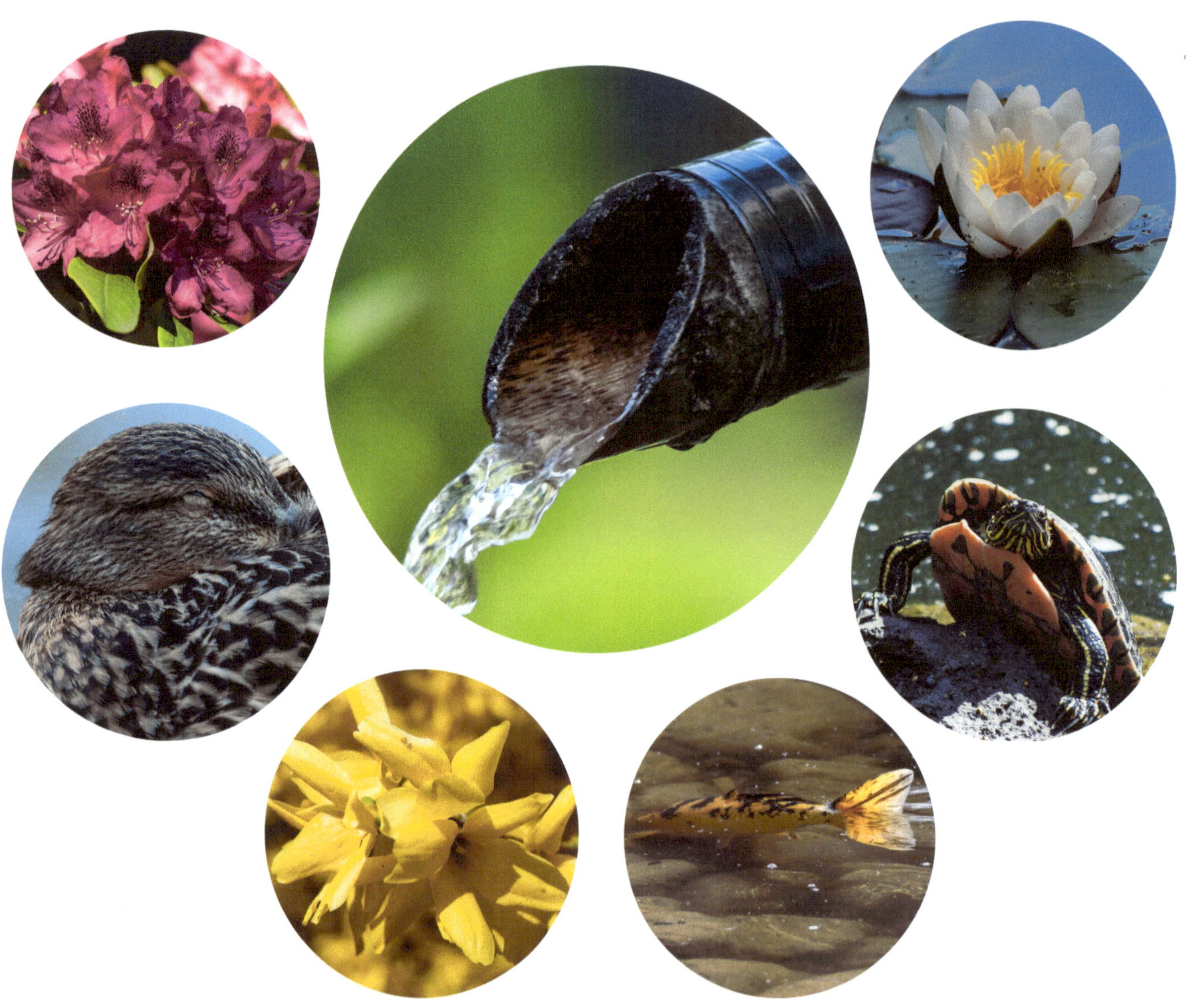

# kasugai's magic is everywhere

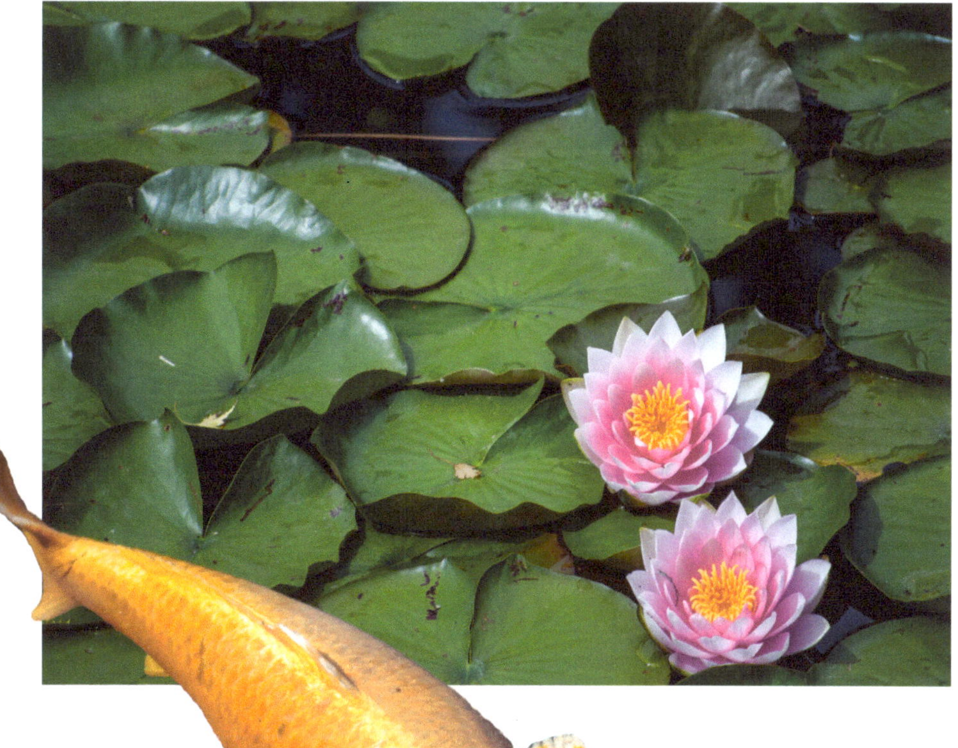

Everything the eye falls on in the garden has been thoughtfully chosen to add to the visitor's enjoyment.

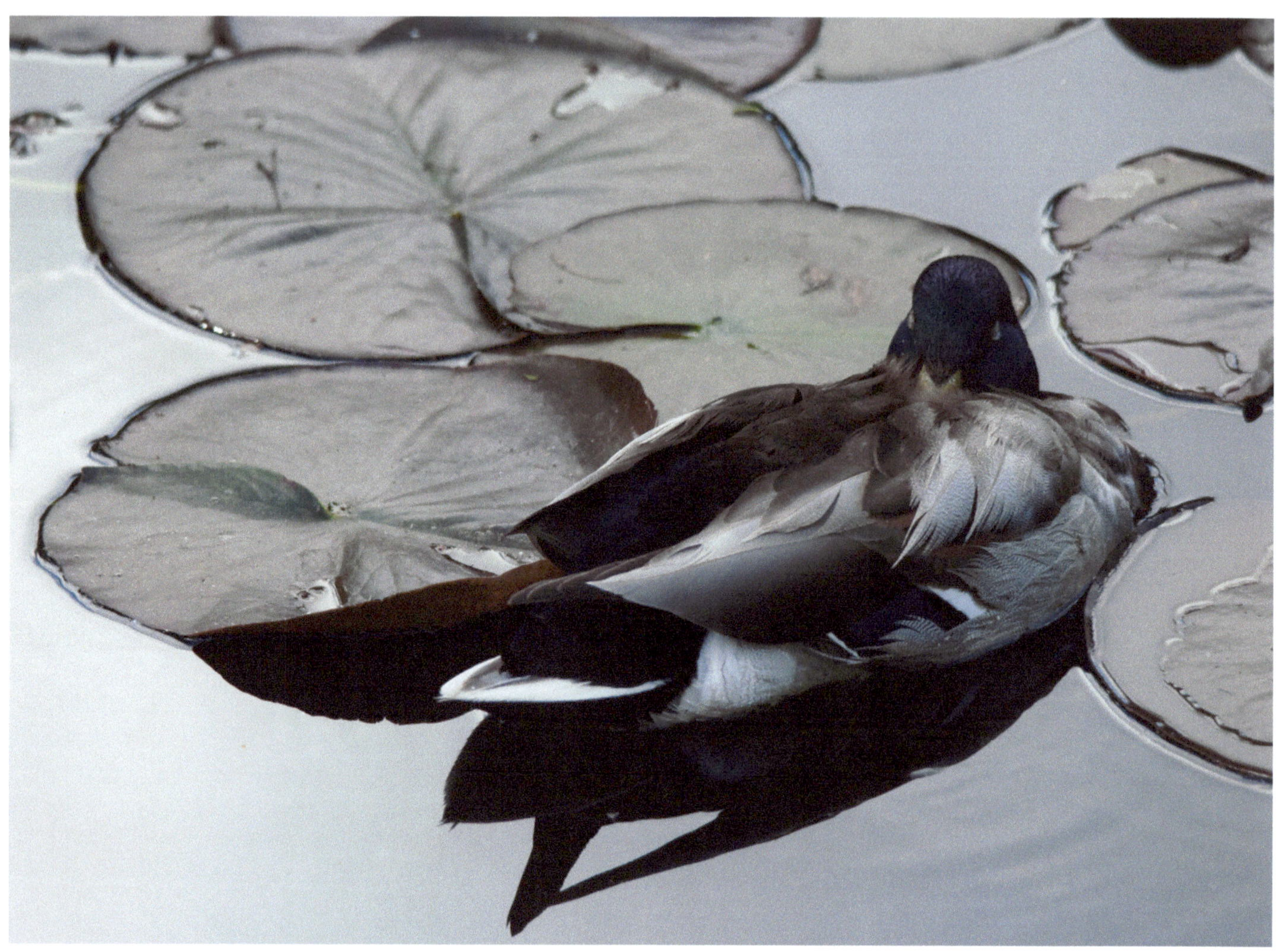

# A few mallards hang out

to nap among the lily pads, feed on succulent insects, and occasionally accept the offerings humans toss their way. (Please hold the bread, friends. That's not healthy duck feed.)

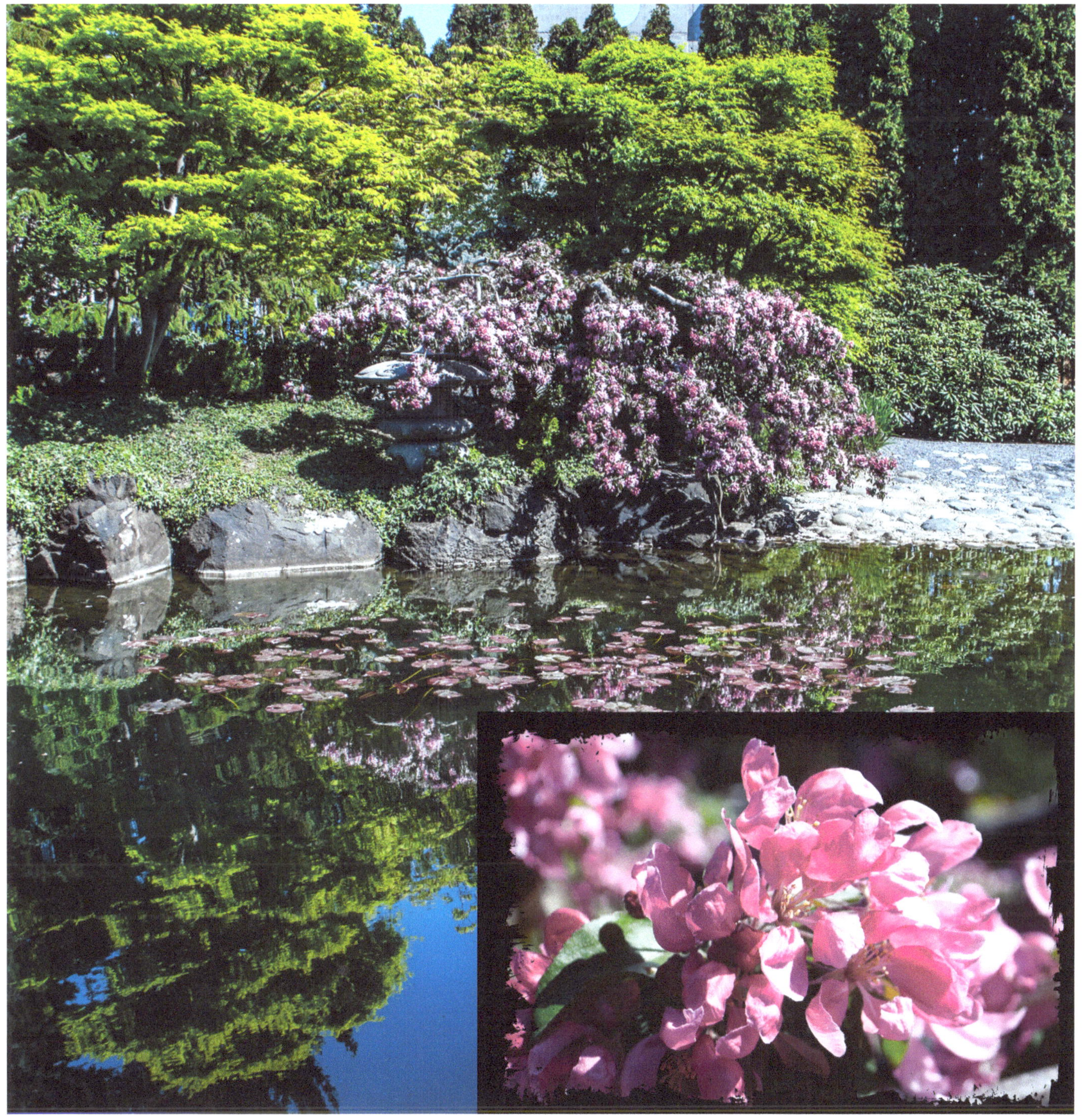

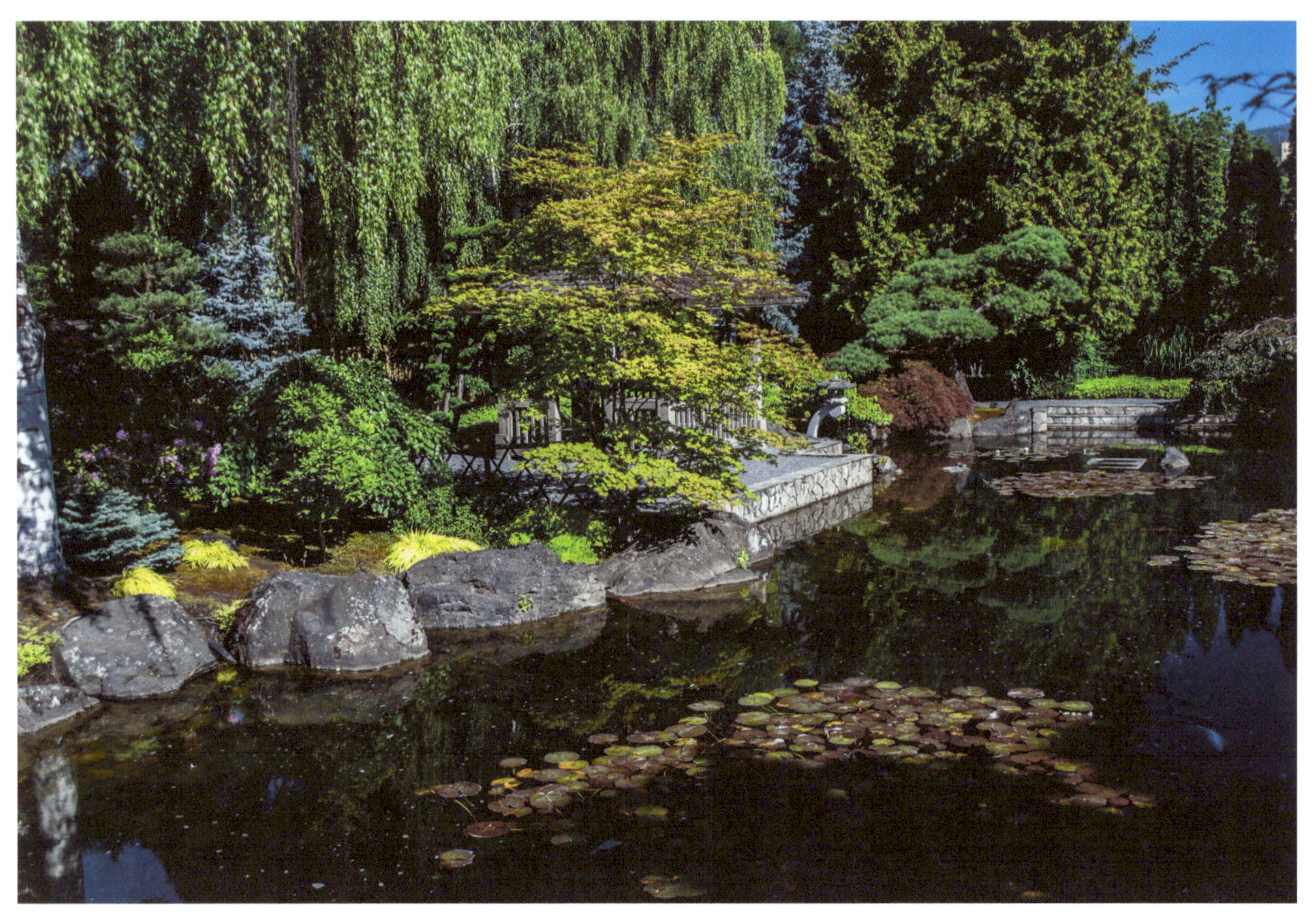

In summer, trees & bushes hide the gazebo

# Reds & oranges herald the coming autumn

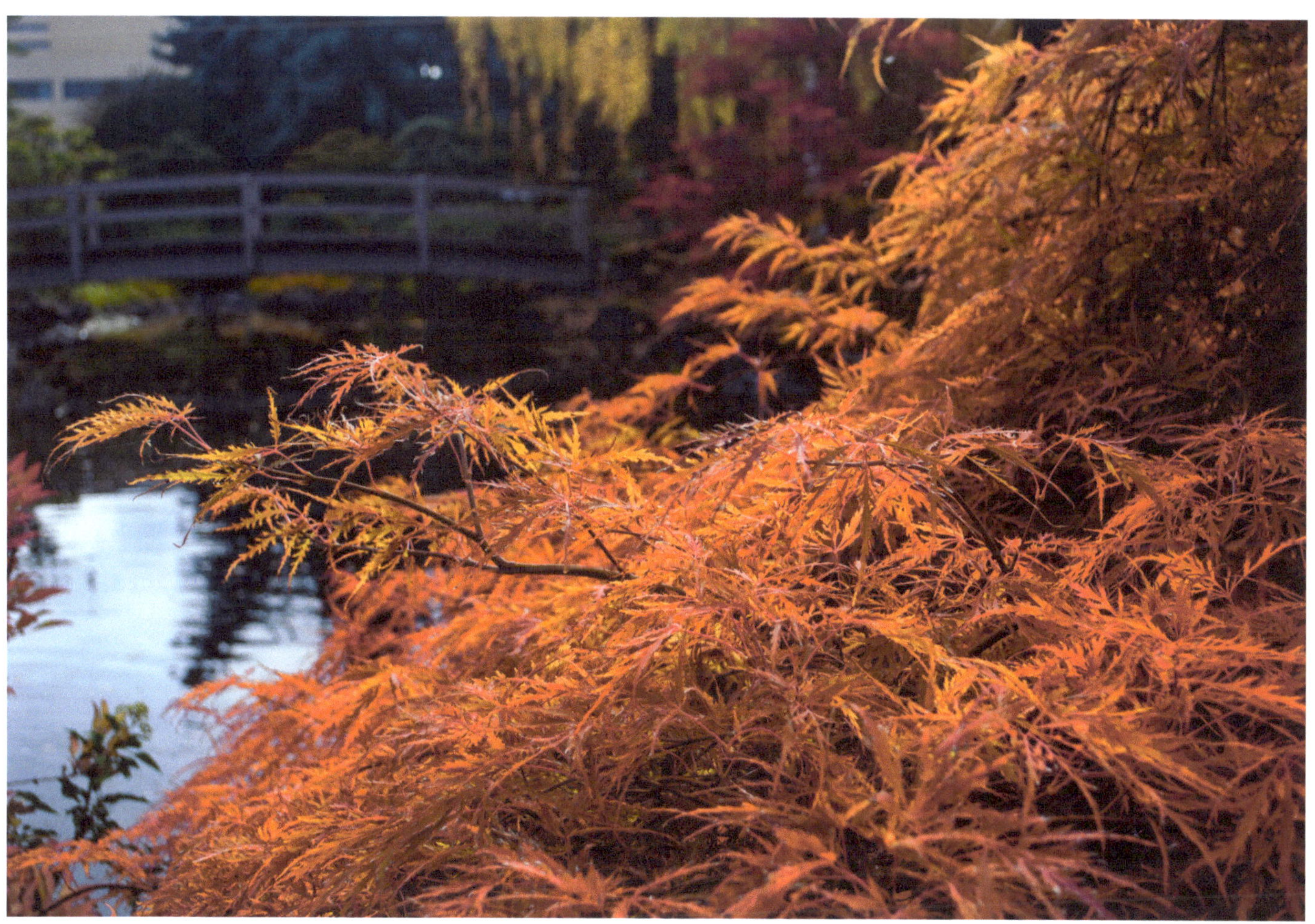

Kasugai garden will soon close its gates for the winter. Part of me wants this gorgeous season to last forever, but the seasons' turnings keep us attuned to the glory around us.

# Back to the Waterfront

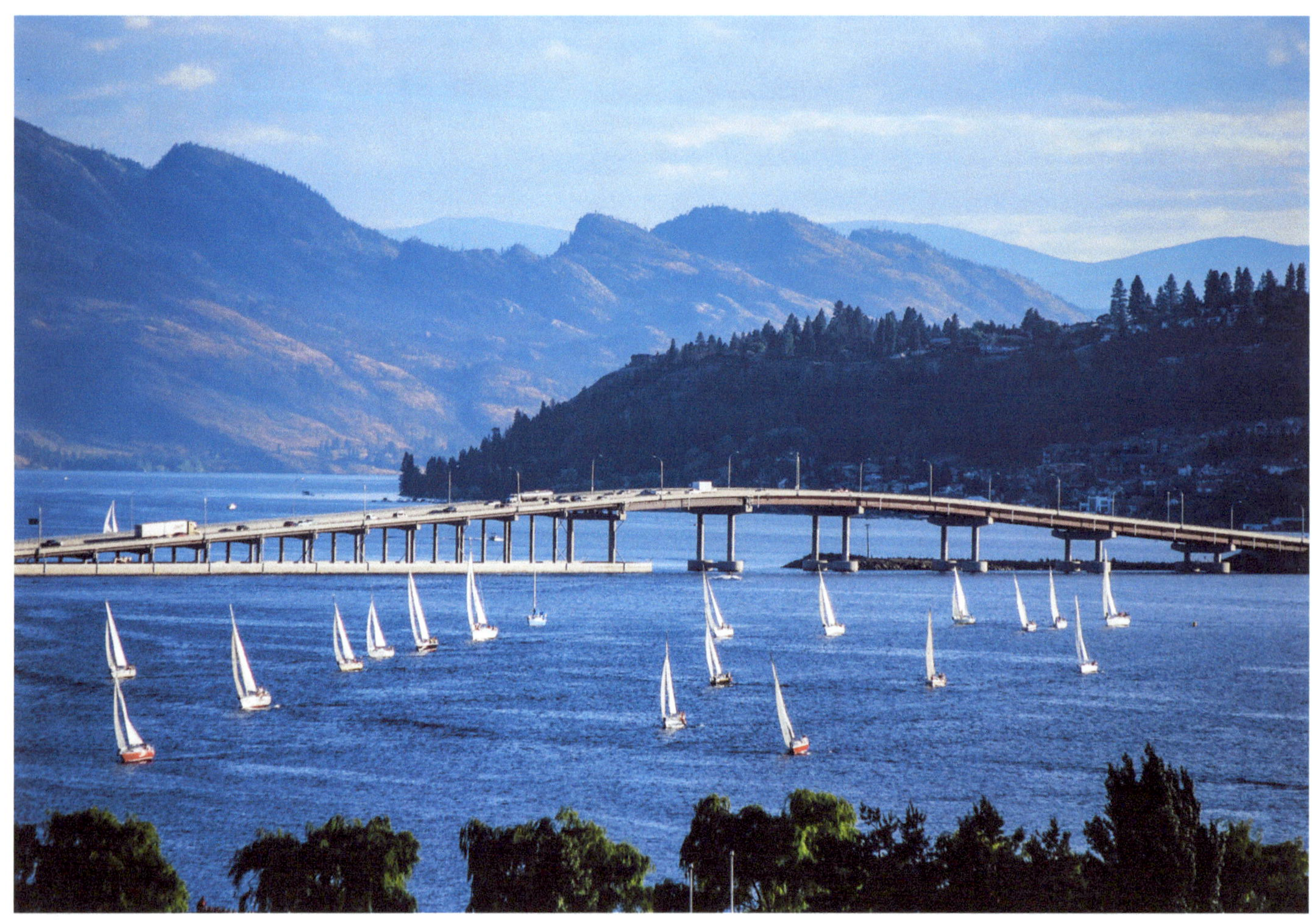

Okanagan Lake stretches 135 kilometers through the hills that form the boundaries of our valley. Power boats are popular on the lake, but, for many, they cannot compete with the romance of wind-filled sails.

# To live by water is joy & responsibility

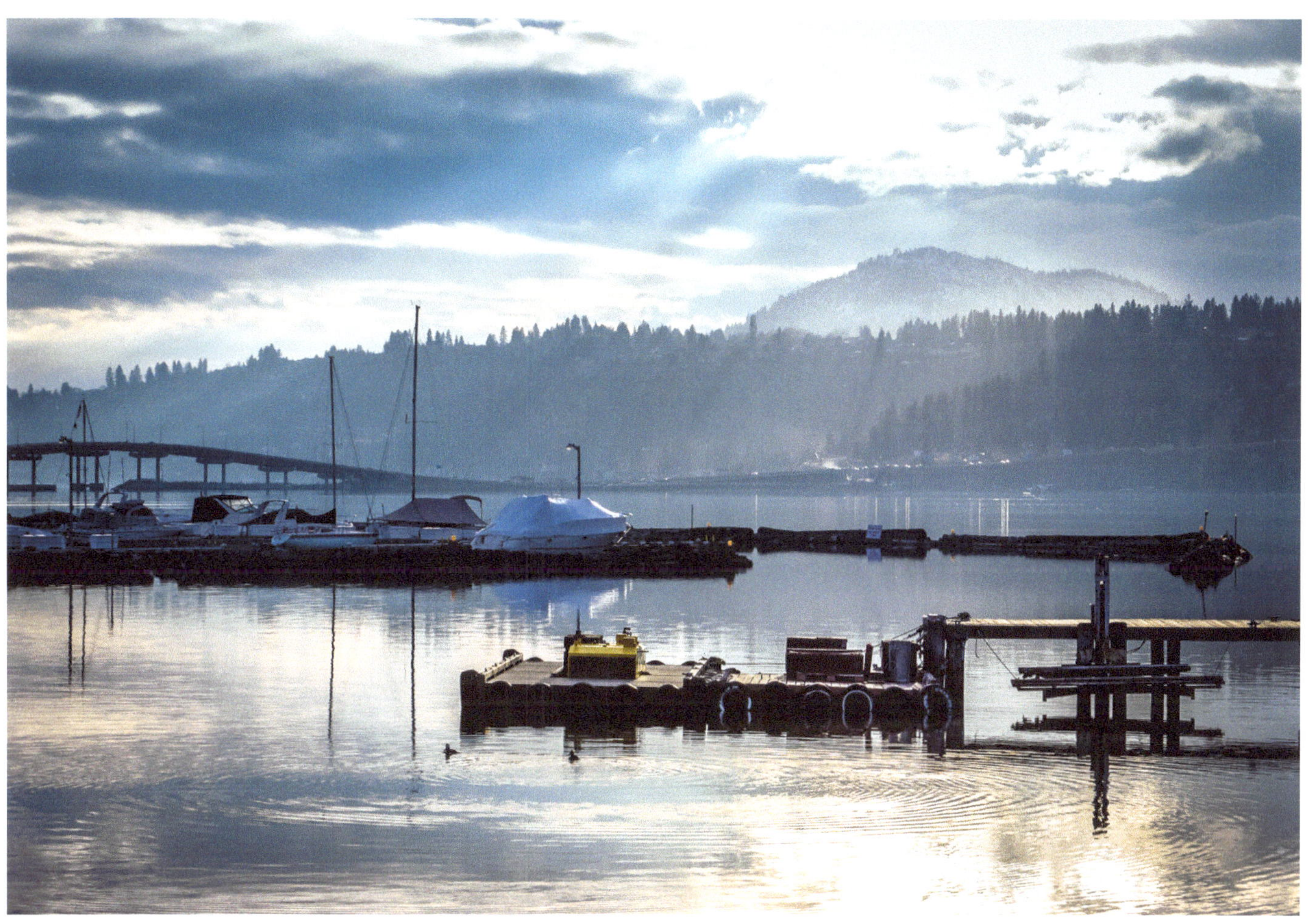

Blessed with such abundance, we sometimes forget the water we use and abuse is one of life's greatest gifts. The lake is part of our common good, to enjoy but also to safeguard.

# Hot summer days bring more than tourists

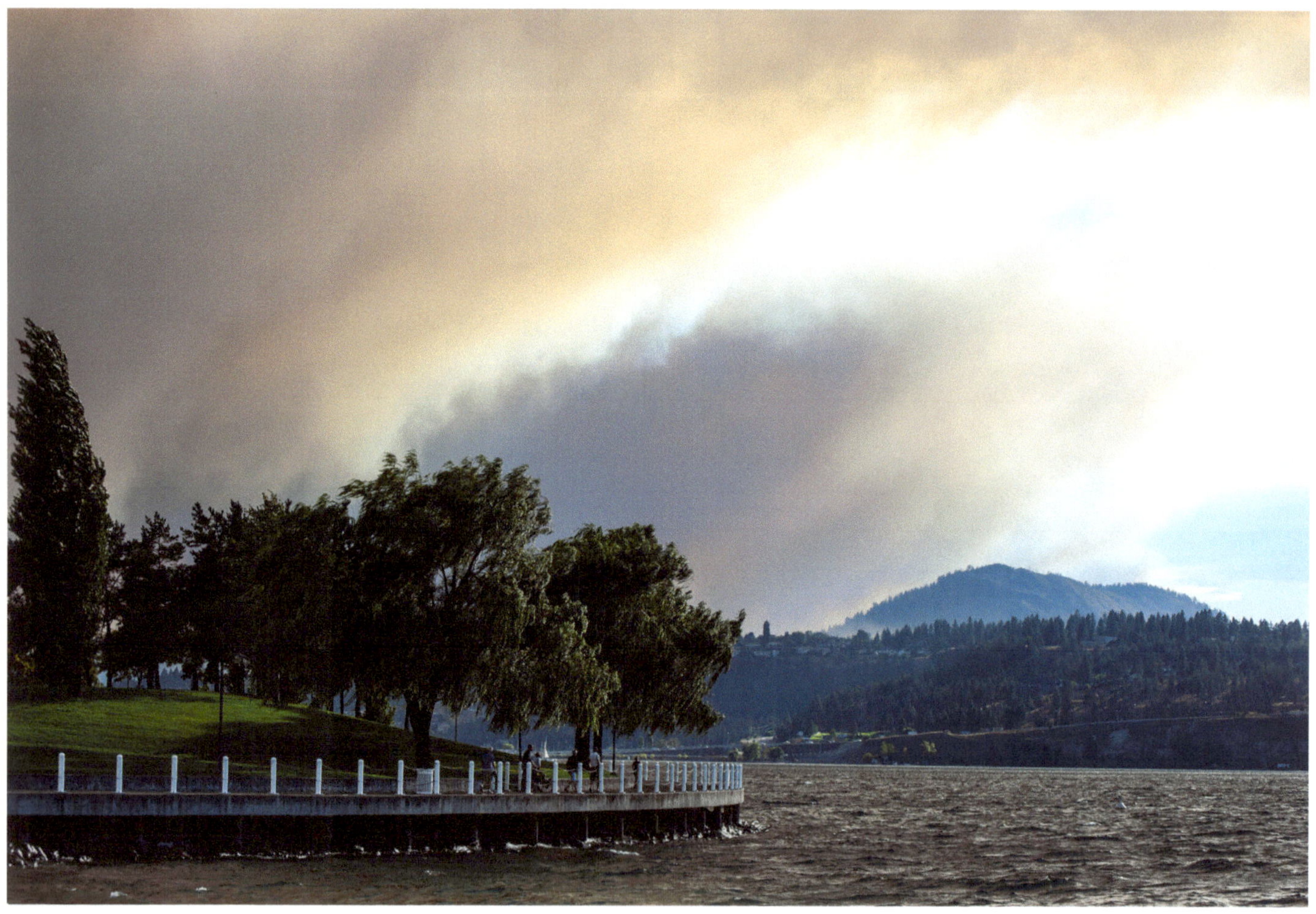

They also increase the risk of forest fires in the nearby hills. With more and more people moving into interface areas in search of rural lifestyles, the likelihood of fires and the cost of keeping them away from human habitation rises. The eerie beauty of smoke-filled skies reminds us of the impacts we humans have on our shrinking areas of true wilderness. Though lightning starts some fires, humans cause many more.

# Kelowna winters are mild

They lack the ferocity of the blizzards and ice of Edmonton or Saskatoon or Toronto. They avoid the drippy days of coastal British Columbia. Instead, clouds clamp down like an iron blanket over the Okanagan Valley, keeping things warmer and only occasionally delivering snow or rain. Still, even on a December day, the clouds can suddenly part, letting the low winter sun gild everything it touches.

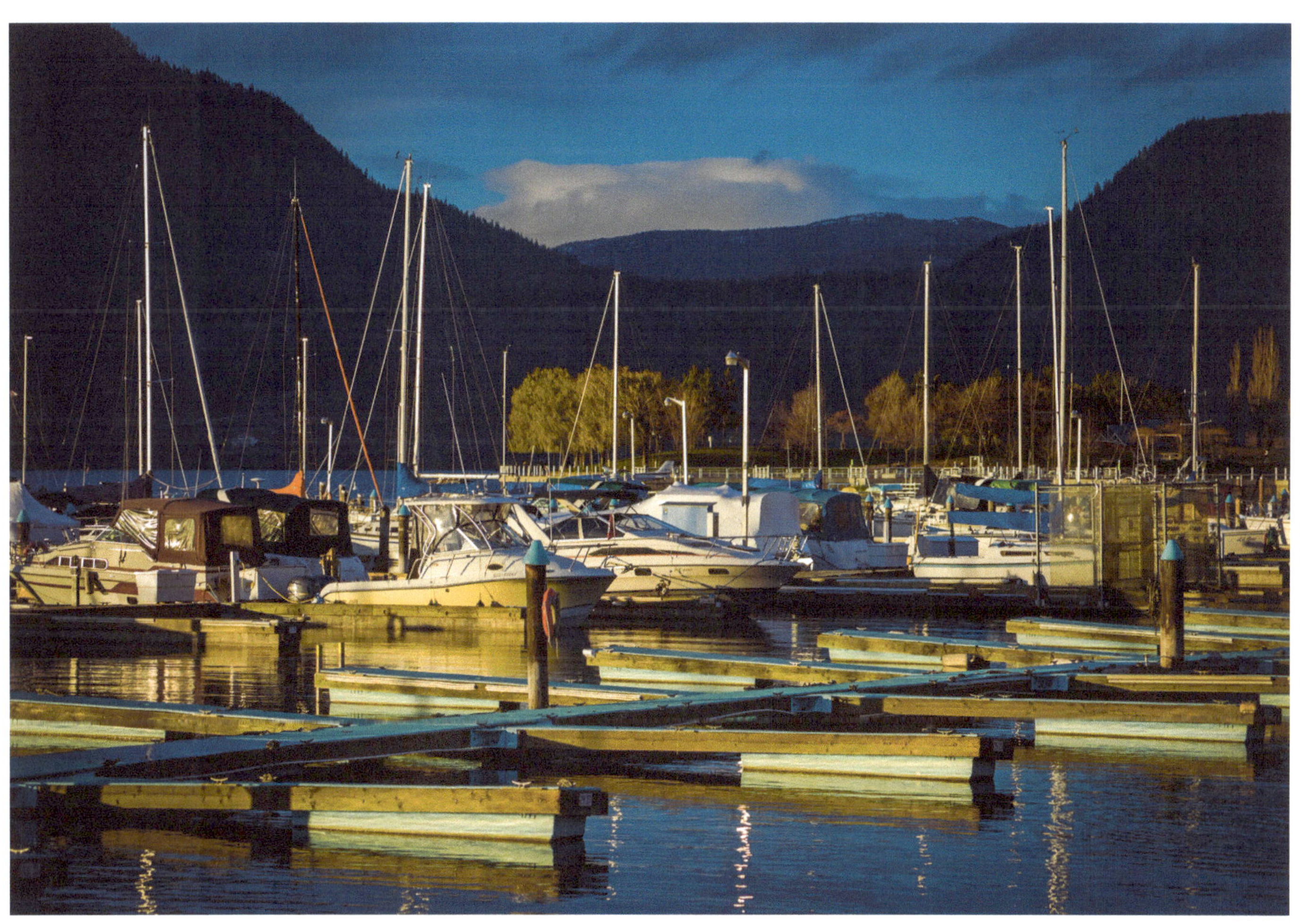

# The big blue bear in Stuart Park

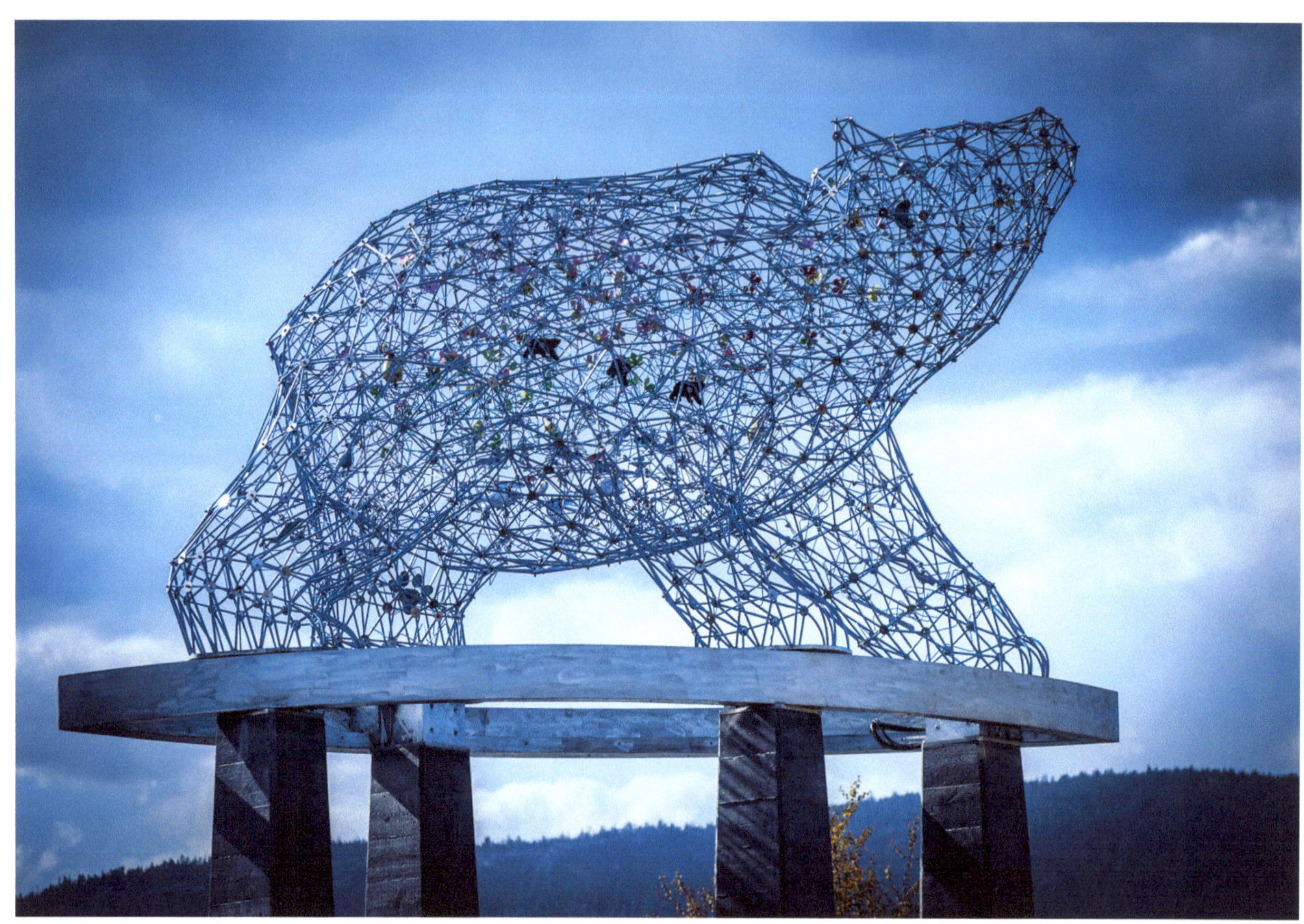

The bear was met with gasps when it was unveiled in September 2010. Designed by Rhode Island artist Brower Hatcher, the female grizzly (Kelowna's namesake) has a belly full of symbols of life and culture in the Okanagan, including fruit trees and blossoms and native wildlife. She stands on a platform shaped like the hull of a boat, connecting her with the lake she stands beside.

# Two stay - two go

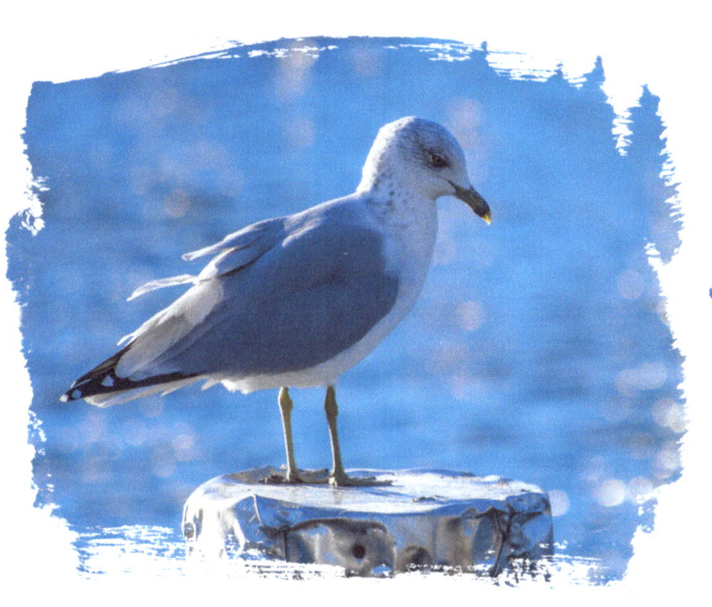

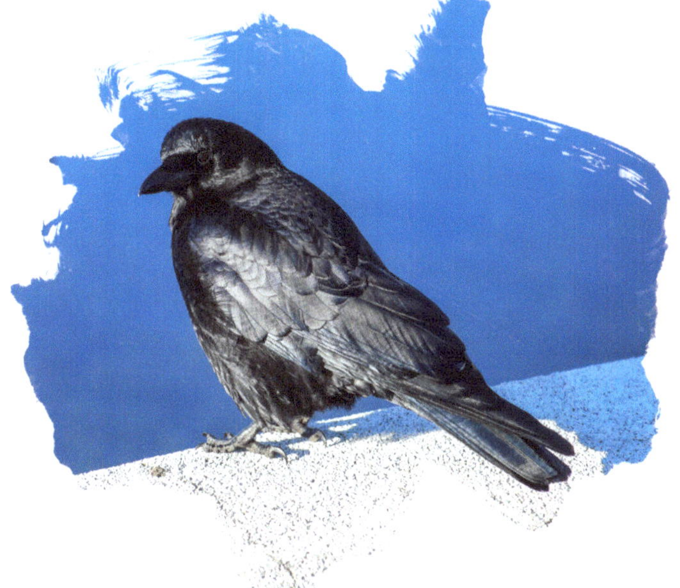

Ring-billed gulls and crows live here year around. The common goldeneye is a winter resident. The merganser to his right raises a family and then moves south.

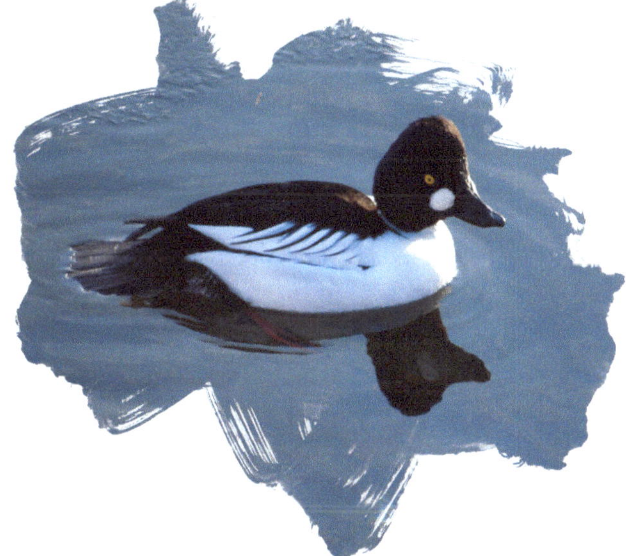

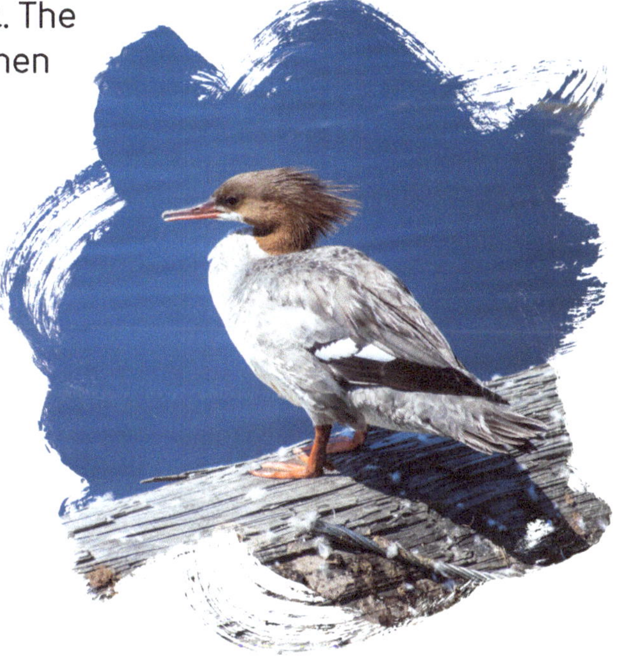

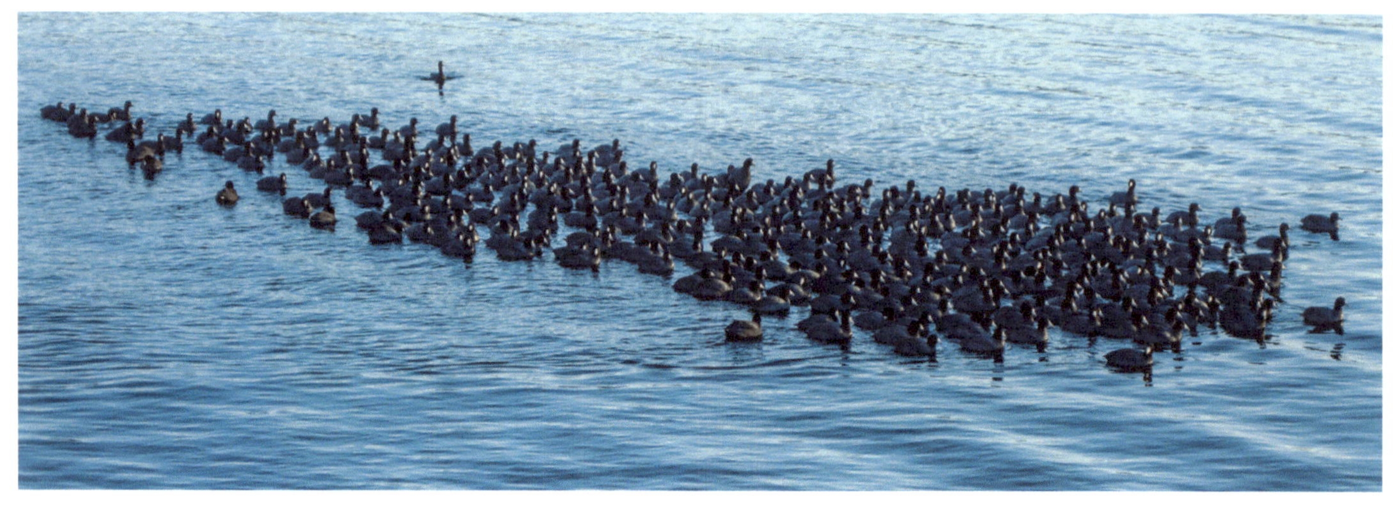

# They are the migrators

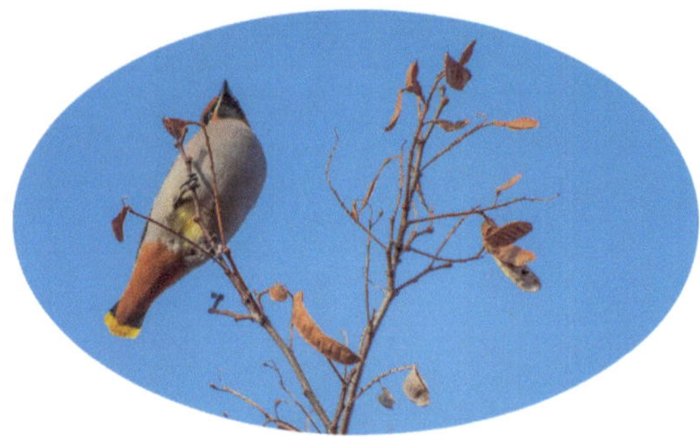

In winter flocks of coots and American wigeons swim on the lake, in the lagoons, on the marsh. The Bohemian Waxwing makes brief visits in fall and spring, harvesting berries on his way north or south.

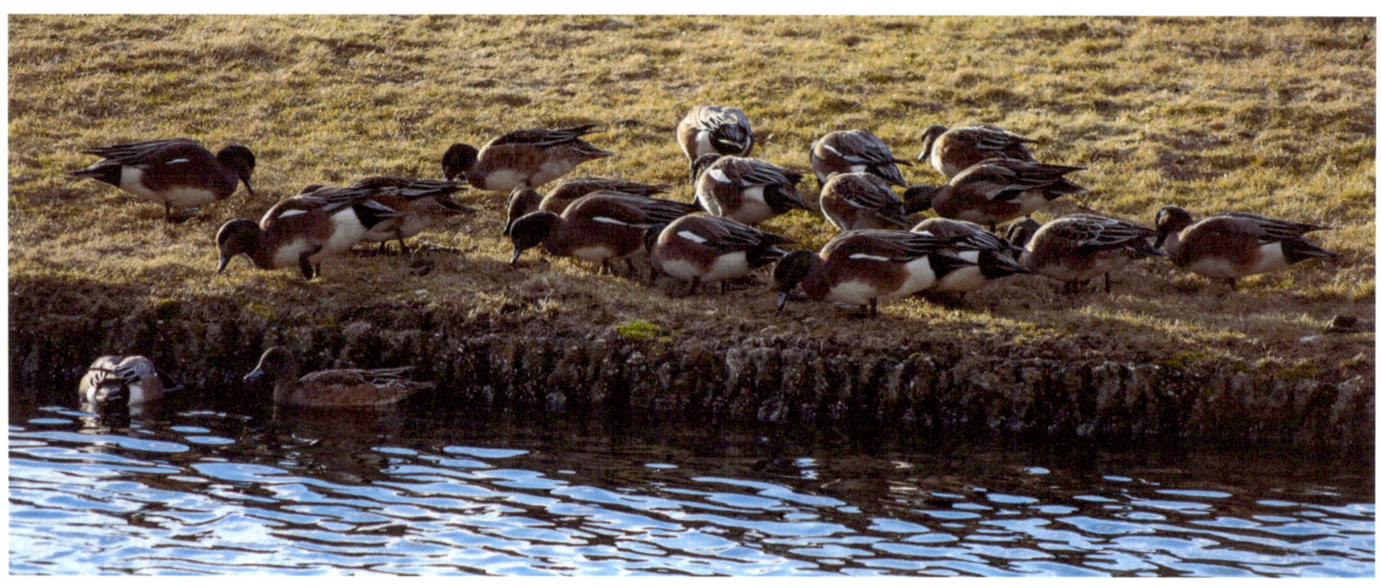

# "sandpiper," I said, but I was wrong

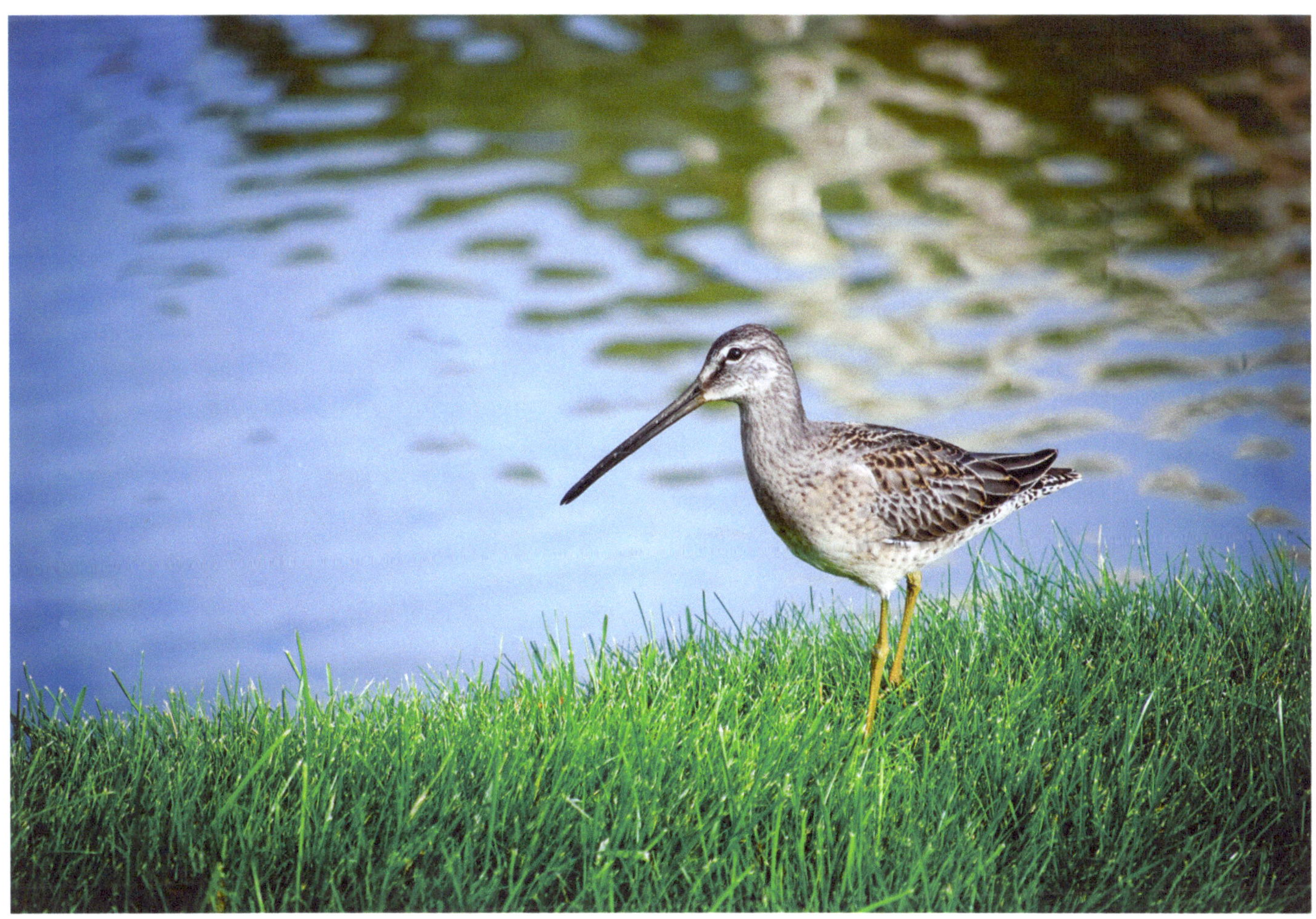

Birder friends told me this early-fall visitor to Waterfront Park was actually a long-billed dowitcher. He was patient with me, letting me watch him search the grass for insects. But he kept looking my way, setting the rules about who could narrow the distance between us.

# Waterfront Park, once part of the lake

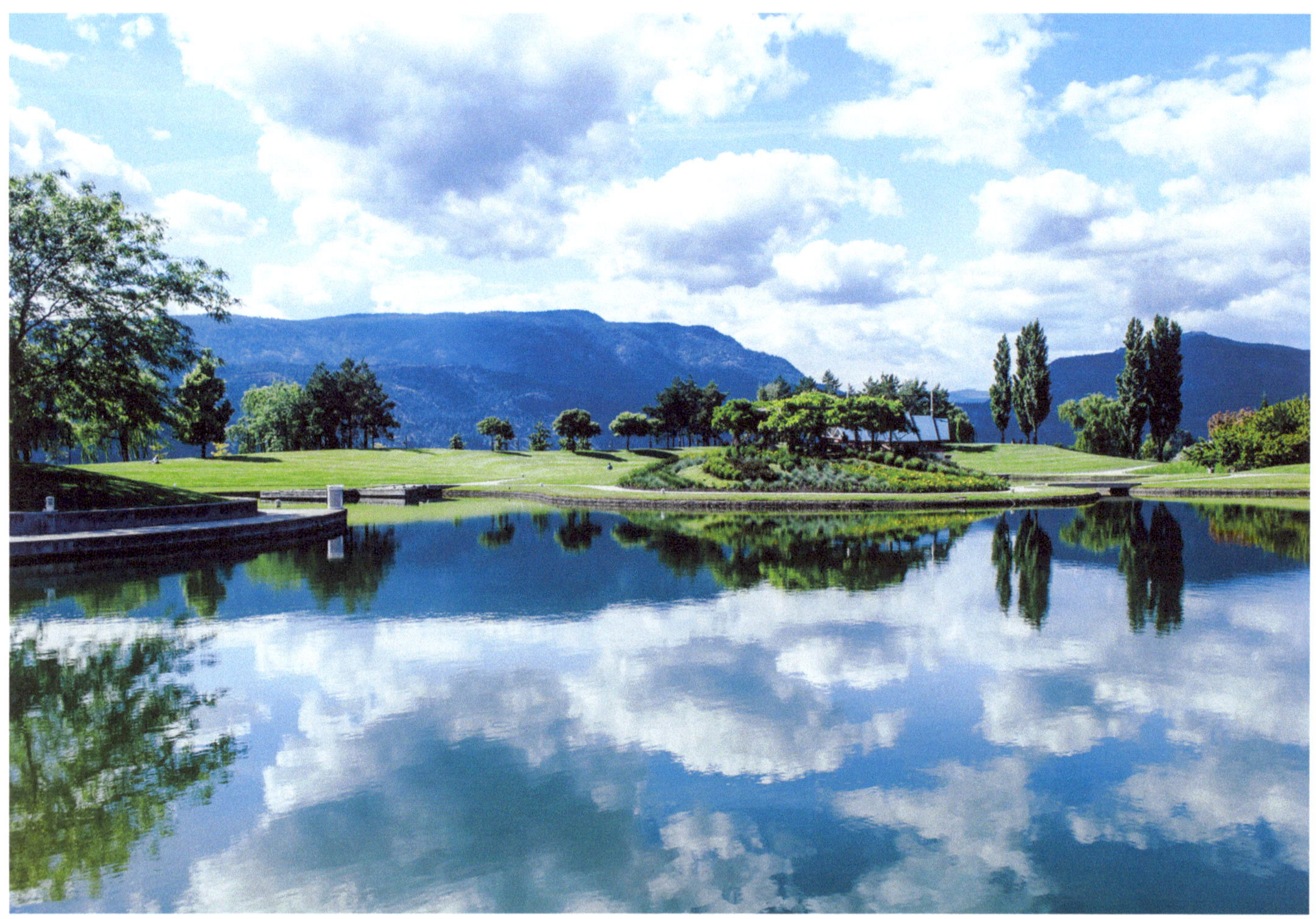

Created to give people more access to the lake, Waterfront Park is one of Kelowna's most popular destinations. In summer bands play beneath the blue roof beyond the small hill where wisteria weaves around a gazebo. Sometimes churches use the stage. Occasionally, couples exchange wedding vows there. All year around the park beckons walkers and cyclists of every age. They wander past the lagoons or walk up the small hill to the right to visit woods and waterfalls.

# A secret forest, cut with waterfalls,

lies atop a knoll in the heart of Waterfront Park. Walk along its paths, and the sound of running water blocks noise from the city that surrounds it.

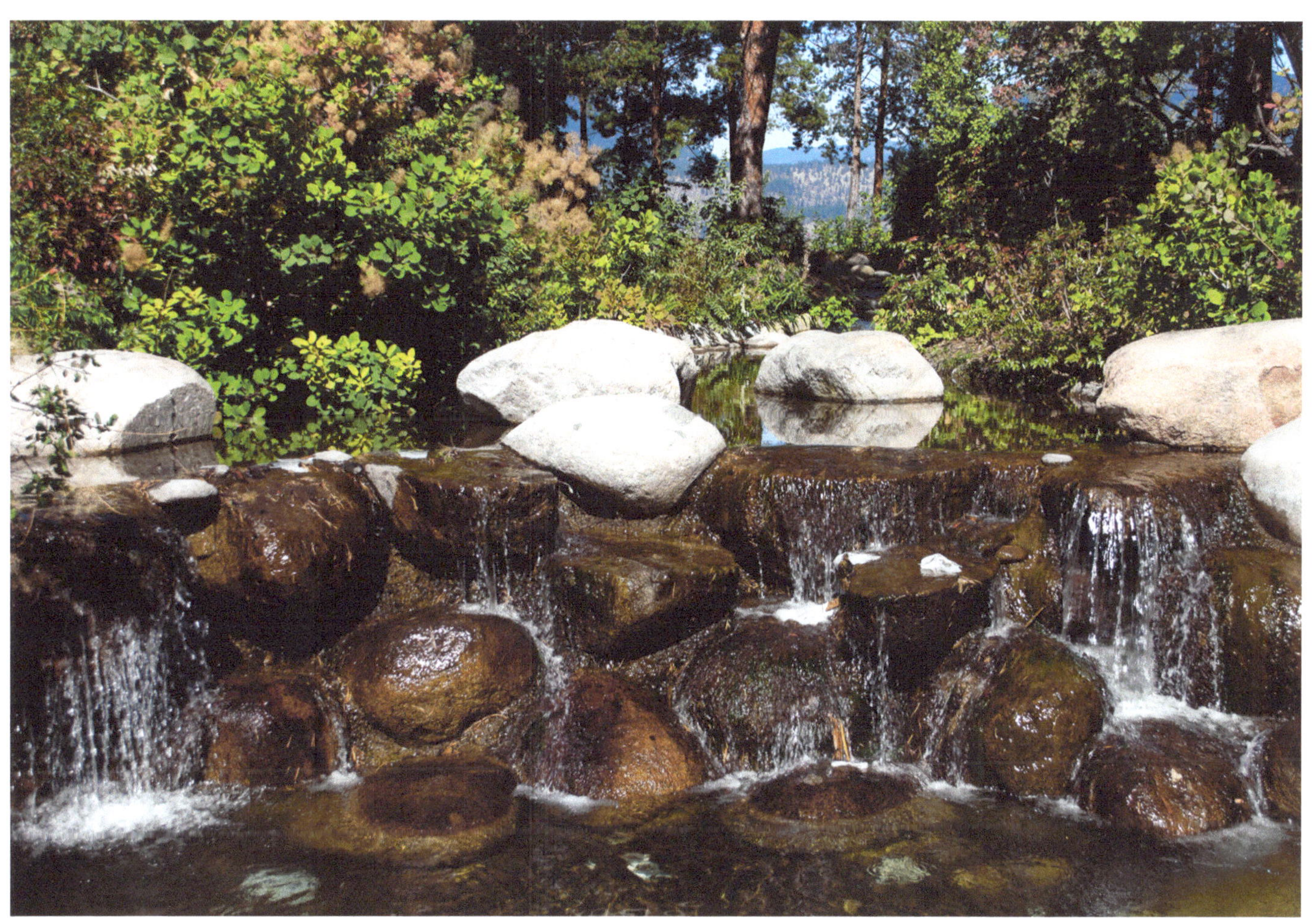

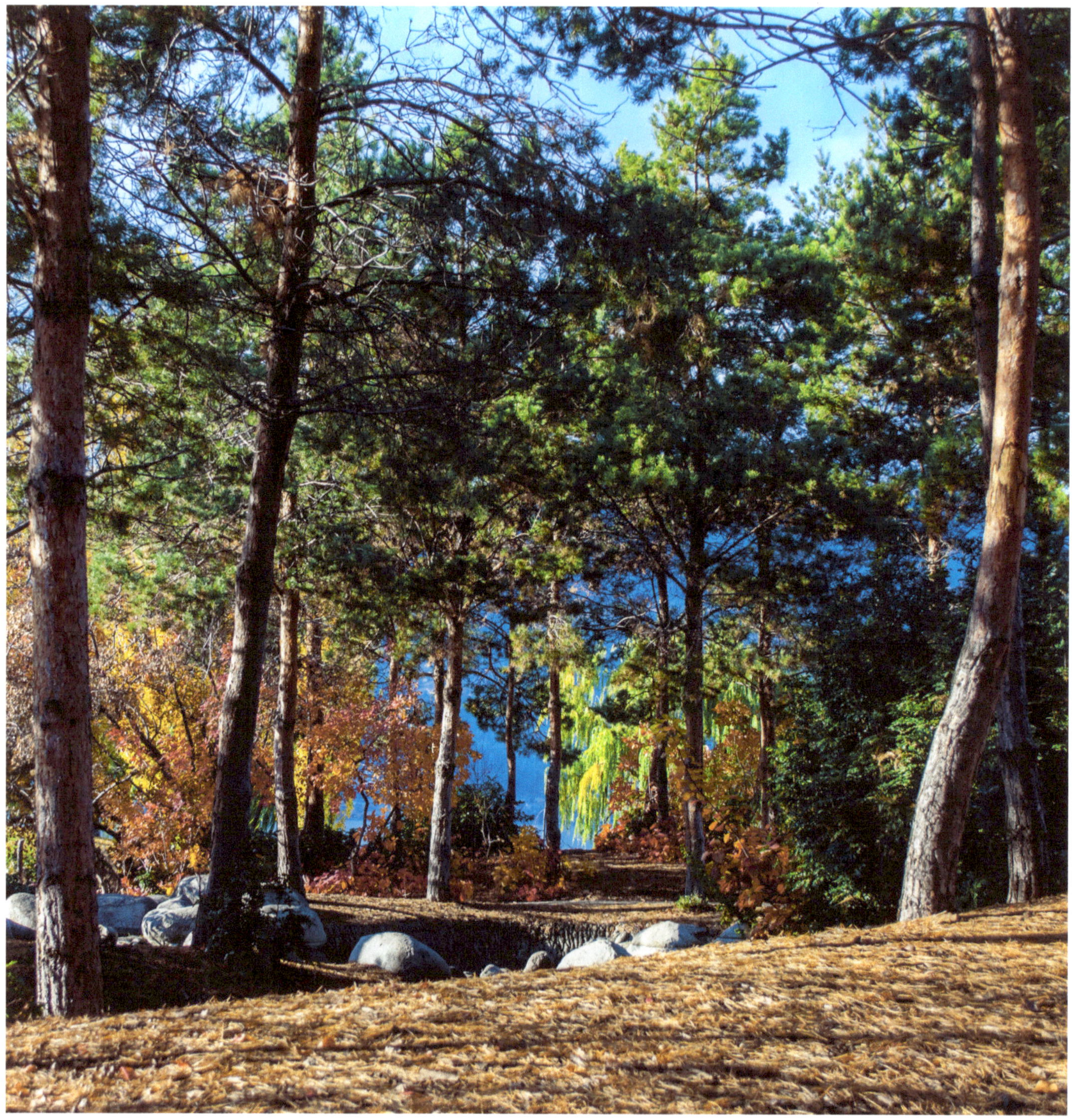

# The path leads by waterfalls

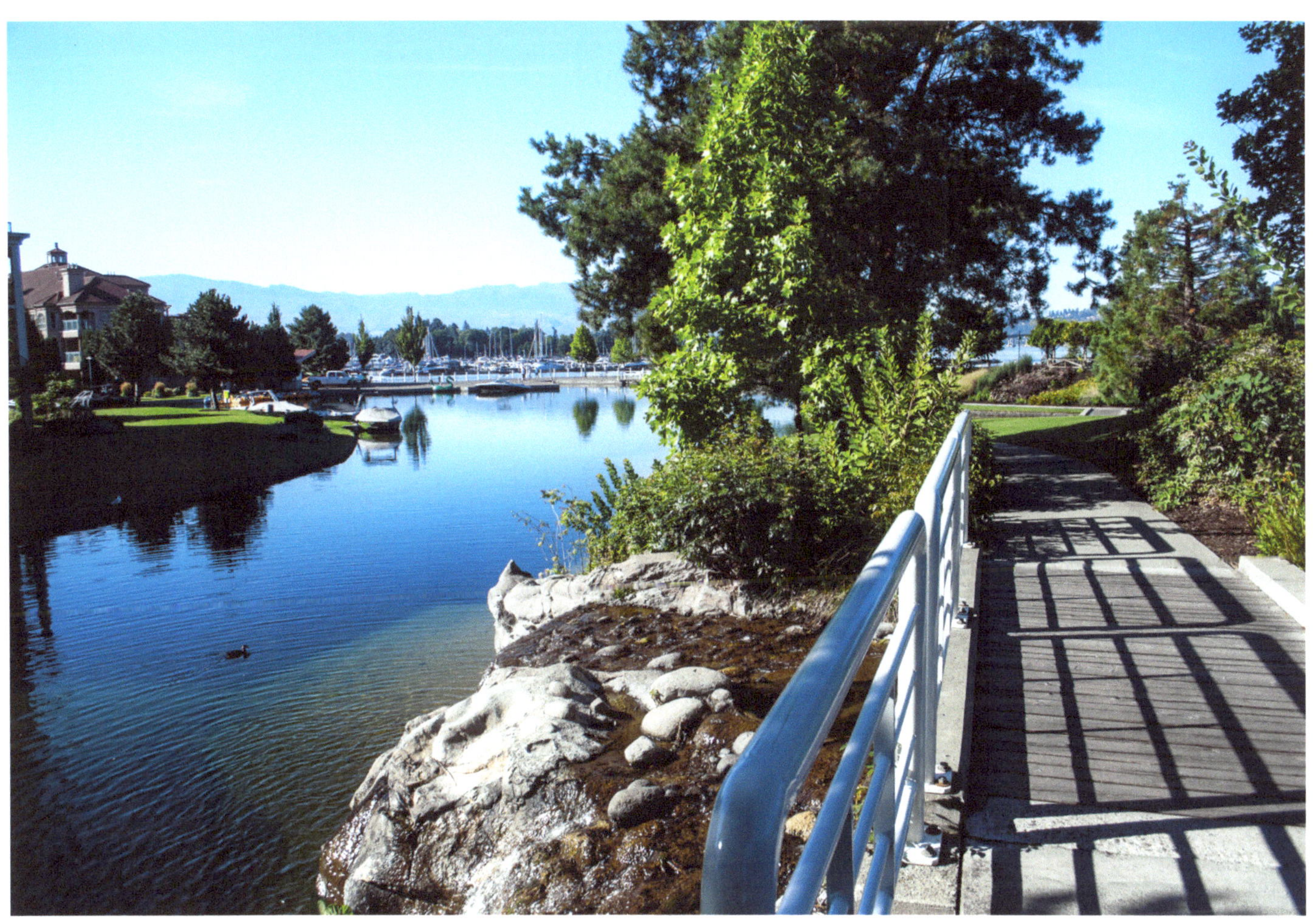

Between lagoons and woodlands, the path leads downward, toward Waterfront Park's gazebo, around to the boardwalk and beyond, to the marina.

# We live in the hug of hills

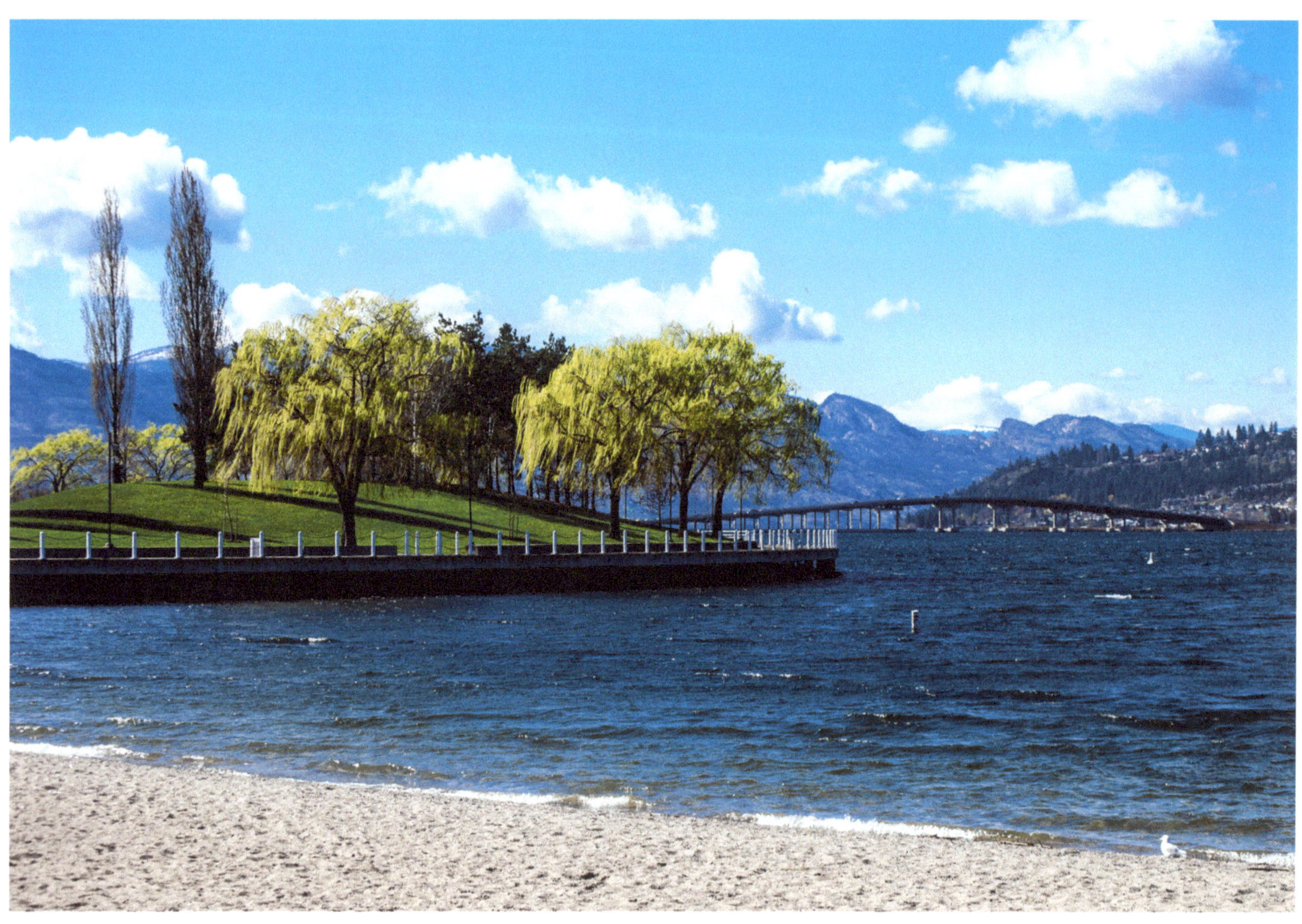

The spring green of willows and the wildness of wind whipping across the lake add drama to a walk along the beach at Tugboat Bay. The grassy knoll that edges Waterfront Park slopes down to the boardwalk along the lake. In the distance rises the graceful span of the Bennett Bridge. The slopes beyond are part of the encircling ranges of mountains. We truly do live in the hug of hills.

# some moments take our breath away

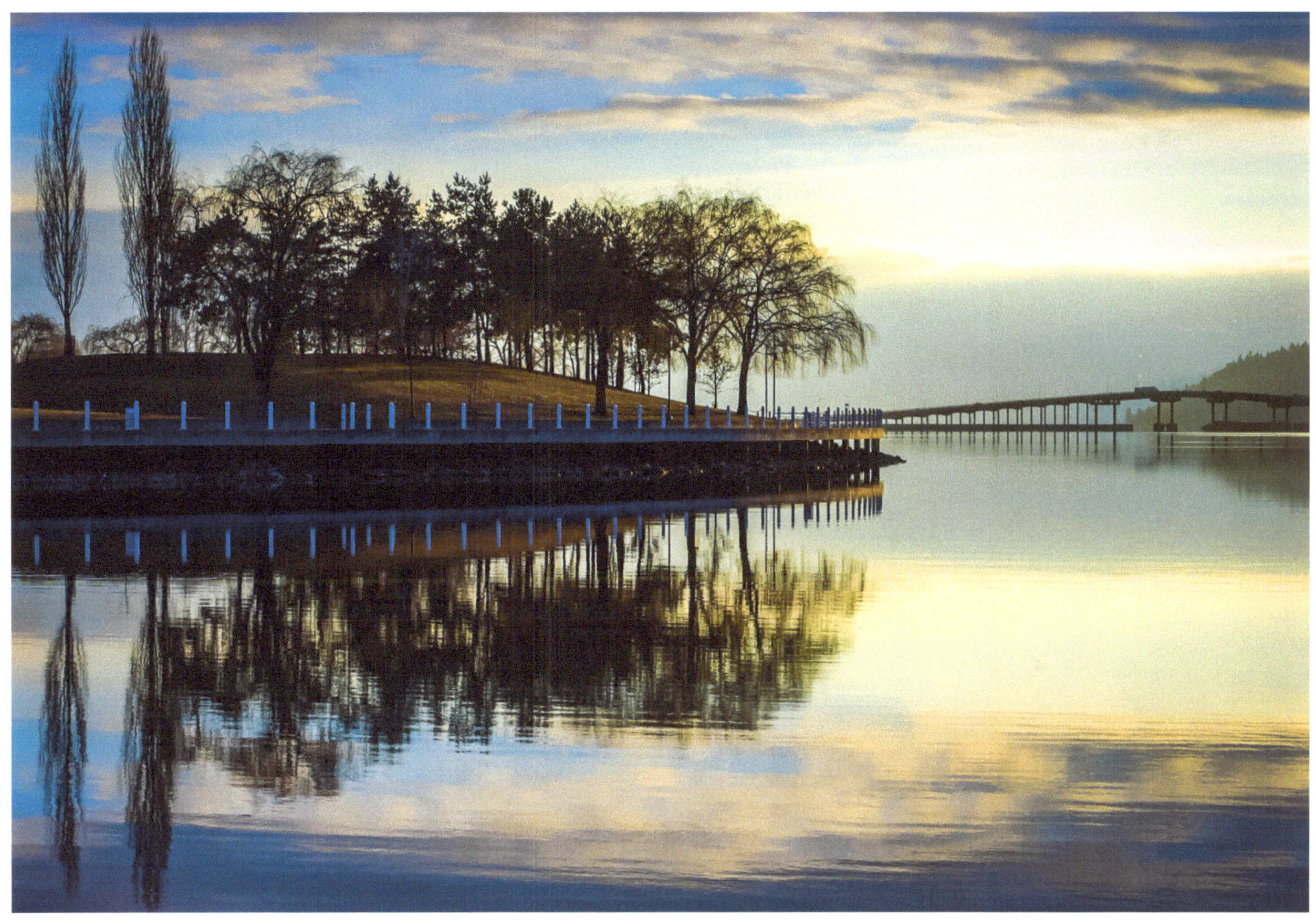

That was true on a day when only a whisper of a breeze ruffled the surface of Okanagan Lake. The sun was going down. Sky and water were painting together on their shared canvas. I had my camera with me so could capture the extraordinary light. On my computer screen, the scene was as jaw dropping as I remembered.

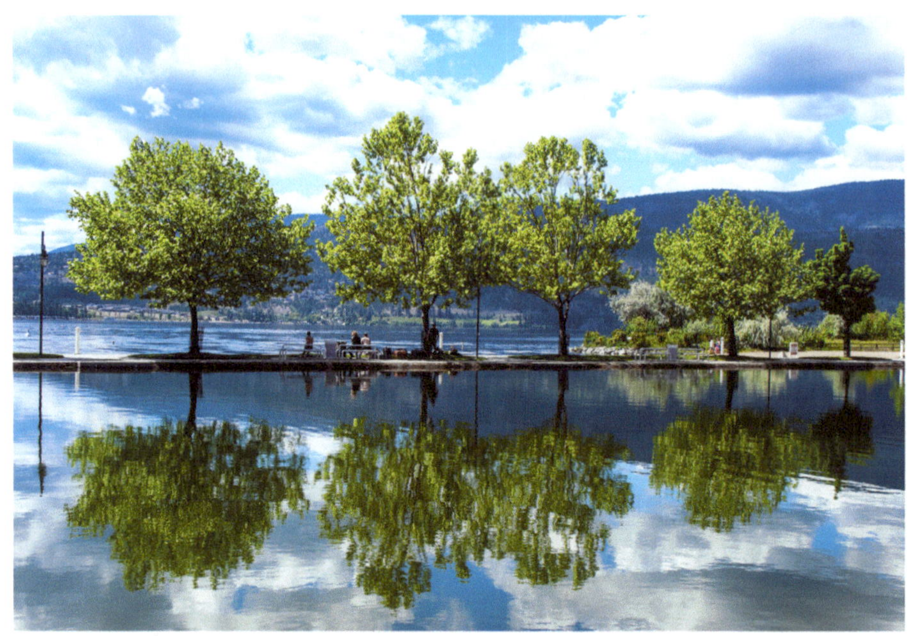

# in every season

the tree sisters cast reflections on the lagoons behind Tugboat Bay

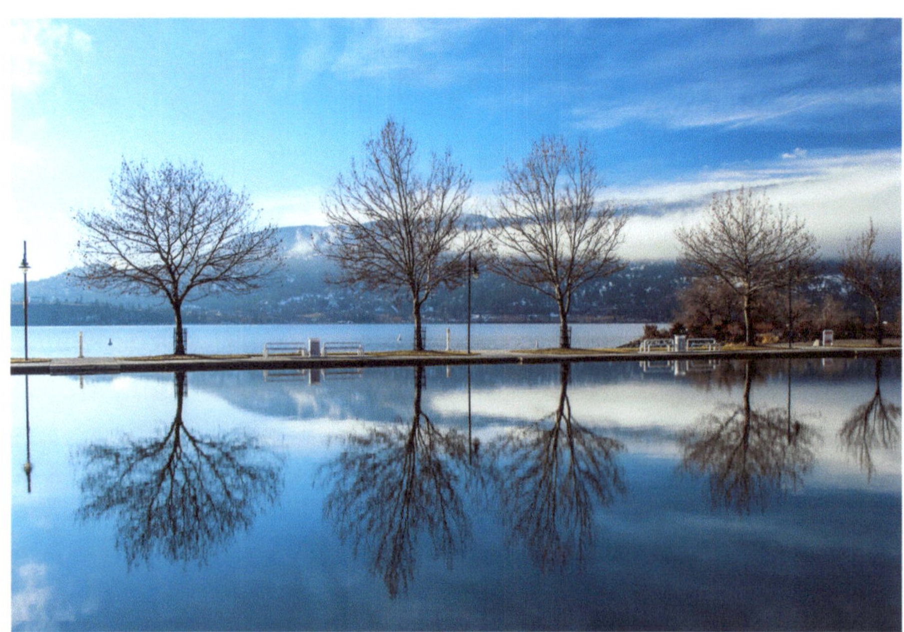

# Muskrat Love

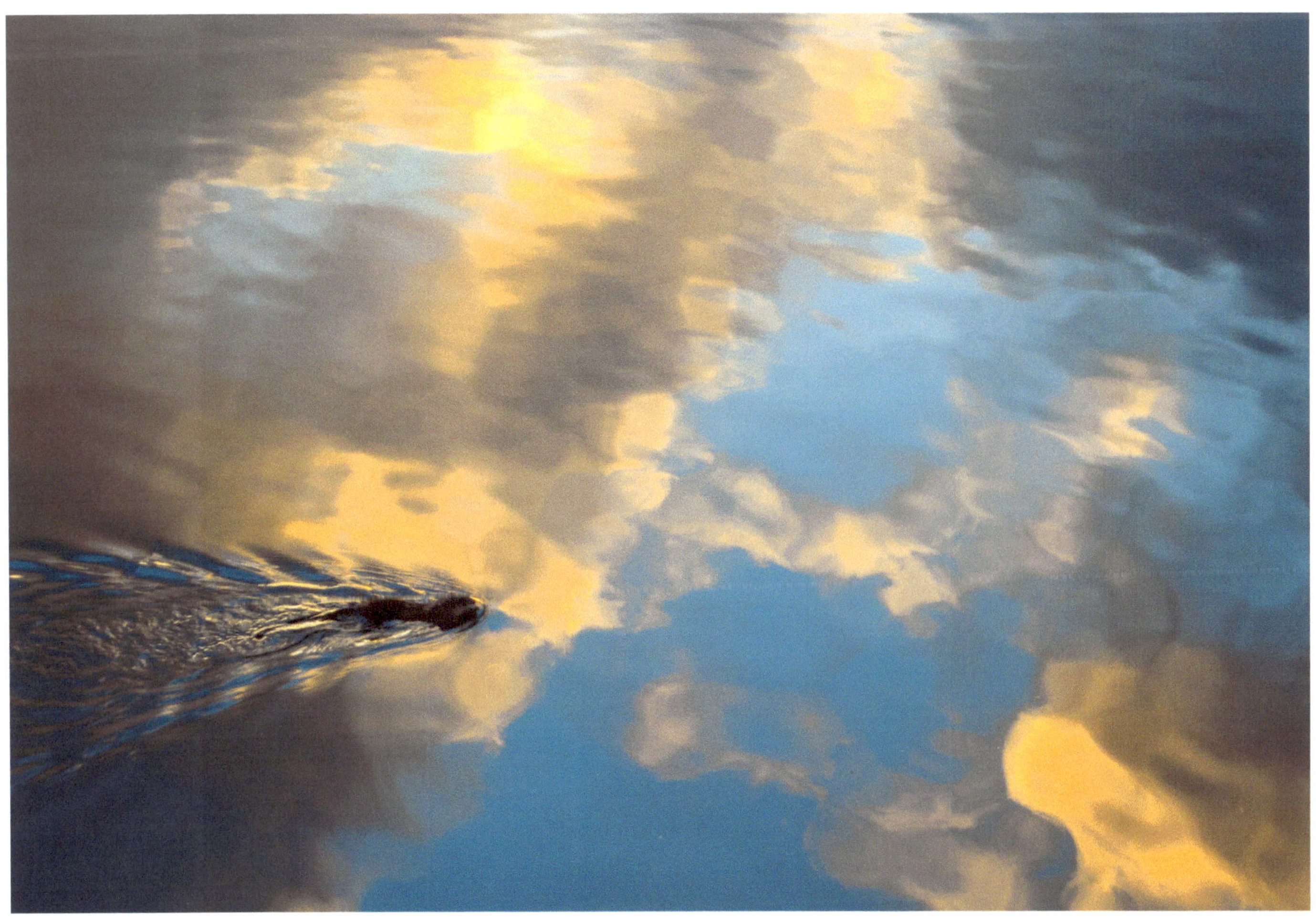

Muskrat swims alone in the Rotary Marsh, in the lagoons behind Tugboat Bay, and in Okanagan Lake. People often mistake him for a beaver, in spite of his smaller size and rat-like tail. At sunset, when he swims through cloud reflections, he looks as if he might be auditioning for the movie, *Life of Pi*. He would be no competition for the tiger, but he cuts a fine swath.

# graceful from any angle

The dolphins swim against ever-changing Okanagan skies. Rhapsody fountain, designed by Robert Dow Reid, has become a beloved Kelowna icon since its creation in 1993.

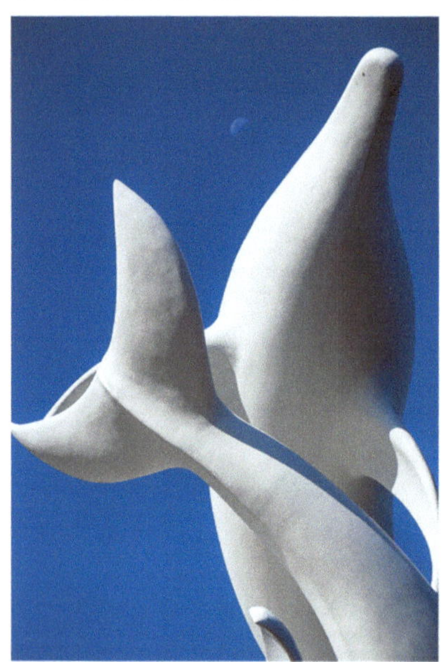

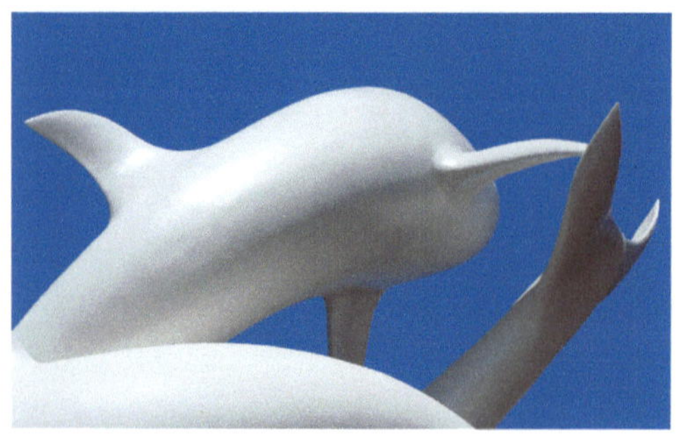

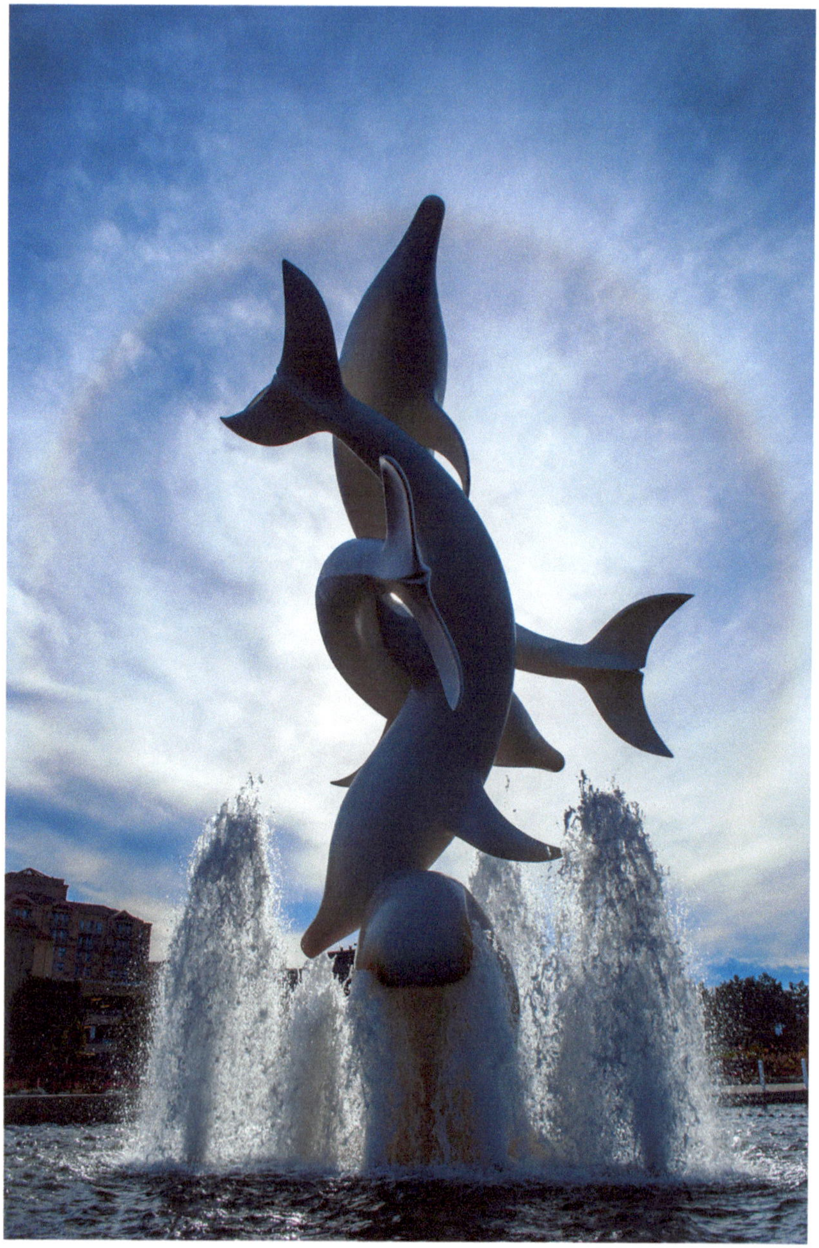

# crashing economies & marmots

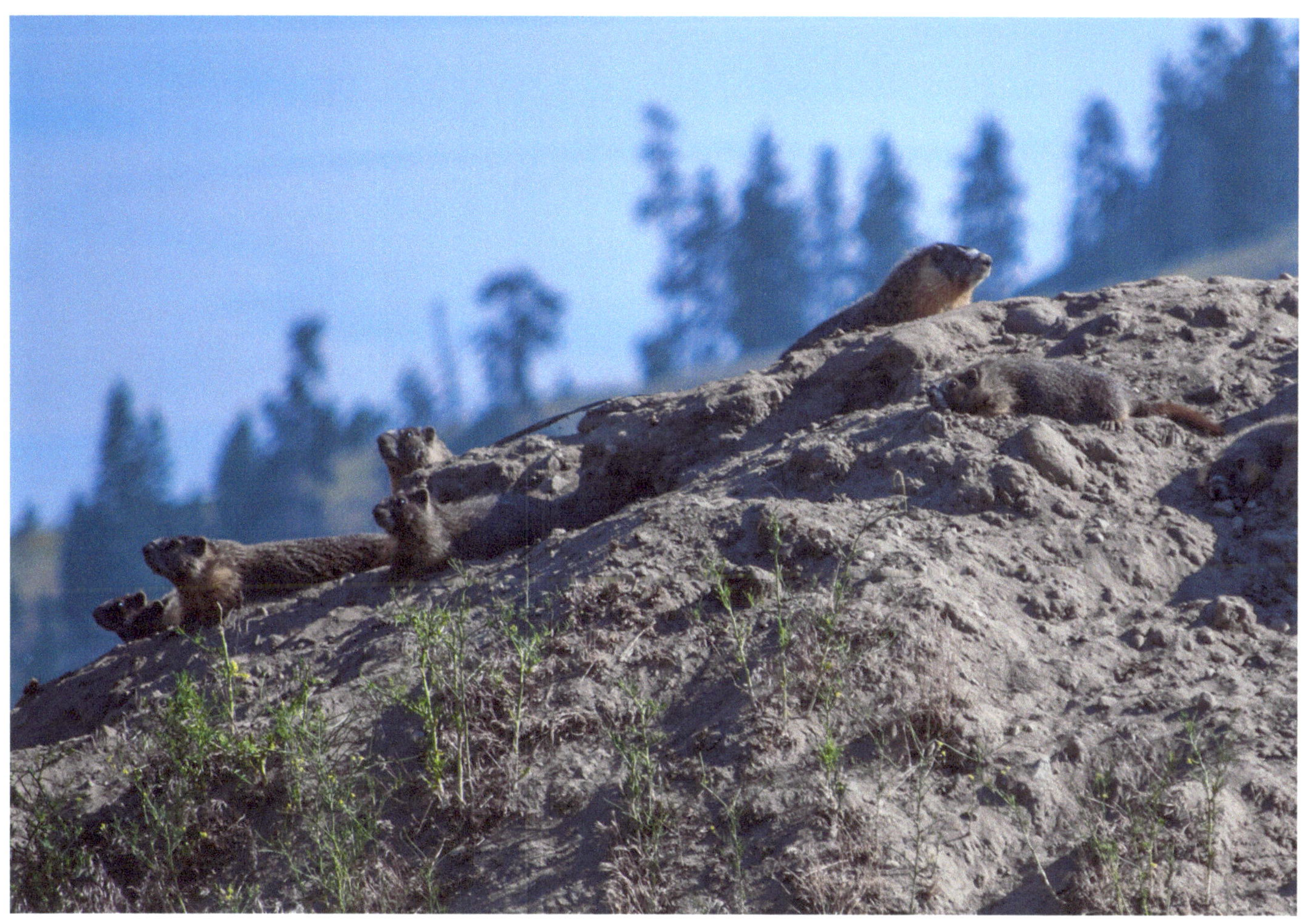

During the global crash of 2008, construction halted on two major condominium developments on Sunset Drive, leaving behind mounds of dirt. It was not long before marmots created their own housing complex. The area was ideal for marmot families. With humans fenced out of the site, they had free rein.

# The Okanagan is not always sunny

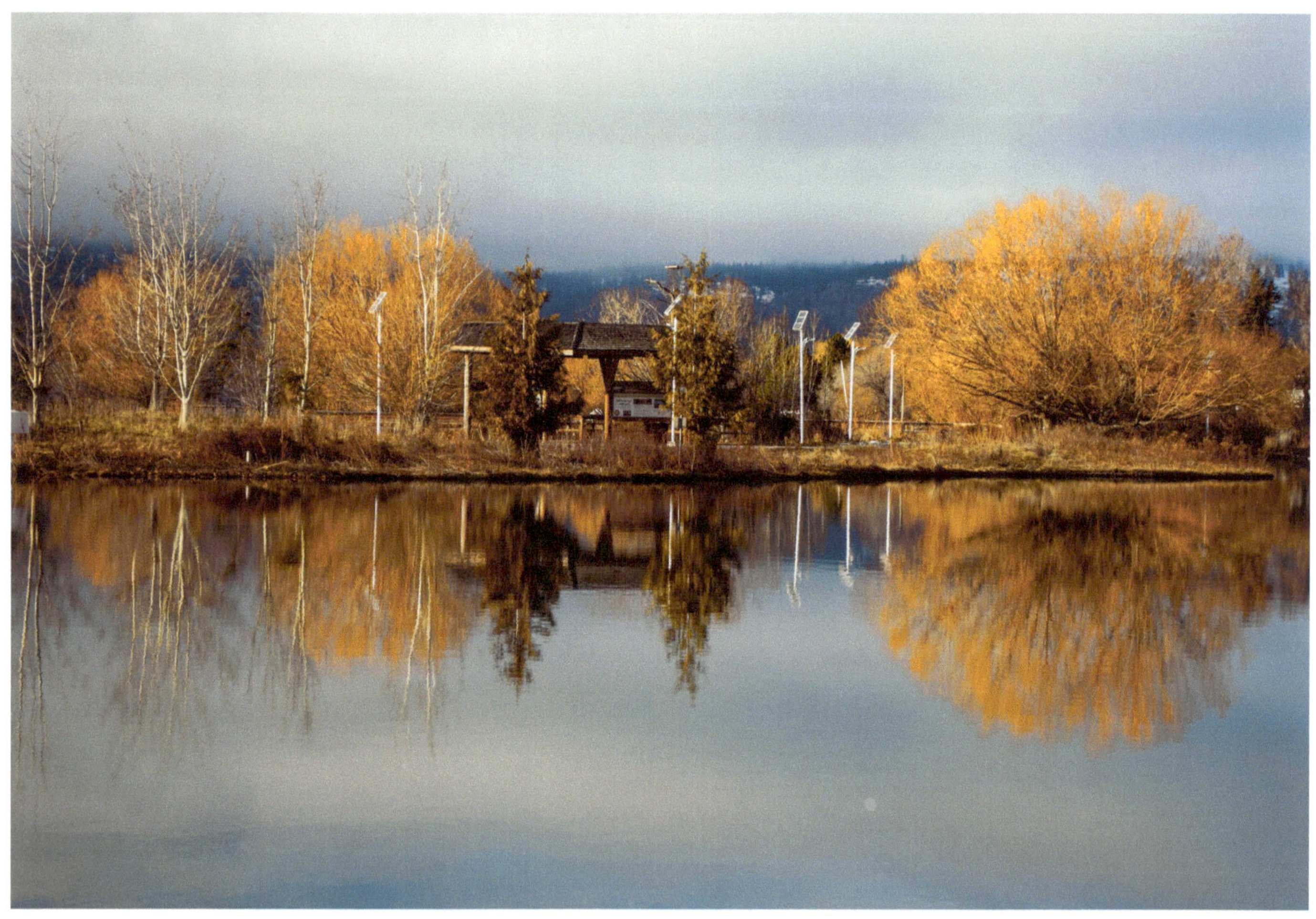

When I moved here, I was surprised to learn the sunny Okanagan can turn dreary when winter clouds clamp down over the valley. Still, winter here is easy, and when the clouds part just enough to let through a shaft of light, the lowering sun turns willow limbs into delicate arms of pure gold.

# new inukshuks every day

They appeared among the rocks that line a point of land that stretches into Okanagan Lake, on the south edge of Rotary Marsh. Others appeared near the boat dock by Rose's Pub. It was mid-winter of 2016. A young man made it his art and his meditation to construct new ones each day. Then he was gone. The inukshuks disappeared. But the memory of their whimsical forms remains.

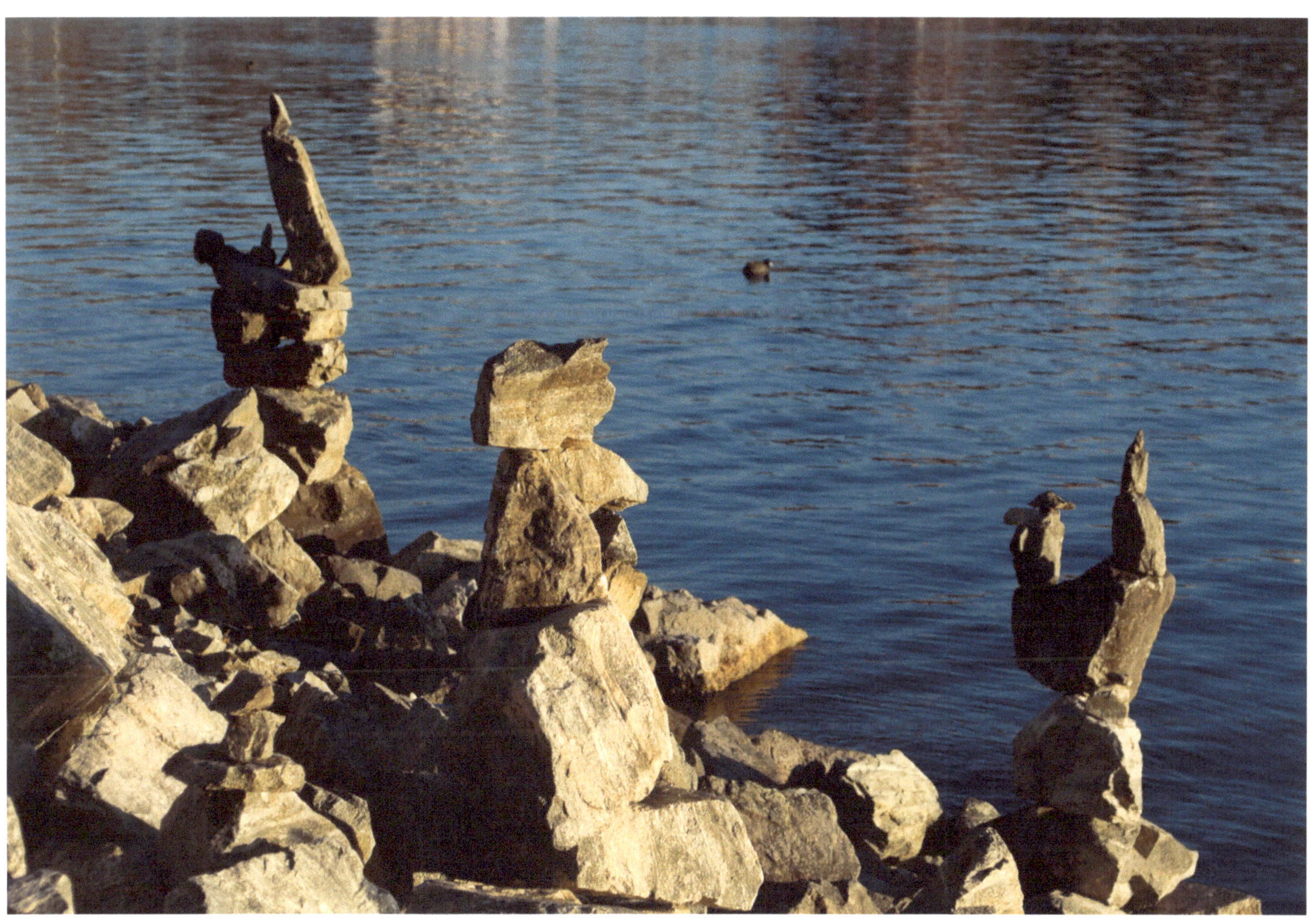

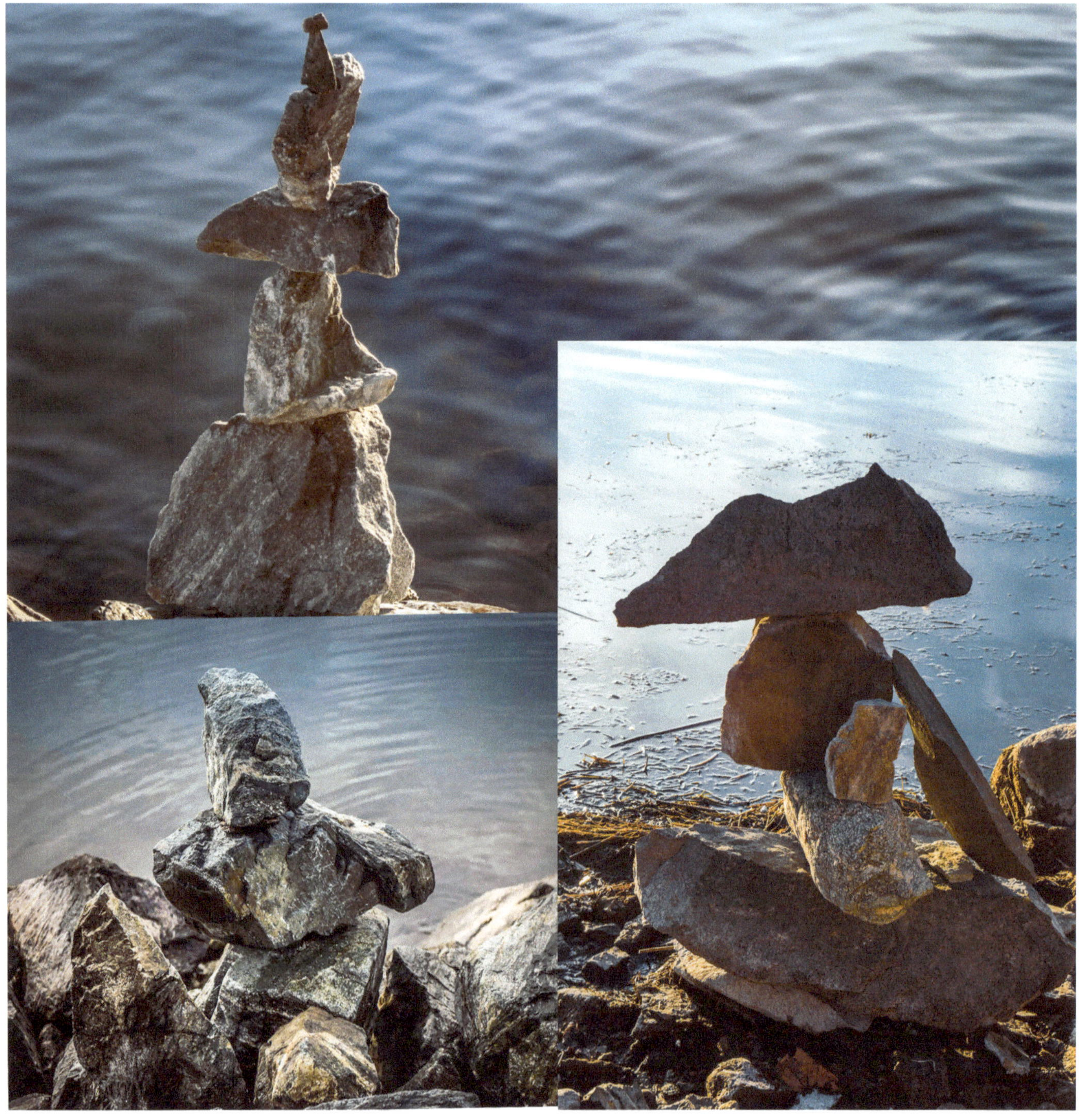

# His heart was sad

and so he tied an eagle feather to a twig at the edge of the marsh. He sang a death song, to send his brother's

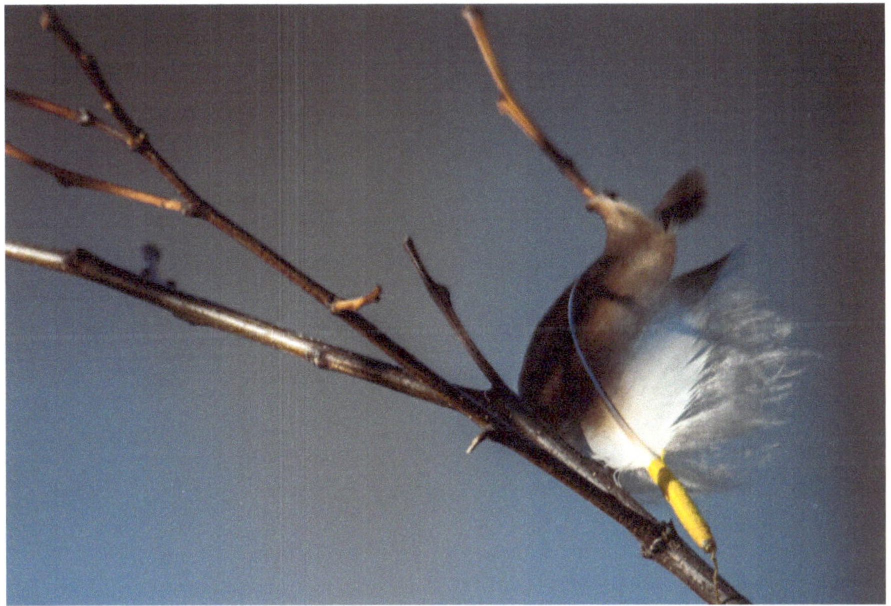

troubled spirit to its final rest. The haunting melody drew me to him. His wife asked me to stay. When he emerged from the woods, he told me the story, then invited me to unburden my own sore heart. No one ever bothered the feather. It lifted my spirit for years.

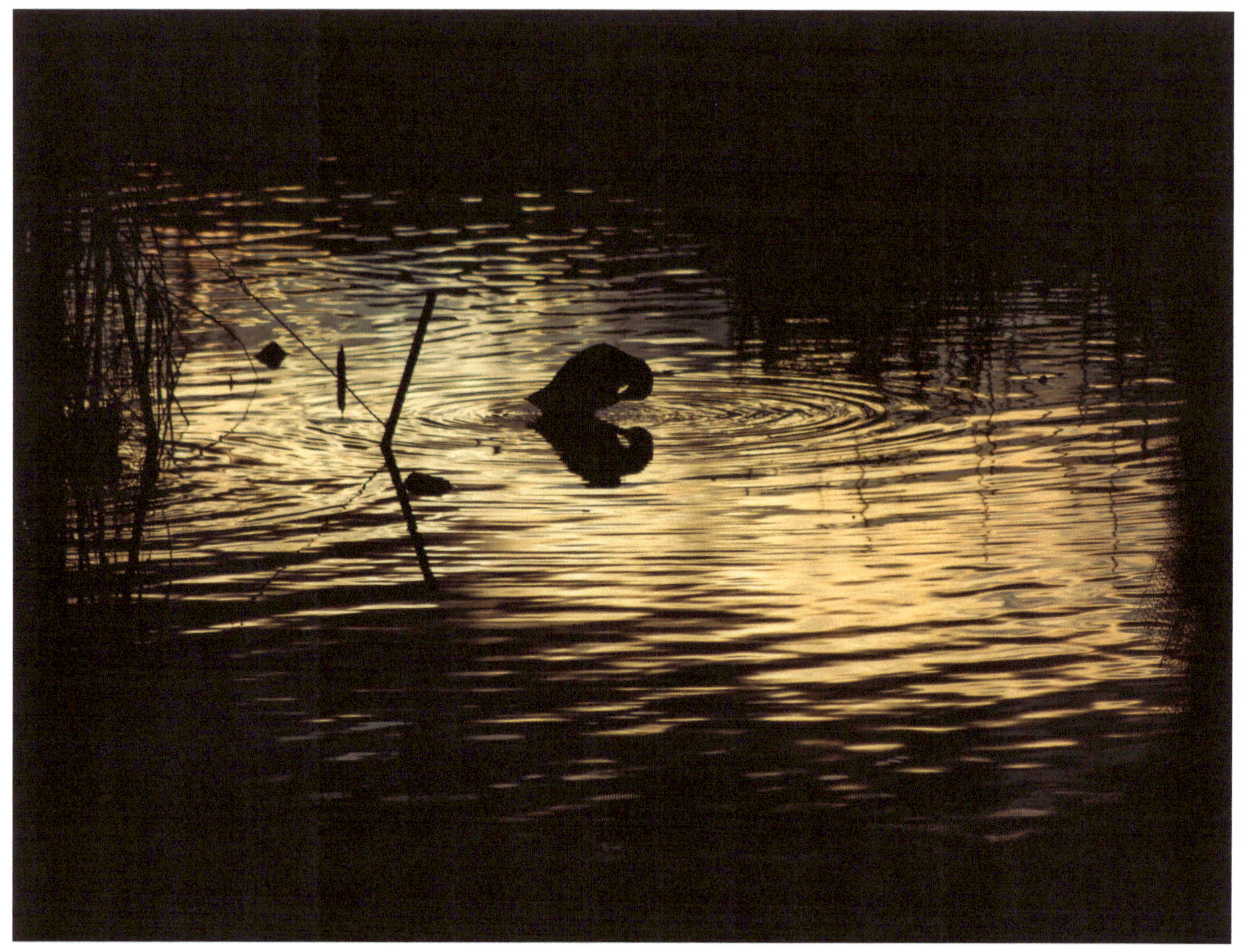

# untroubled by humans who stop and stare,

a mallard hen grooms her feathers in the light of a setting sun. Her reflection forms a sideways heart, on the water and in the spirits of those who watch.

# Lean on me

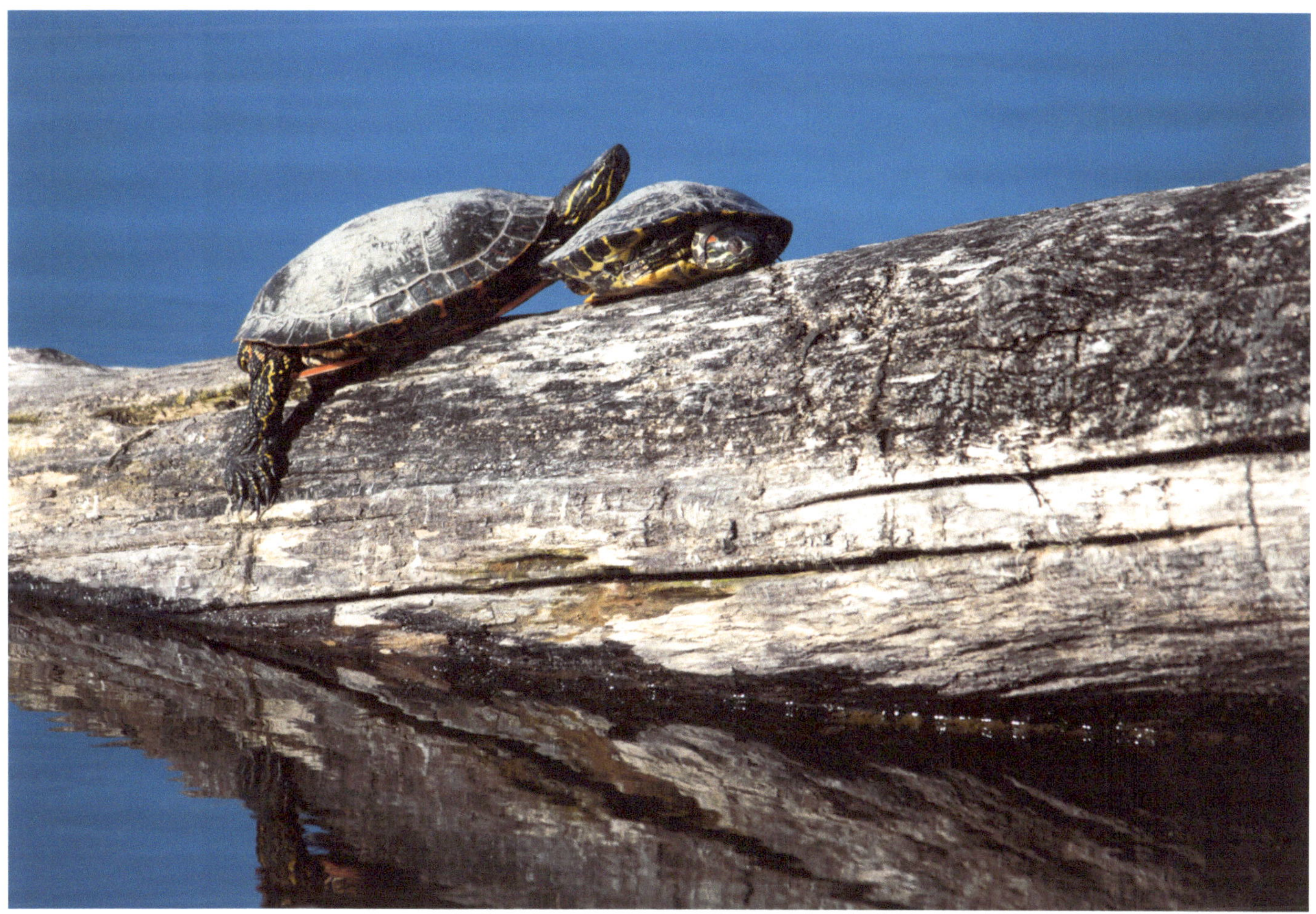

When the weather is warm and sunny, the marsh turtles emerge from their muddy, watery home to warm themselves on the logs. The native, western painted turtles share space with their invader cousins, the red-eared sliders. The alliance appears peaceful, but the native species has trouble competing with the sliders. That is not apparent here, where the slider acts as a head rest for a larger painted turtle.

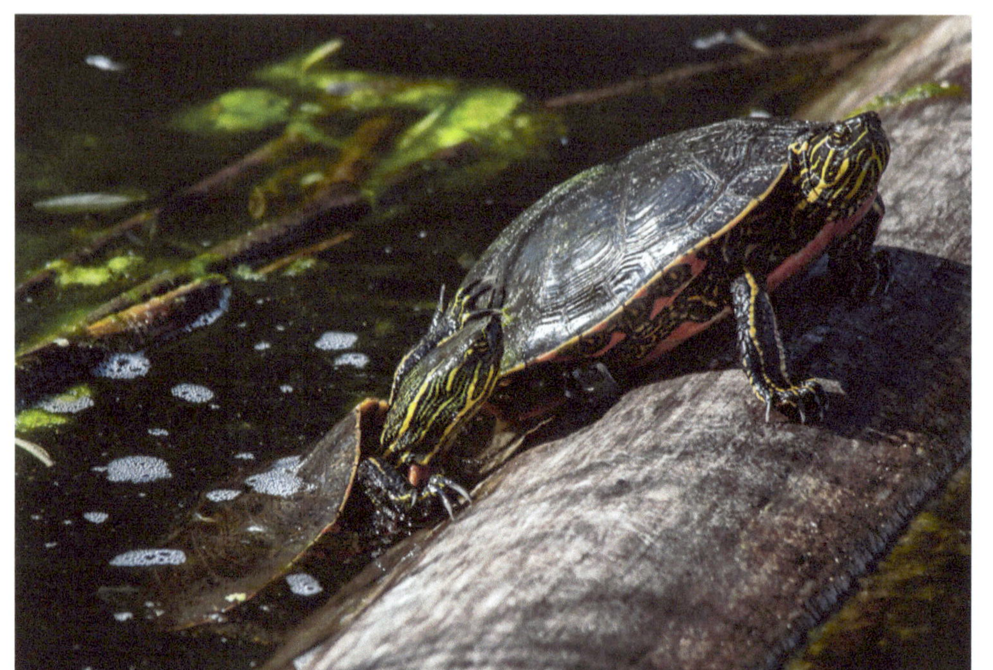

western
painted
turtles

Red-
eared
slider

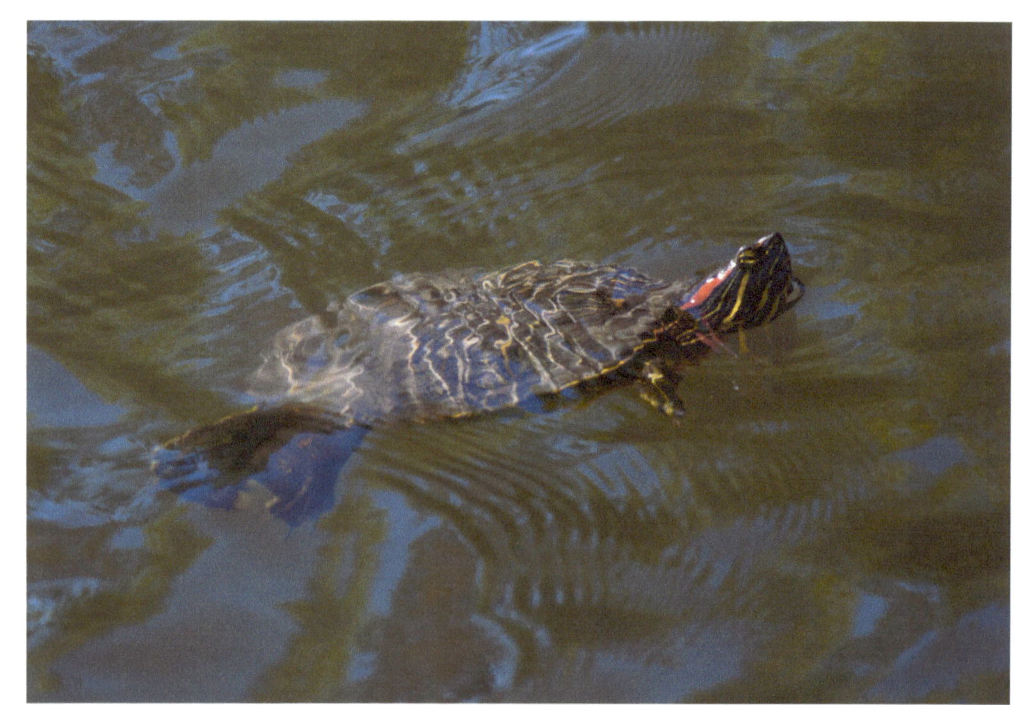

# A Great Blue Heron

stands still and alert, patiently watching for the silvery flash of young carp. He ignores the small head of a turtle swimming his way. With only a handful of favourite fishing perches in the marsh, he is easy to spot when he stops by for dinner.

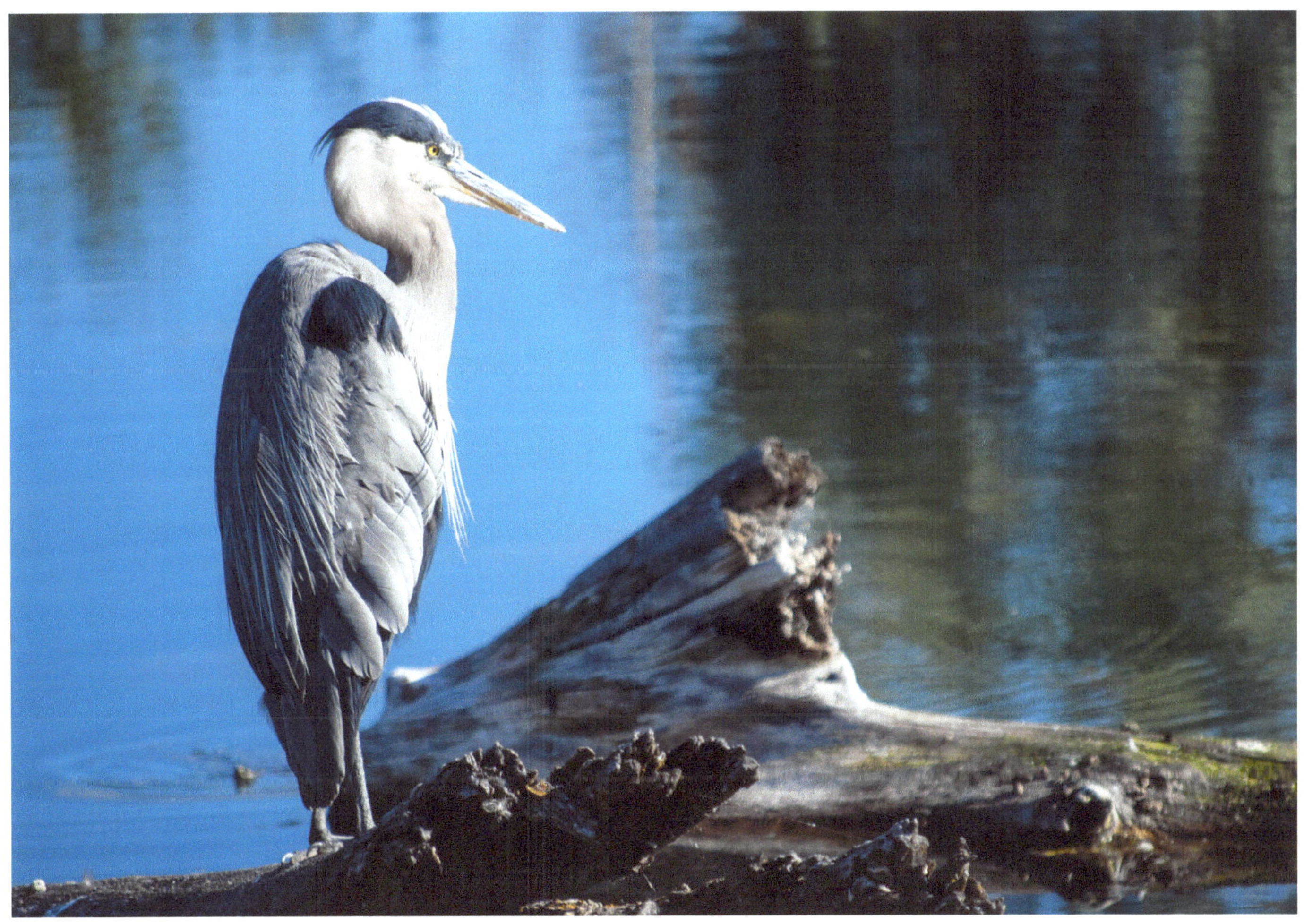

# The doe is a regular visitor

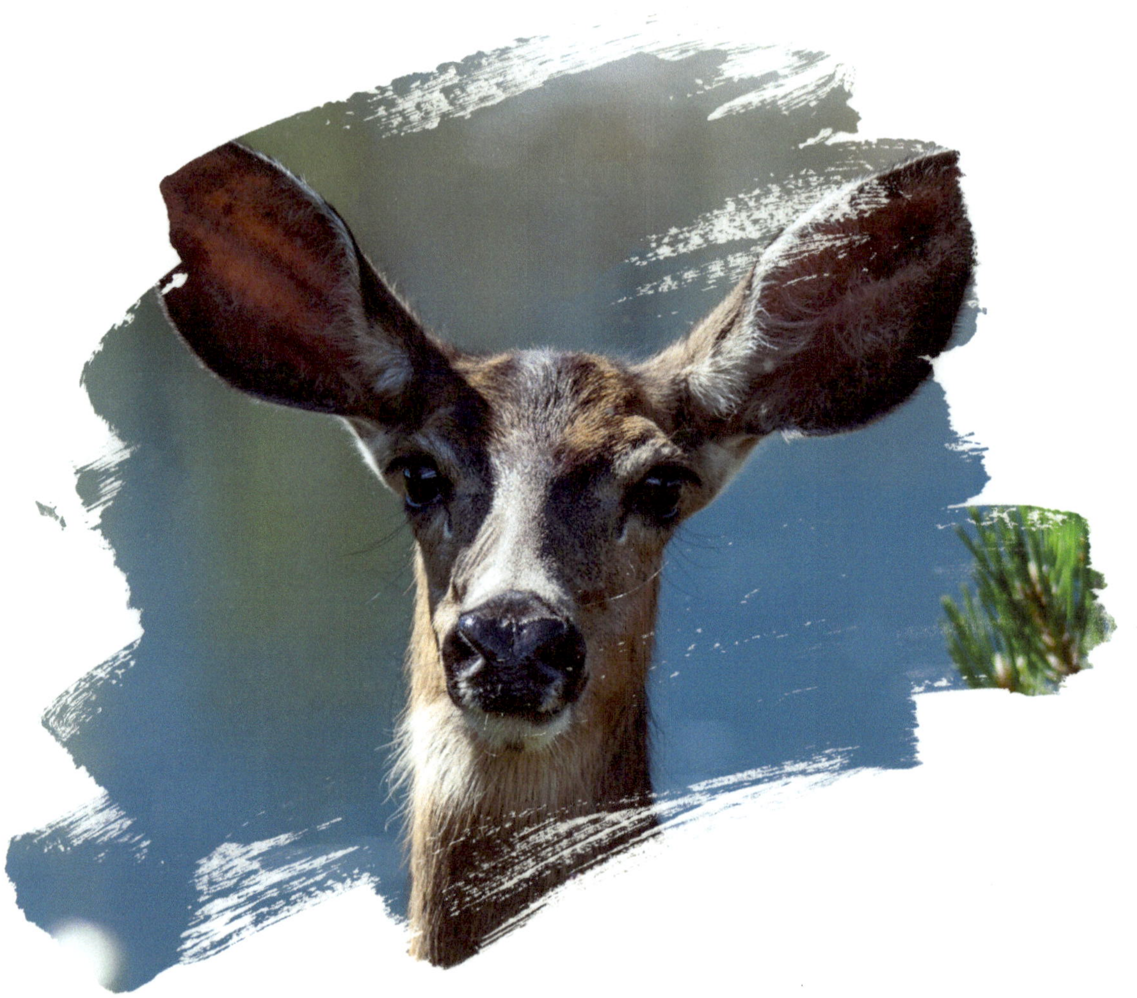

She comes to the marsh, sometimes alone, sometimes with fawns or a handsome buck. Oh, wait, I am the visitor. She is a wild relative who gazes at me, alert, ready to flee, yet not truly afraid. She has known too many humans in her life to take us overly seriously. She regards us as a necessary nuisance in her pursuit of a good meal.

# The friendly mallard

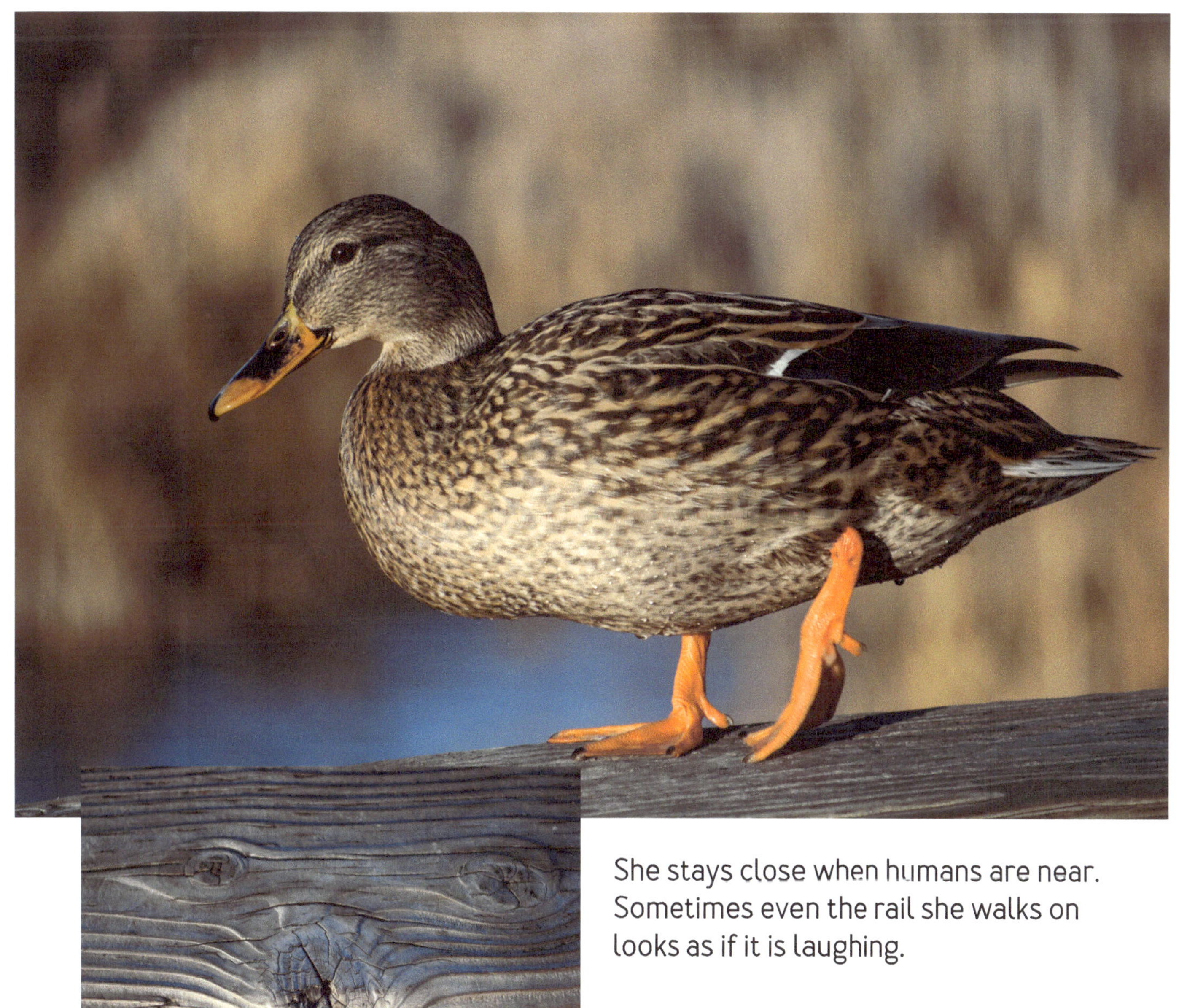

She stays close when humans are near. Sometimes even the rail she walks on looks as if it is laughing.

# Majestic Ospreys

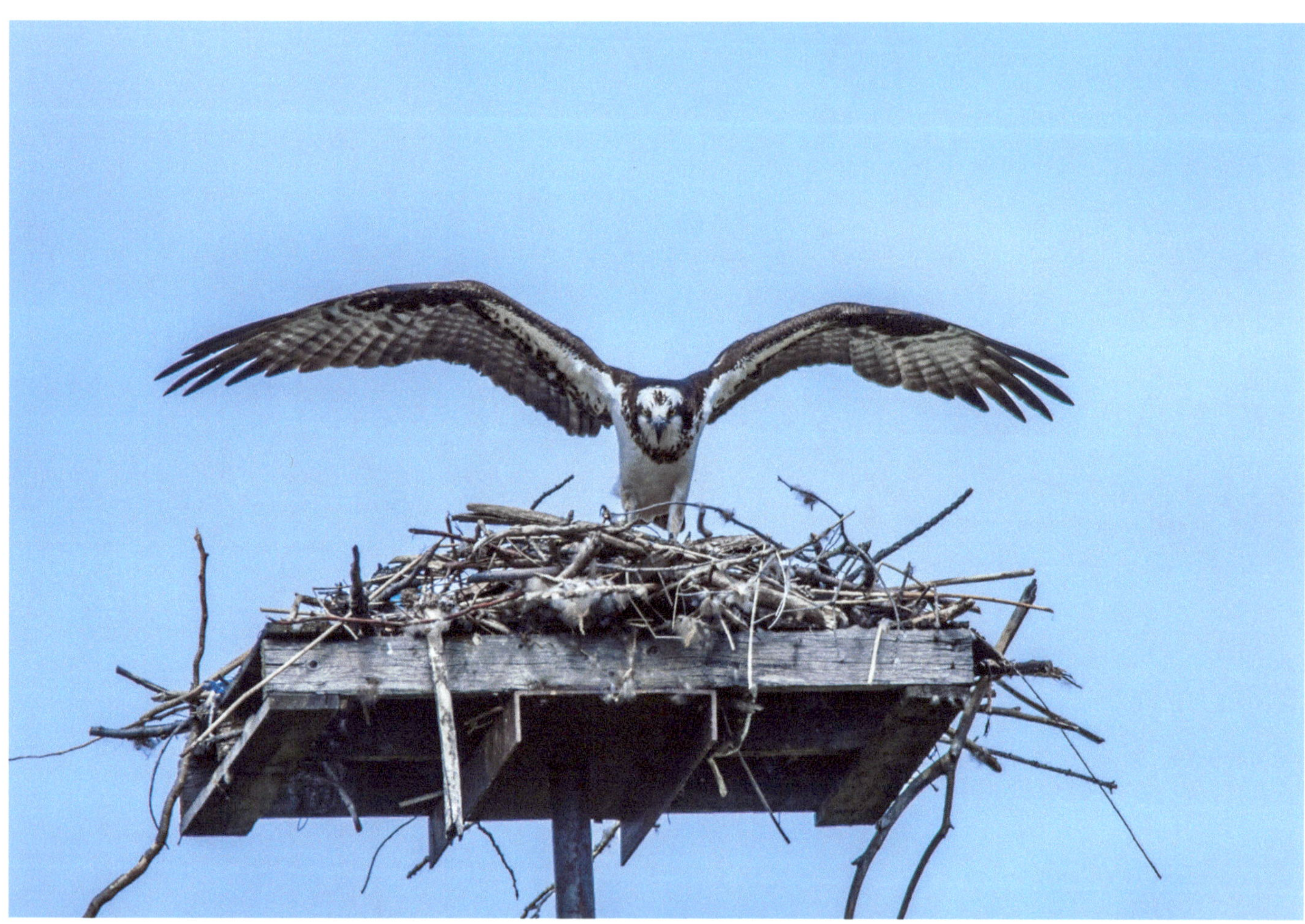

The ospreys raise a family here each summer. Atop their high platform, they hatch one or two chicks. All summer we watch the youngsters grow, stretch their wings, and flap madly. Then one mysterious day, they know they are ready. They feel the wind beneath their wings, and, for the first time, they trust it to hold them.

# One determined goose & her six chicks

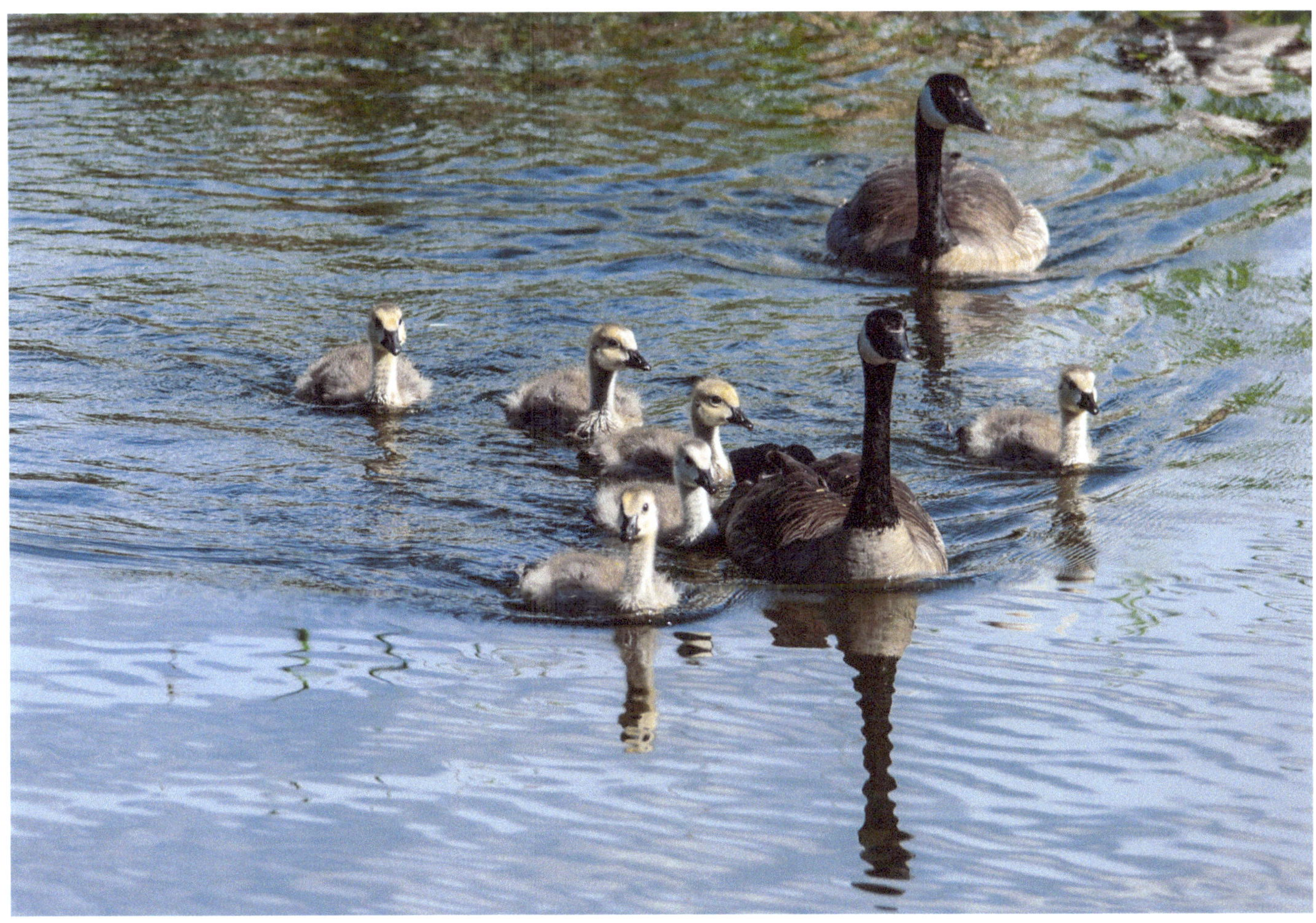

She laid her eggs on the osprey nest, high above the ground. For weeks I watched her and her loyal mate. Knowing the goslings would need to reach food and water as soon as they hatched, I worried. I feared they would plummet to their death. The ospreys came. The goose refused to move. For two weeks the osprey pair flew around looking for a new home. Then the goose eggs hatched. Six fuzzy chicks and their mother jumped off the nest...and survived. Within an hour, the ospreys were back, tidying their nest and preparing to start a new family. Nature is grand.

# cattails - a lovely challenge

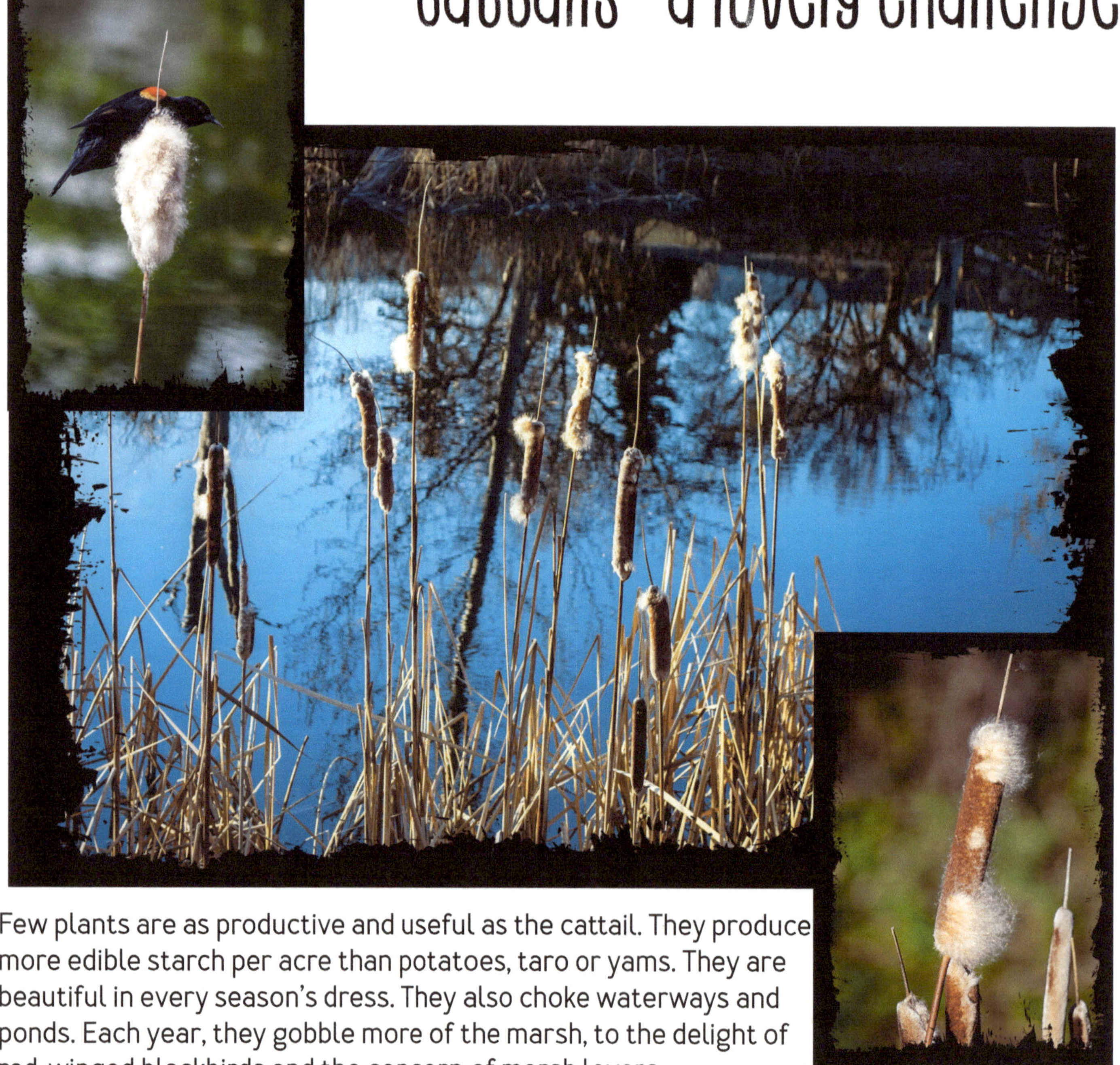

Few plants are as productive and useful as the cattail. They produce more edible starch per acre than potatoes, taro or yams. They are beautiful in every season's dress. They also choke waterways and ponds. Each year, they gobble more of the marsh, to the delight of red-winged blackbirds and the concern of marsh lovers.

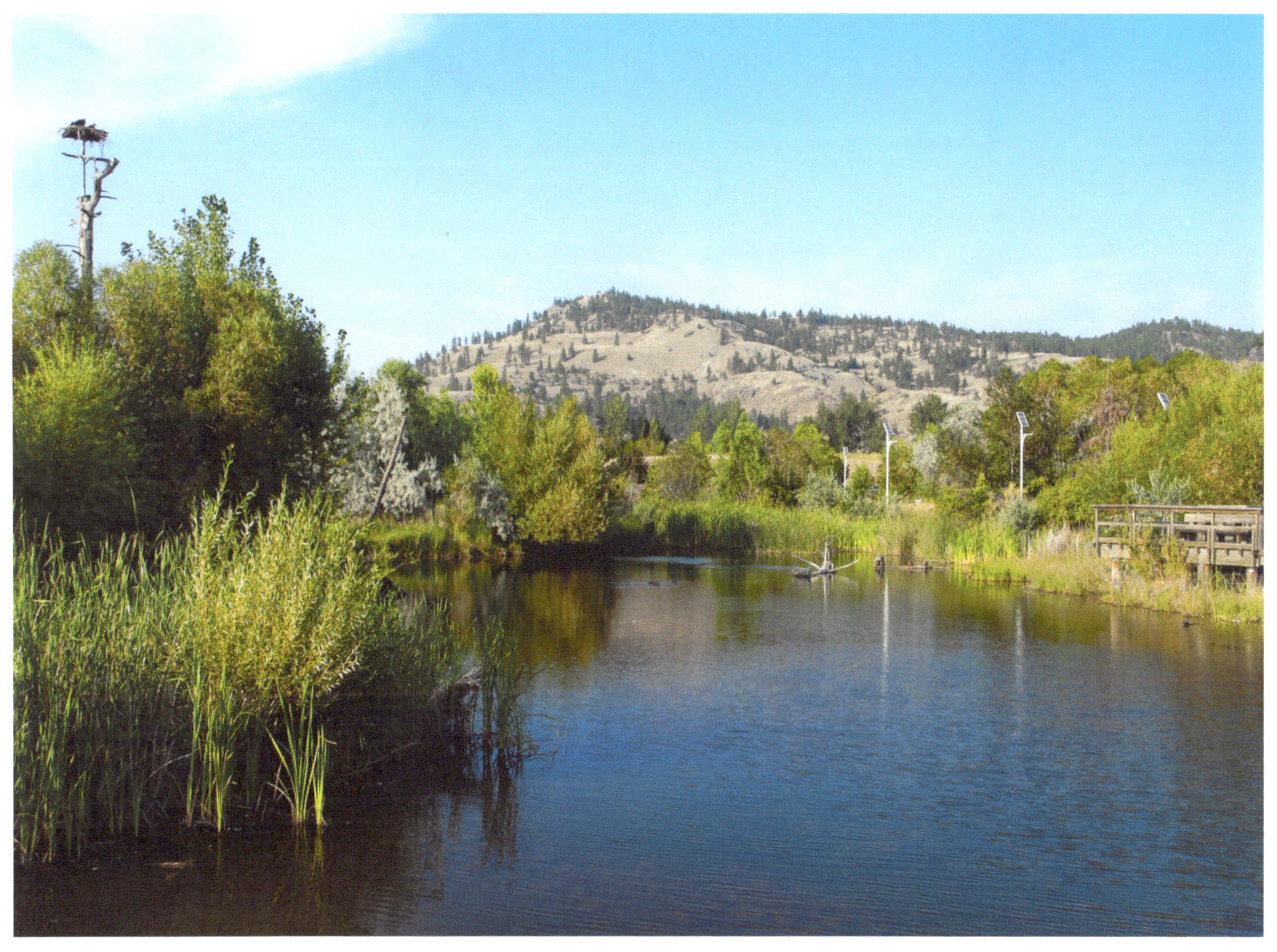

# The Slopes of Knox Mountain

line the horizon as we walk along the boardwalk that leads from Rotary Marsh, across a bridge, to Sunset Drive. Most of the year, the slopes are covered with dry grass. The grass is green for only a brief time in spring, but pines always form a patchy green carpet along the sides and tops of the hills. After a brief foray along Brandt's Creek, we'll head that way.

# Brandt's Creek Linear Walkway

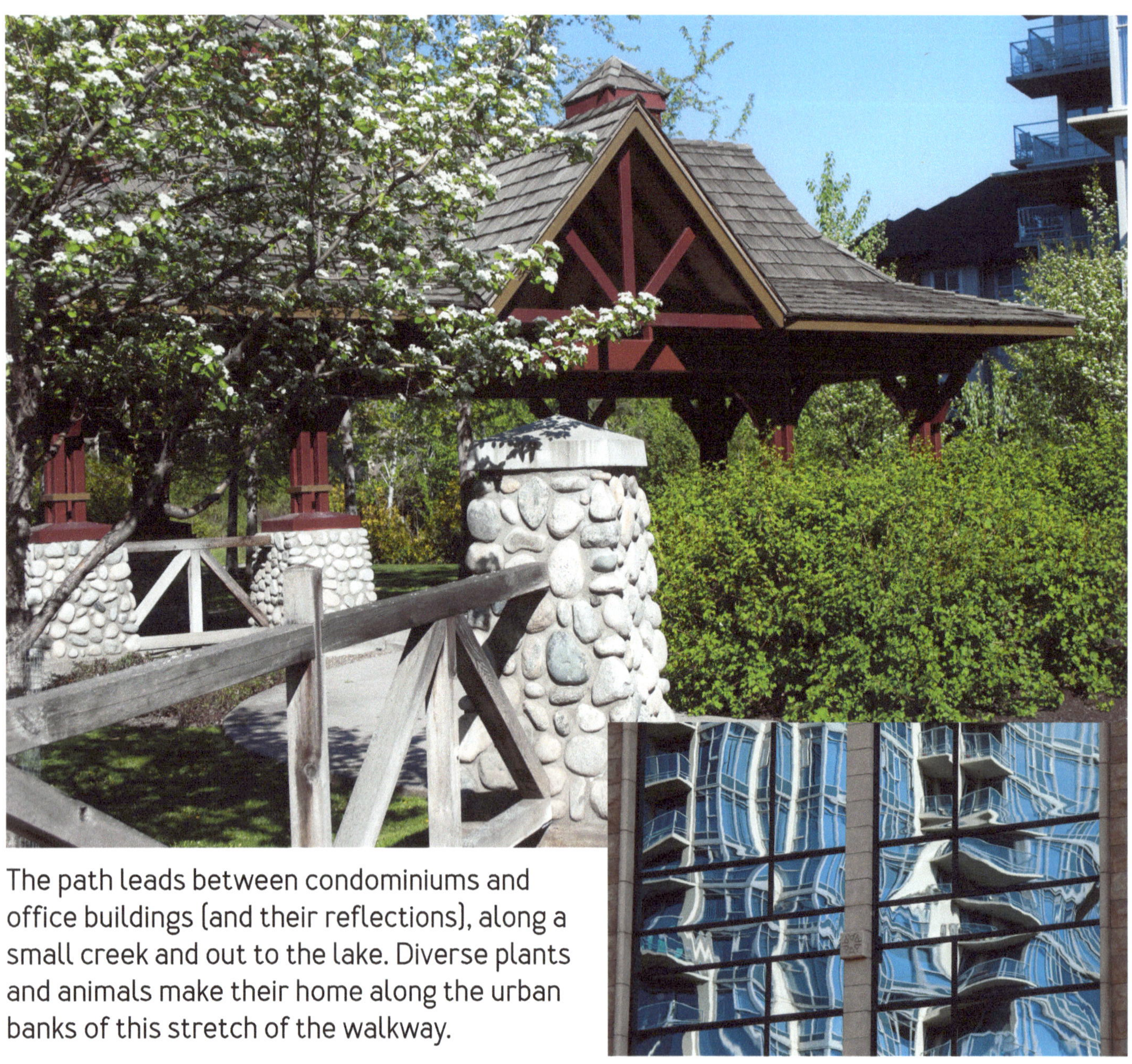

The path leads between condominiums and office buildings (and their reflections), along a small creek and out to the lake. Diverse plants and animals make their home along the urban banks of this stretch of the walkway.

# oregon grape, pines, lilacs & more line the path

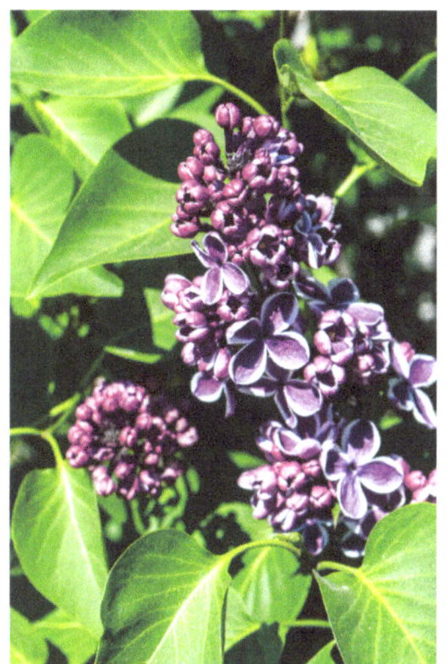

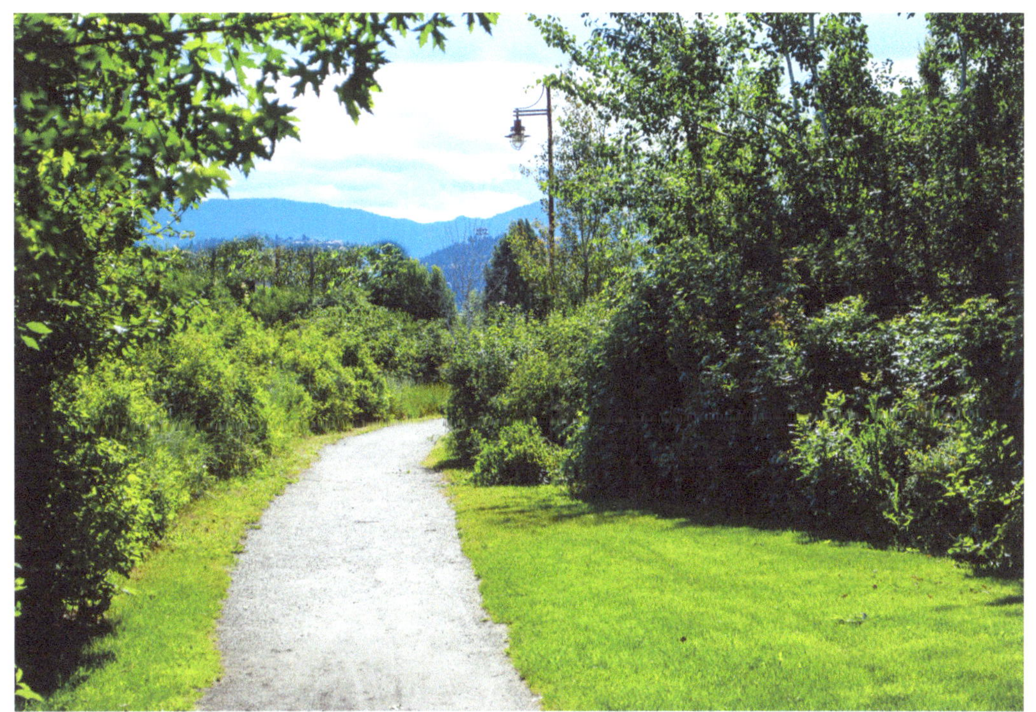

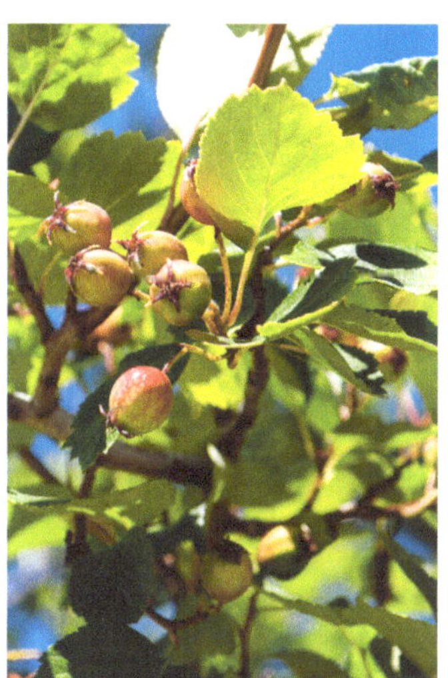

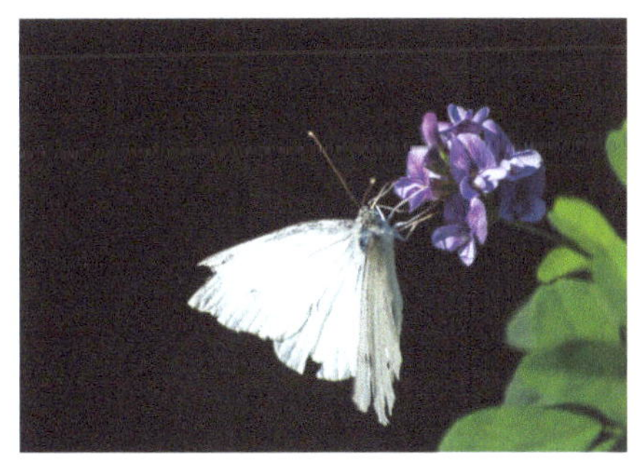

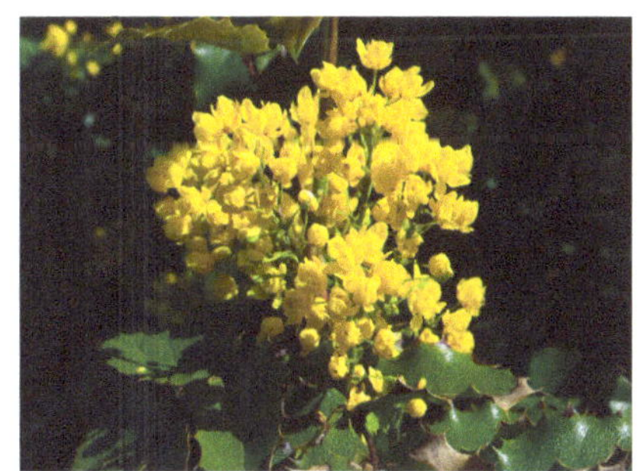

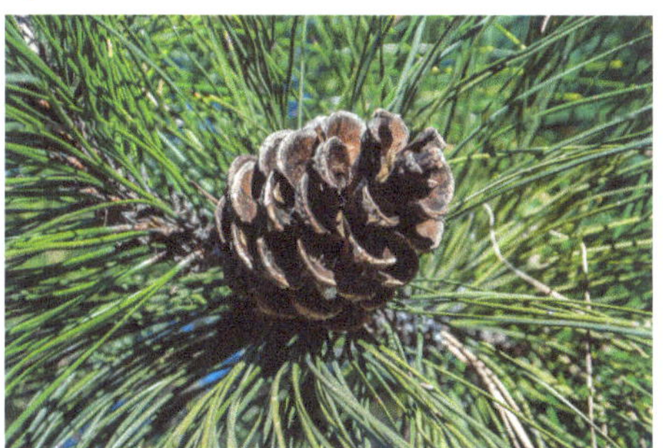

# Beaver has a taste for young trees

Beaver tends his dams with great care. Many young trees in the Rotary Marsh and along Brandt's Creek fall to his gnawing. City workers put wire mesh or cages around trees they most want to save. They can't protect them all. Beaver needs materials for his dams and is a fast worker. He can fell a five-inch tree in as little as three minutes. With oil from his scent glands, Beaver keeps his coat waterproof and warm even in the harshest weather, but he still needs dams and a winter home.

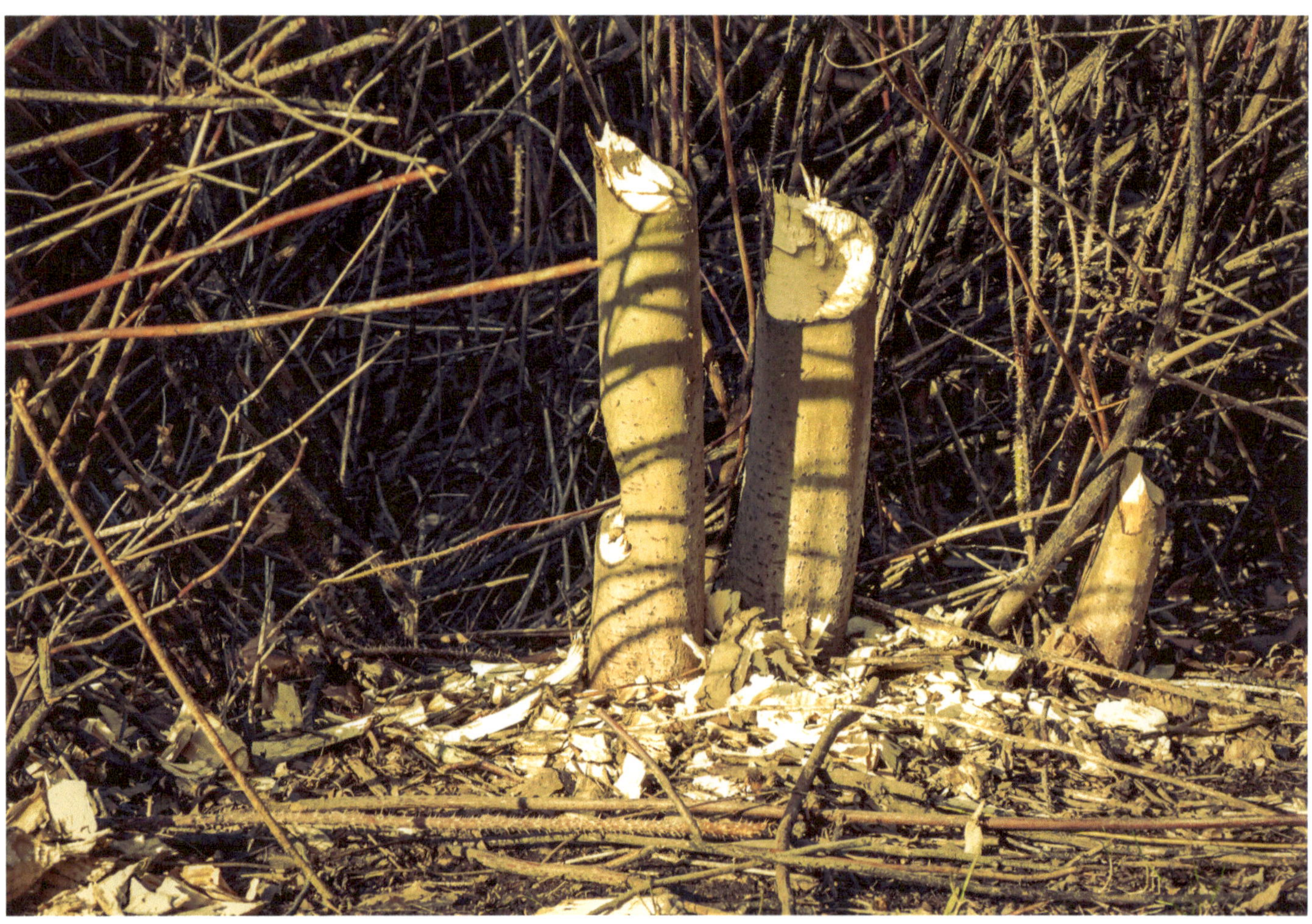

# grandfather beaver

His coat glistens, but his eyes are rheumy and clouded by cataracts. He has munched through many of our young trees. He has fathered youngsters, built dams, and swum the marsh waters. He makes me understand why his gorgeous pelt attracted early explorers to Canada. No wonder he was chosen as a symbol for Canada, with his industriousness, intelligence and beauty.

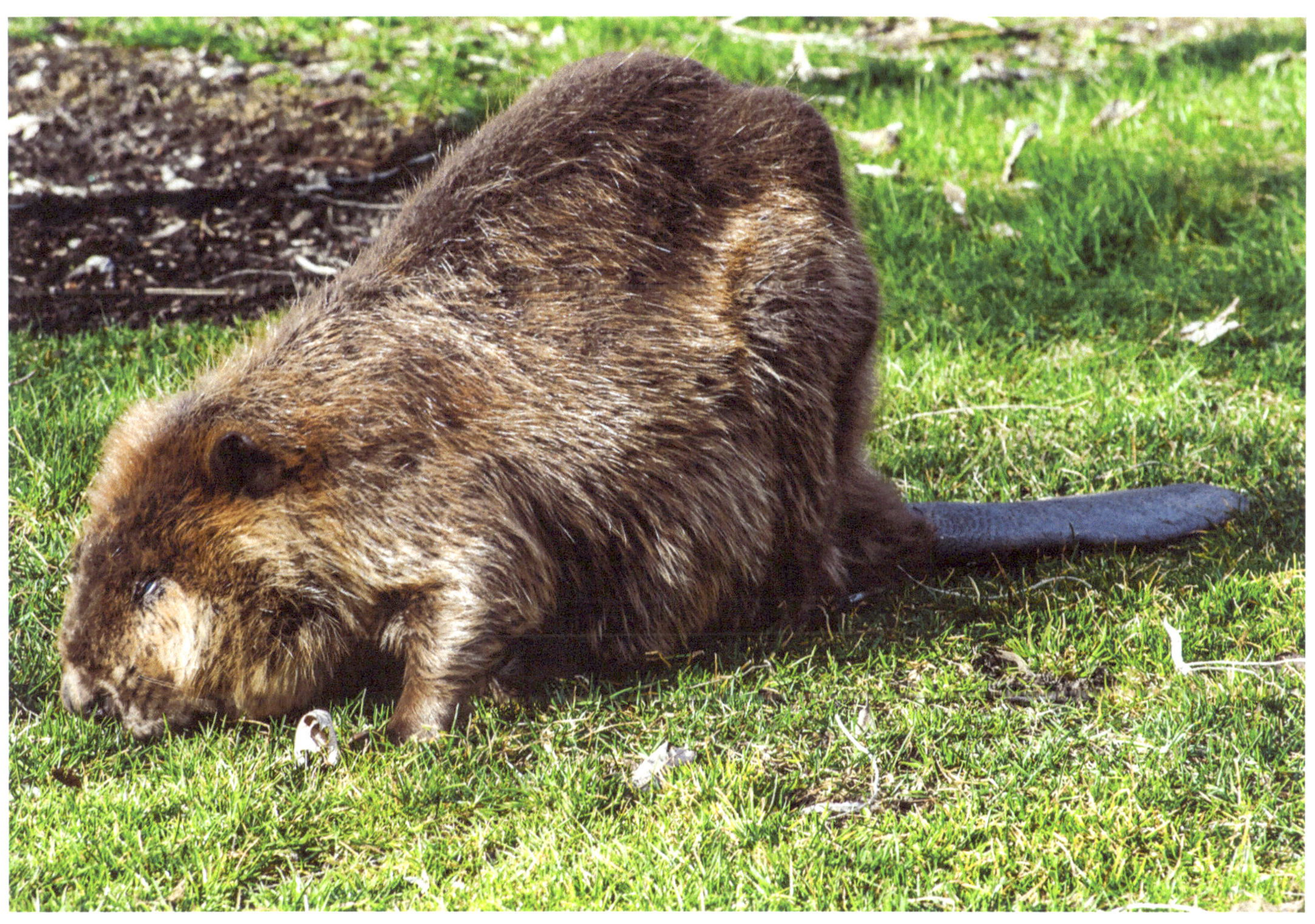

# Another Kind of Creature on the Path

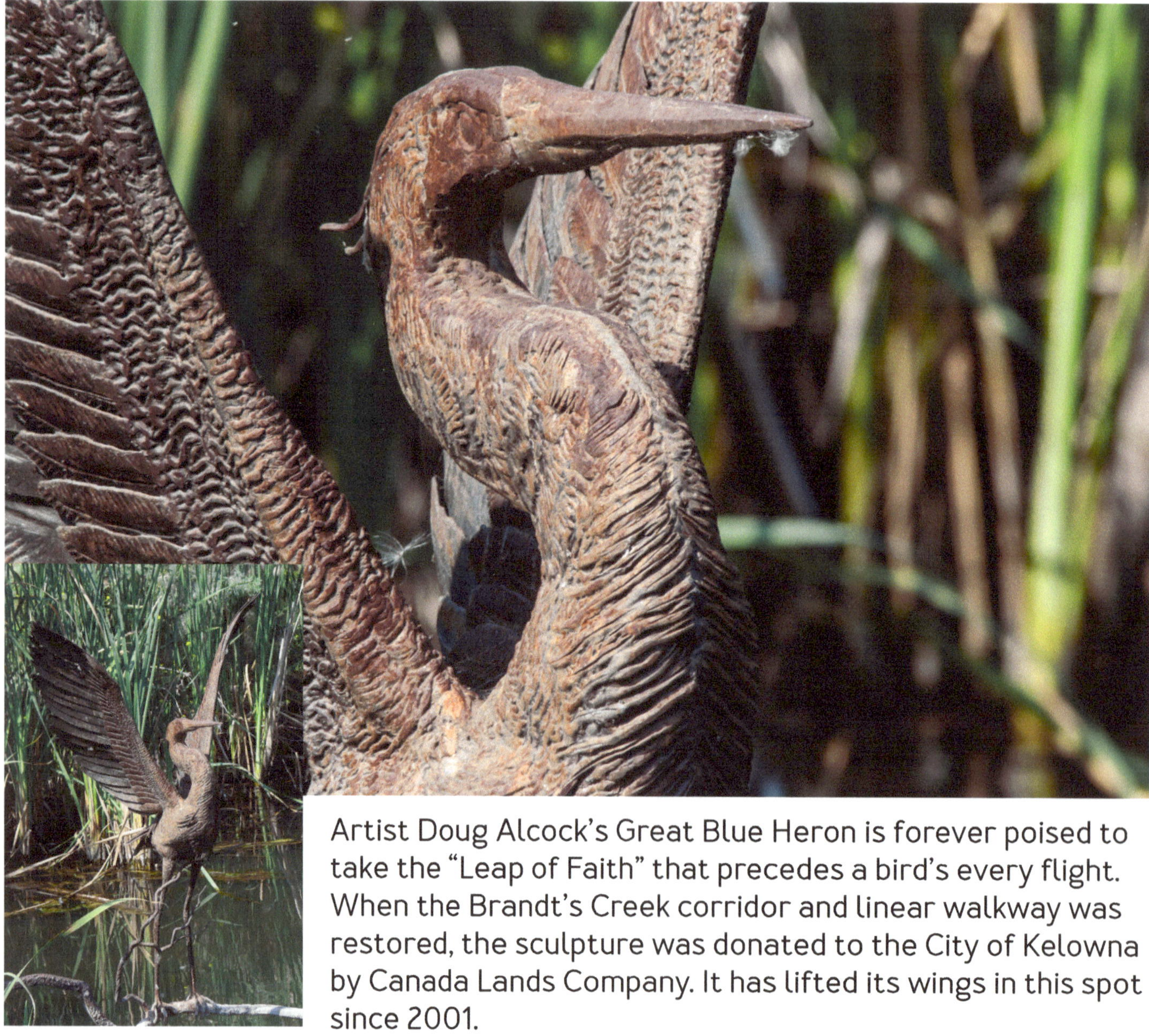

Artist Doug Alcock's Great Blue Heron is forever poised to take the "Leap of Faith" that precedes a bird's every flight. When the Brandt's Creek corridor and linear walkway was restored, the sculpture was donated to the City of Kelowna by Canada Lands Company. It has lifted its wings in this spot since 2001.

# Deer and squirrels feed along the banks

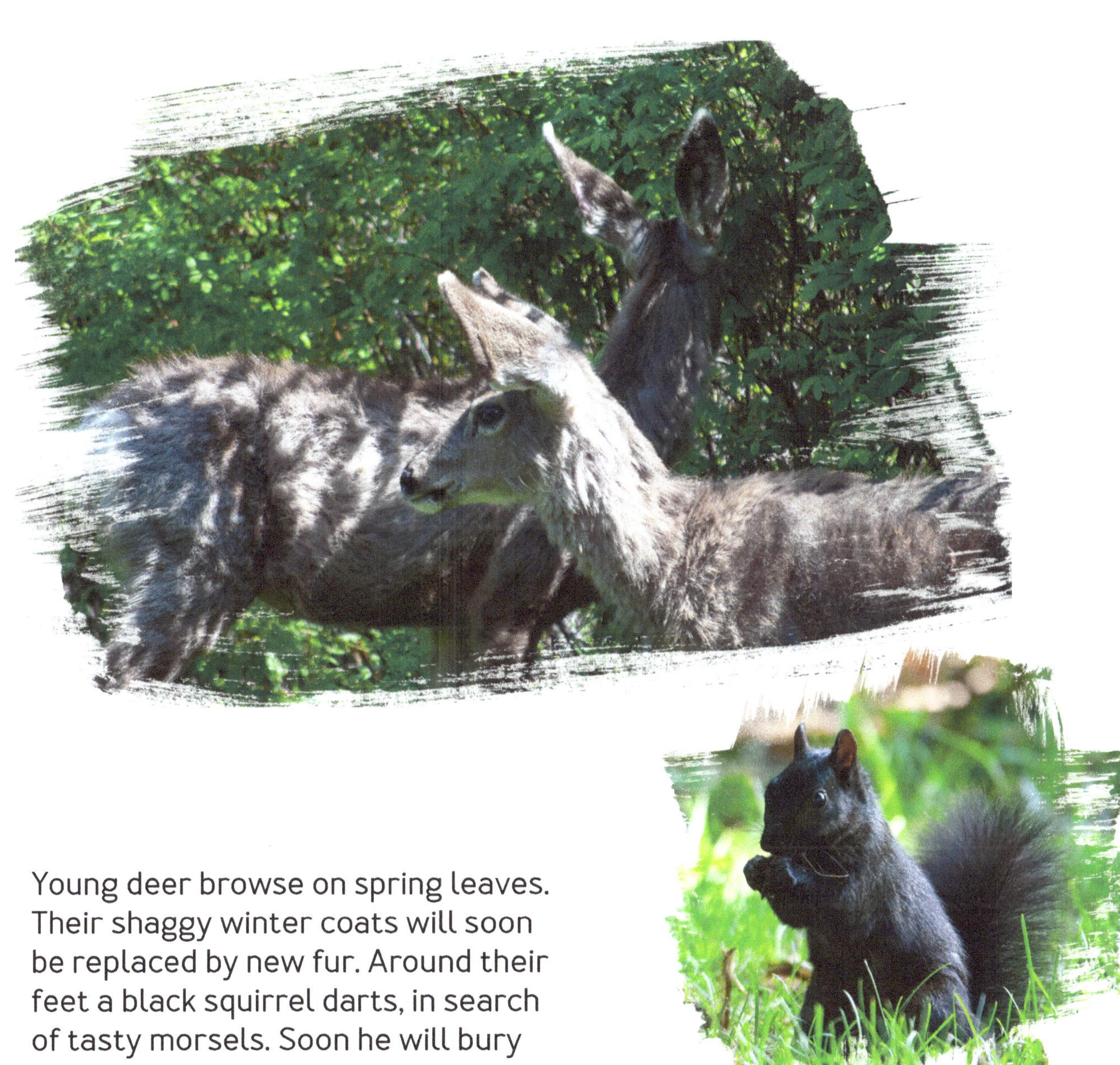

Young deer browse on spring leaves. Their shaggy winter coats will soon be replaced by new fur. Around their feet a black squirrel darts, in search of tasty morsels. Soon he will bury his winter supply.

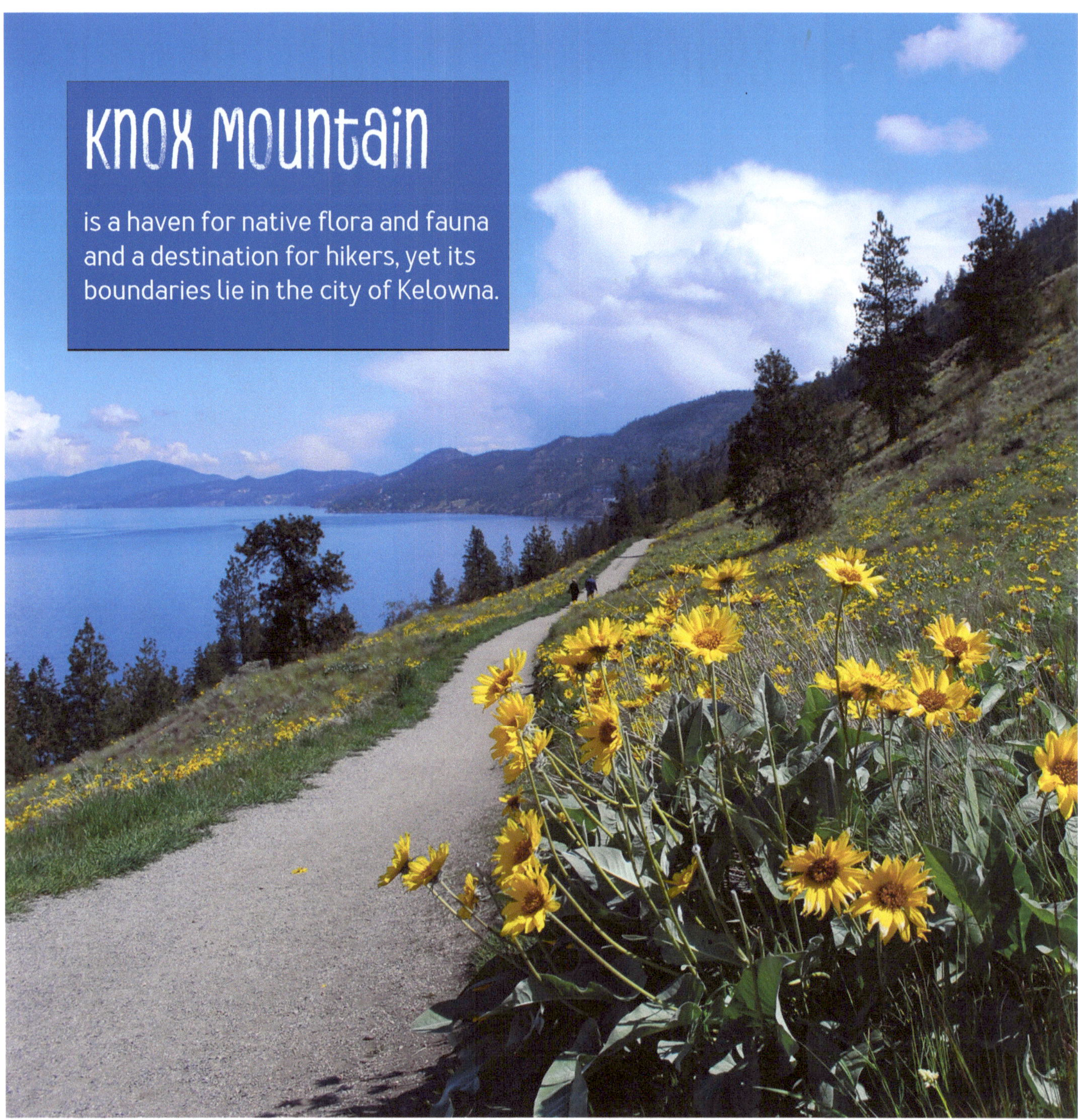

knox mountain
is a haven for native flora and fauna and a destination for hikers, yet its boundaries lie in the city of Kelowna.

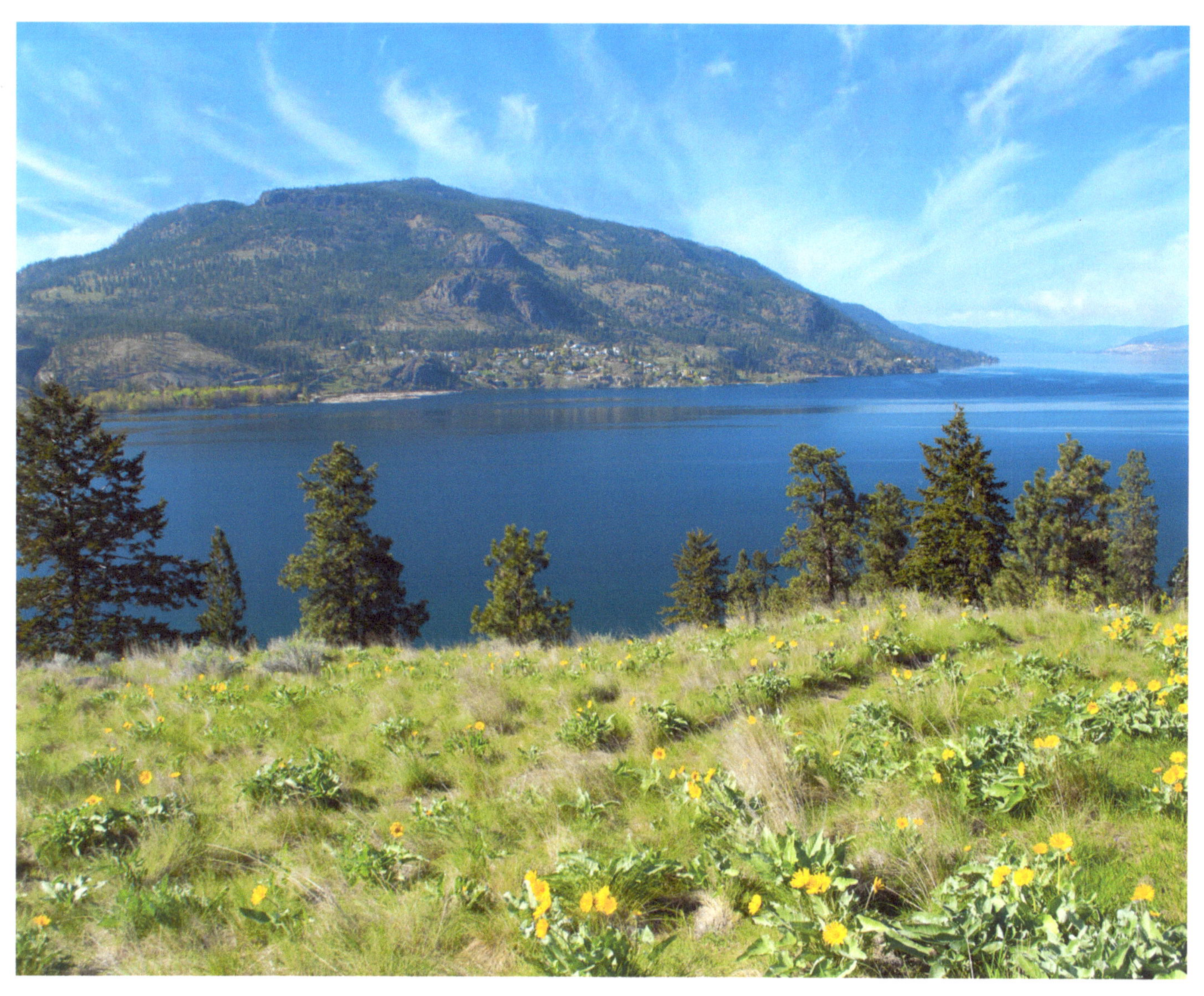

Views of lake, sky, & water everywhere

# cups of sunshine

Arrowleaf Balsamroot flowers lift their heads toward the sun, covering the hillsides in spring. They are beloved of locals, who call them Okanagan

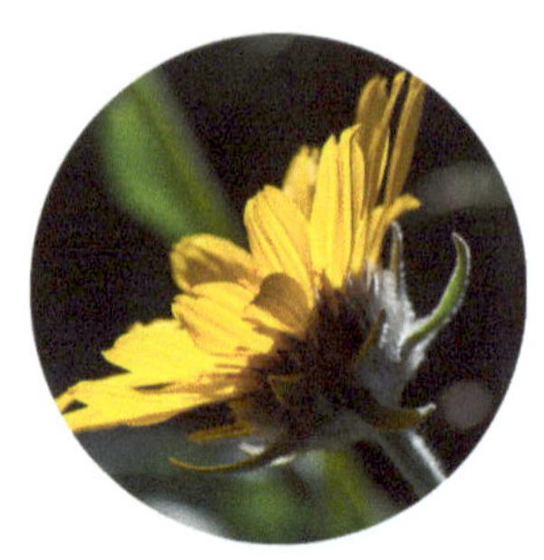

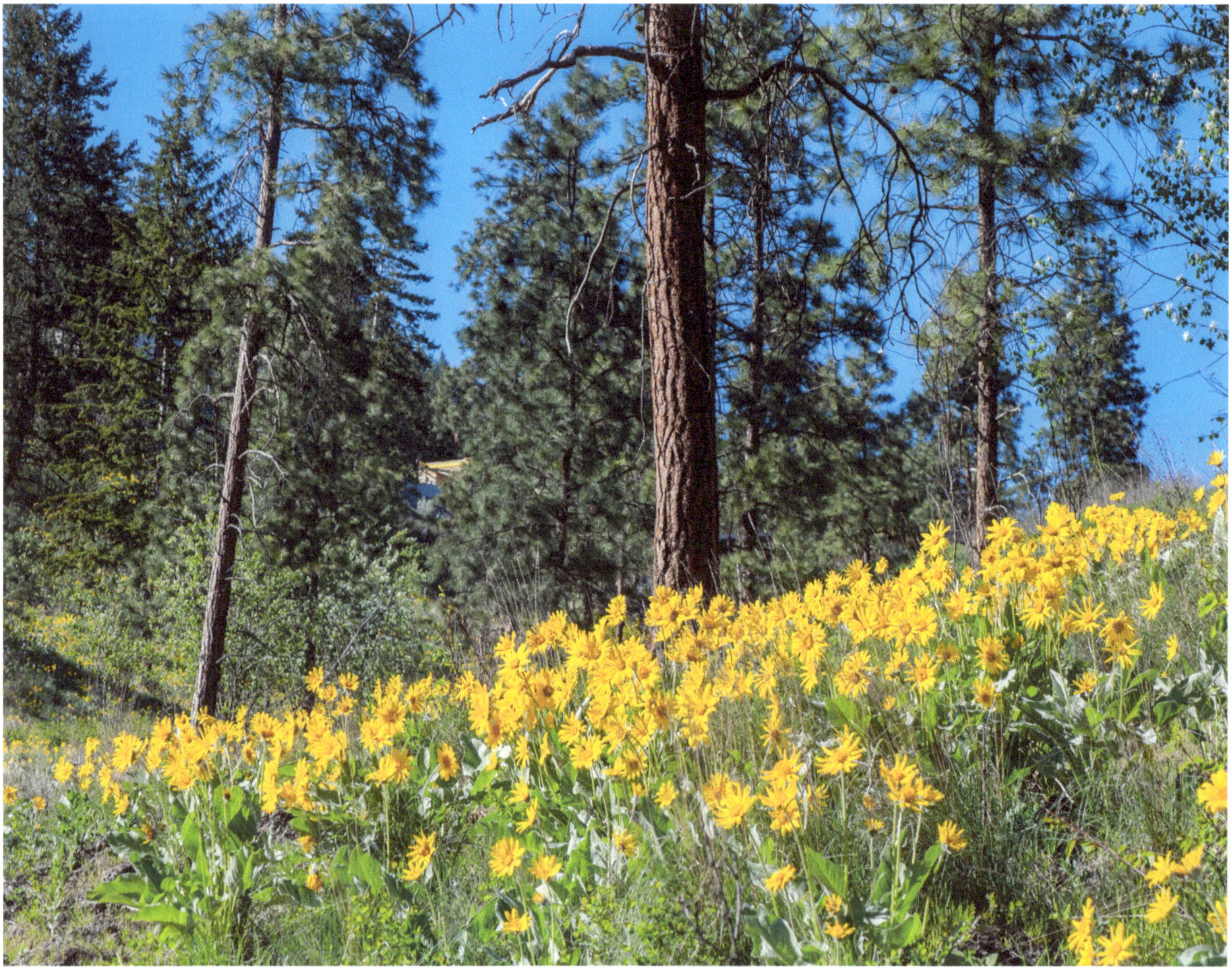

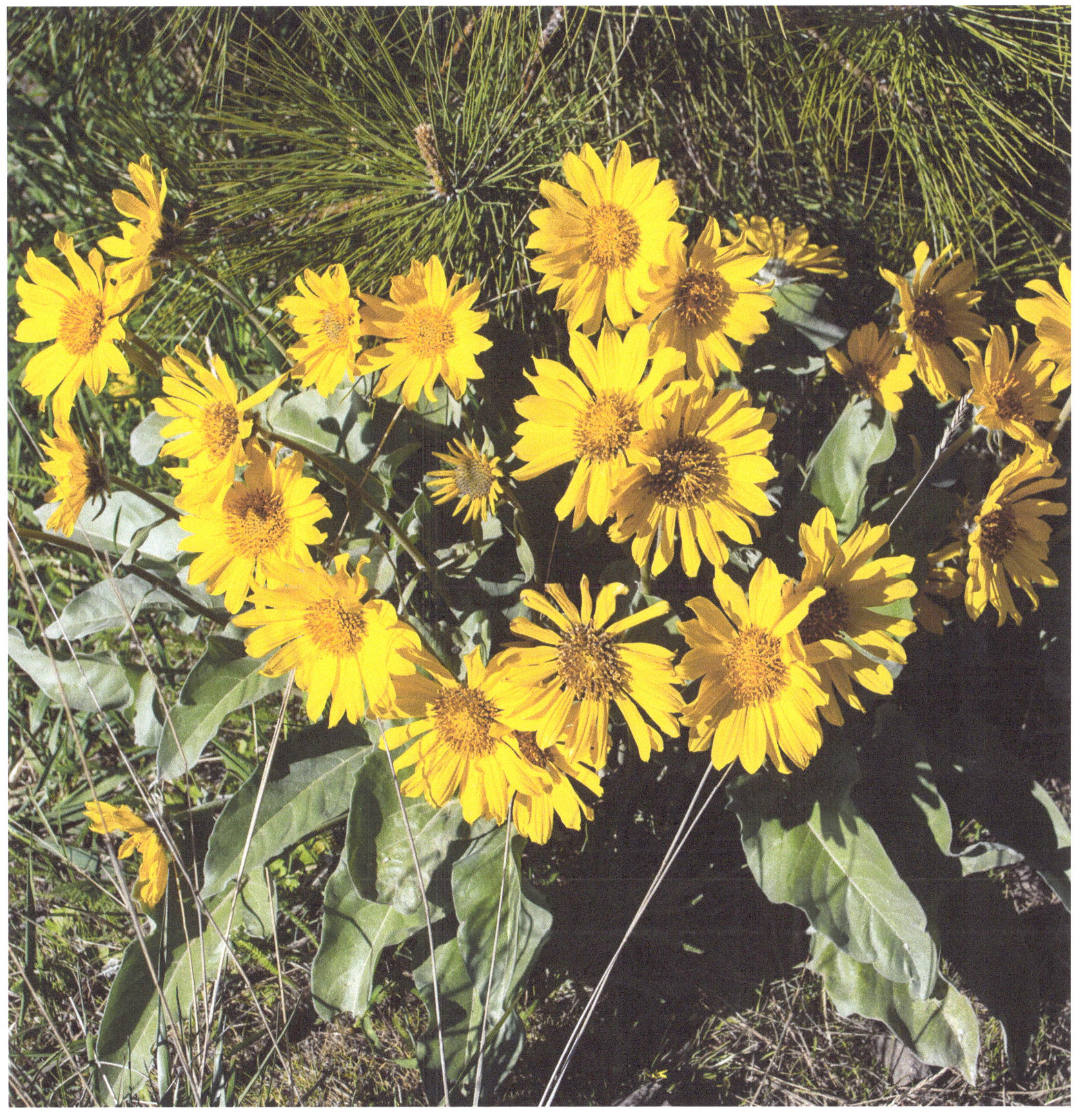

# Tiny Shooting Stars

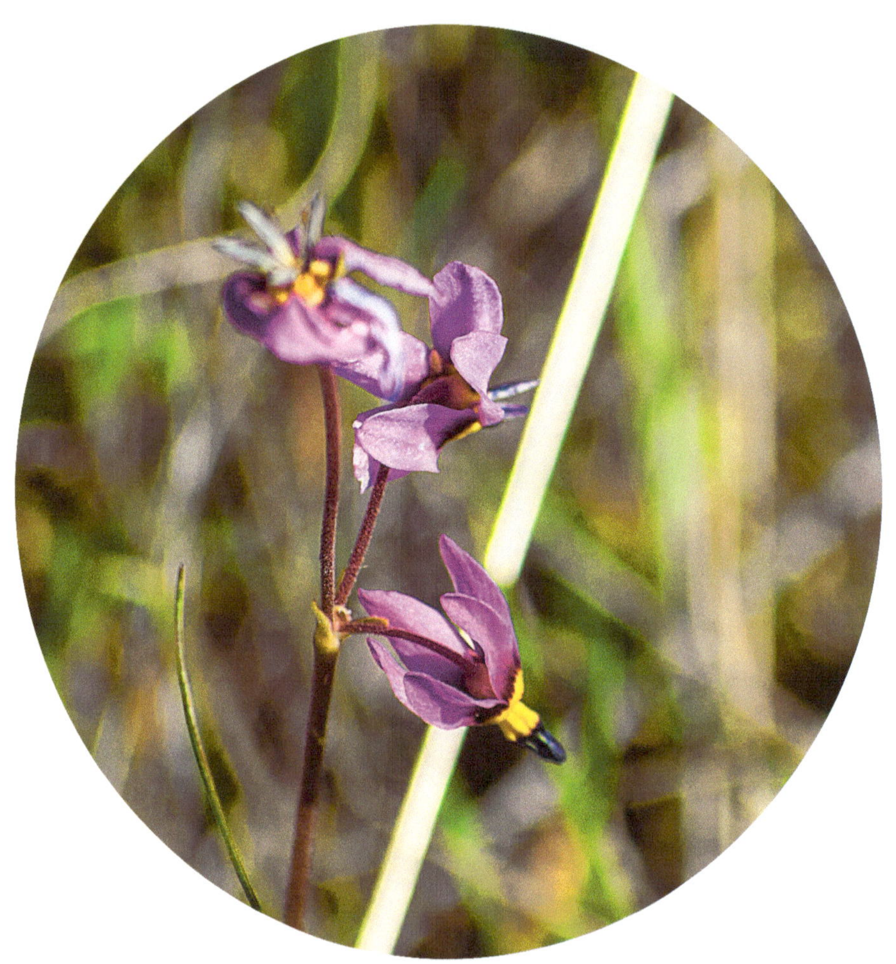

Smaller and more delicate than the showy Okanagan sunflowers, shooting stars reward observant hikers. Their purple petals flare back like the bright trails of the meteroids for which they are named.

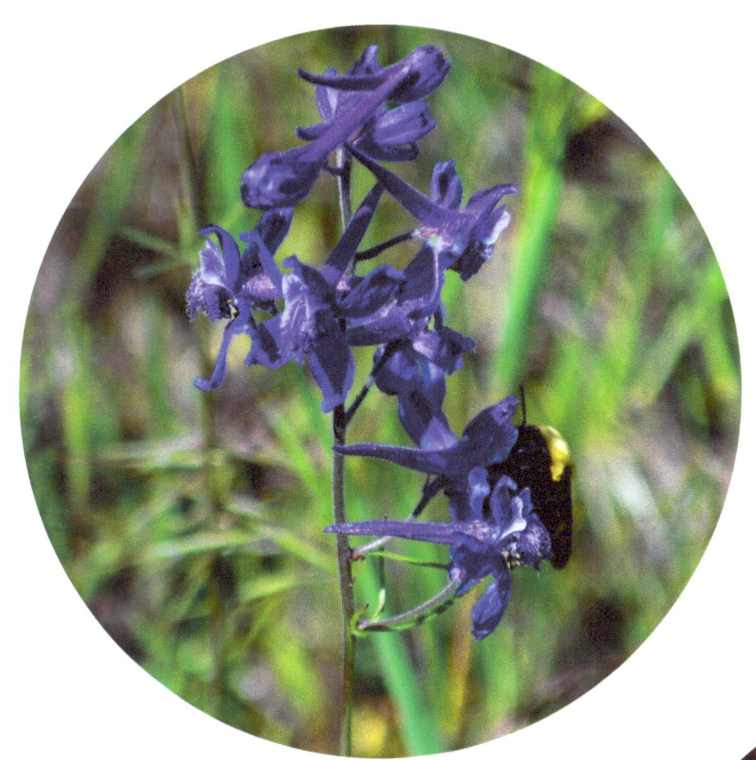



A stalk of delphinium (also called larkspur) attracts a fat, golden bee. Further on, in a dry, gravel patch, penstamon needs very little water to produce dozens of blossoms.

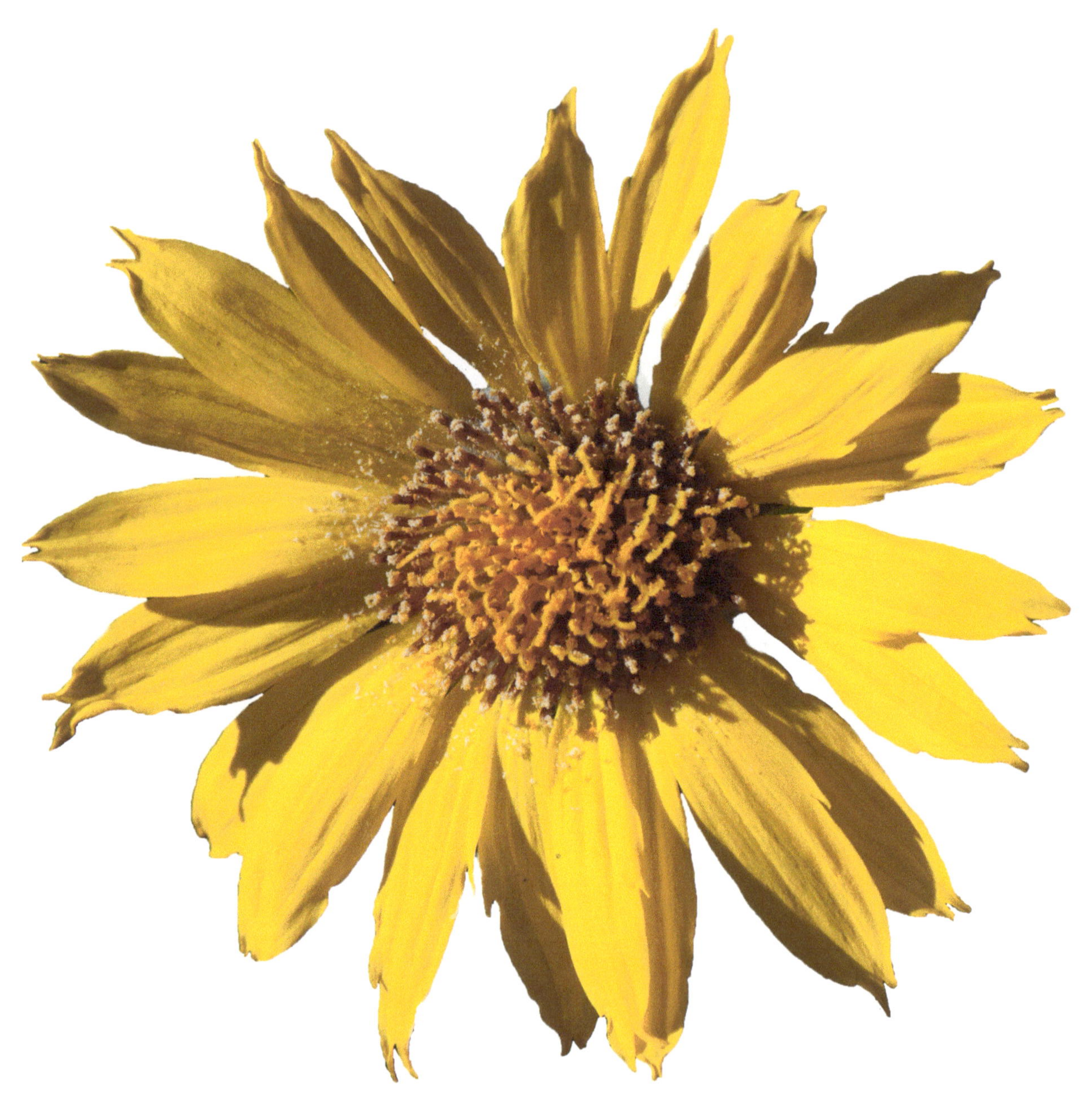

still, in spring, okanagan sunflowers
are the main attraction

# A legacy

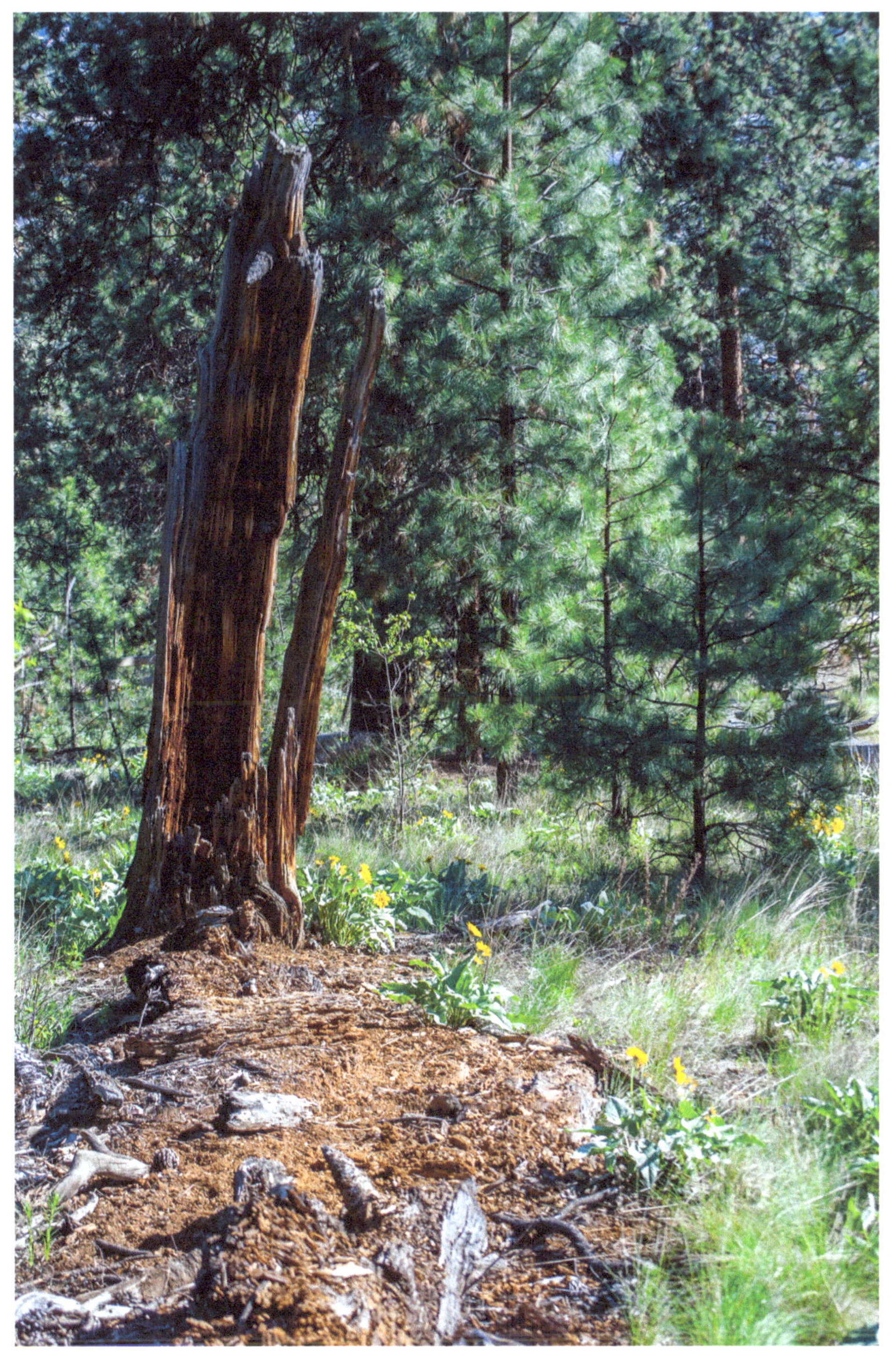

Winds sigh through the limbs of pines that dot the slopes of Knox Mountain. When one of these stately trees falls, it becomes a nurse tree for seedlings that find fertile ground in rotting wood.

Trees grow slowly in this northern climate. In the years between seedlings and tall trees, many insects and plants will make their homes in the remains of the tree whose branches once waved in the breezes.

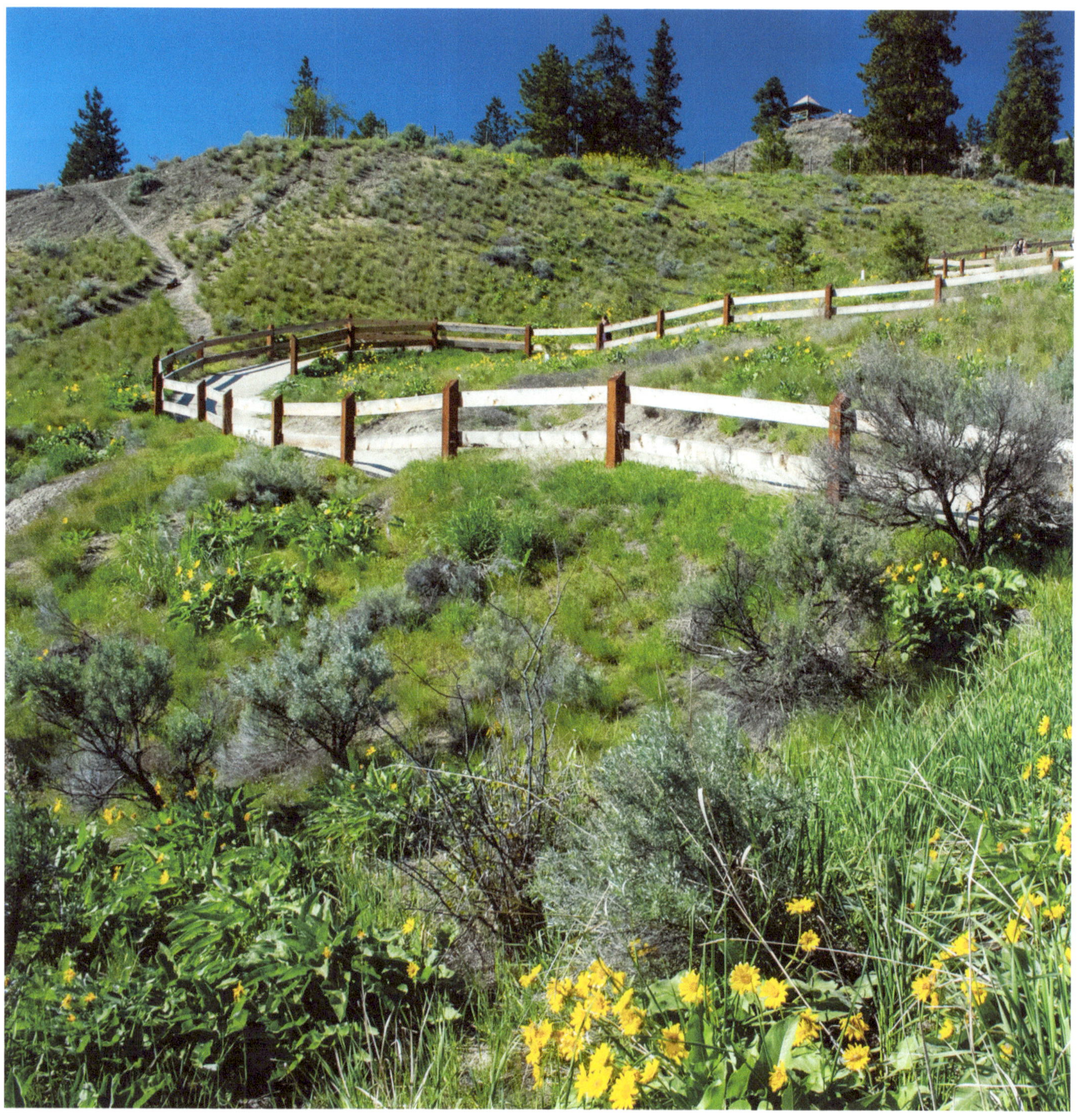

# The tomb of a wanderer

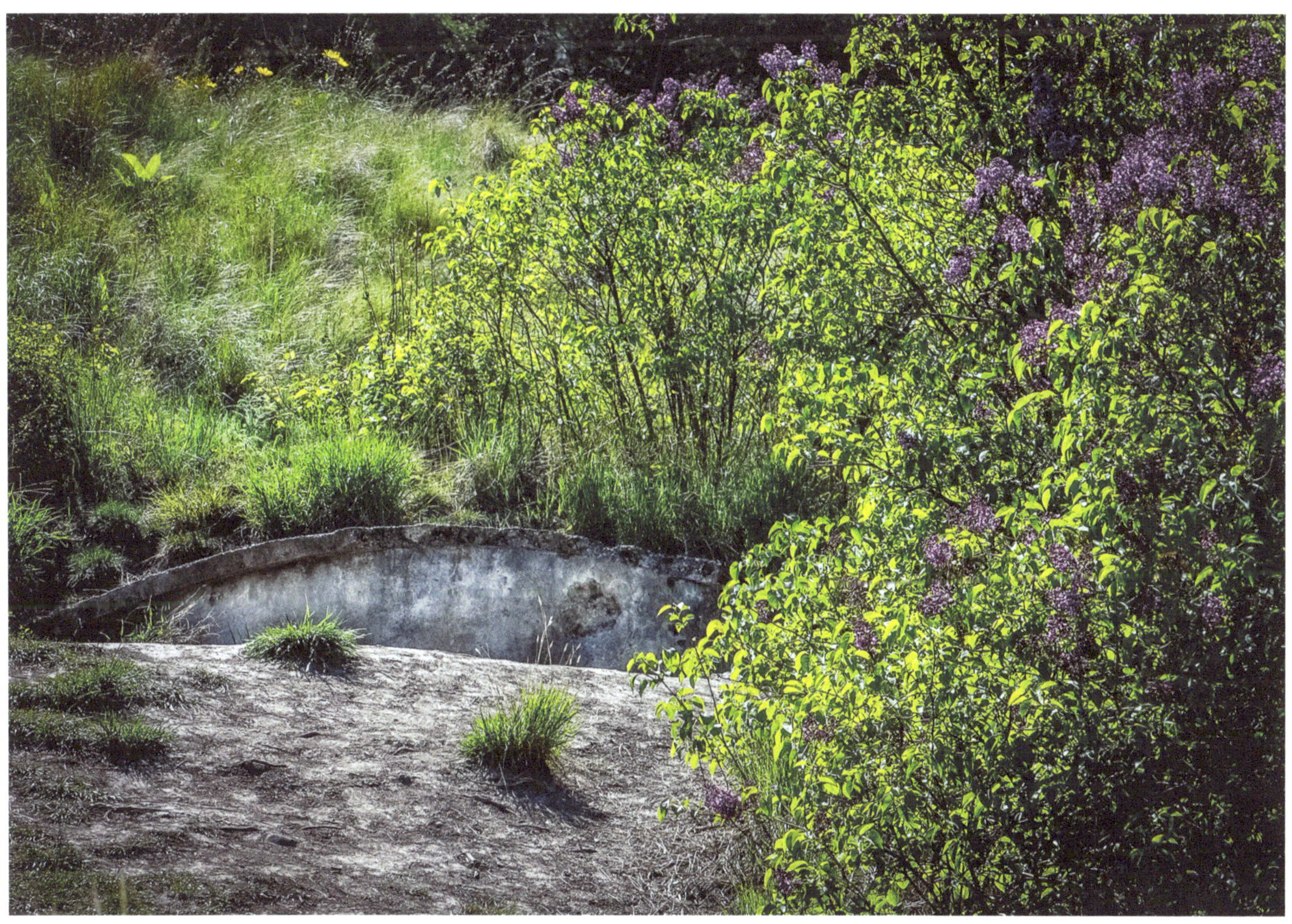

Rembler Paul was an entrepreneur and adventurer. In 1905 he and his wife Elizabeth moved to Kelowna. Although they lived downtown, they built a summer cottage in this spot on what is now called Knox Mountain. Elizabeth visited only once before cancer took her life. Rembler built a tomb for her here and a few years later was buried beside her. The cottage is gone, but the tomb remains, as do the lilacs he planted around their summer home.

# End of the trail

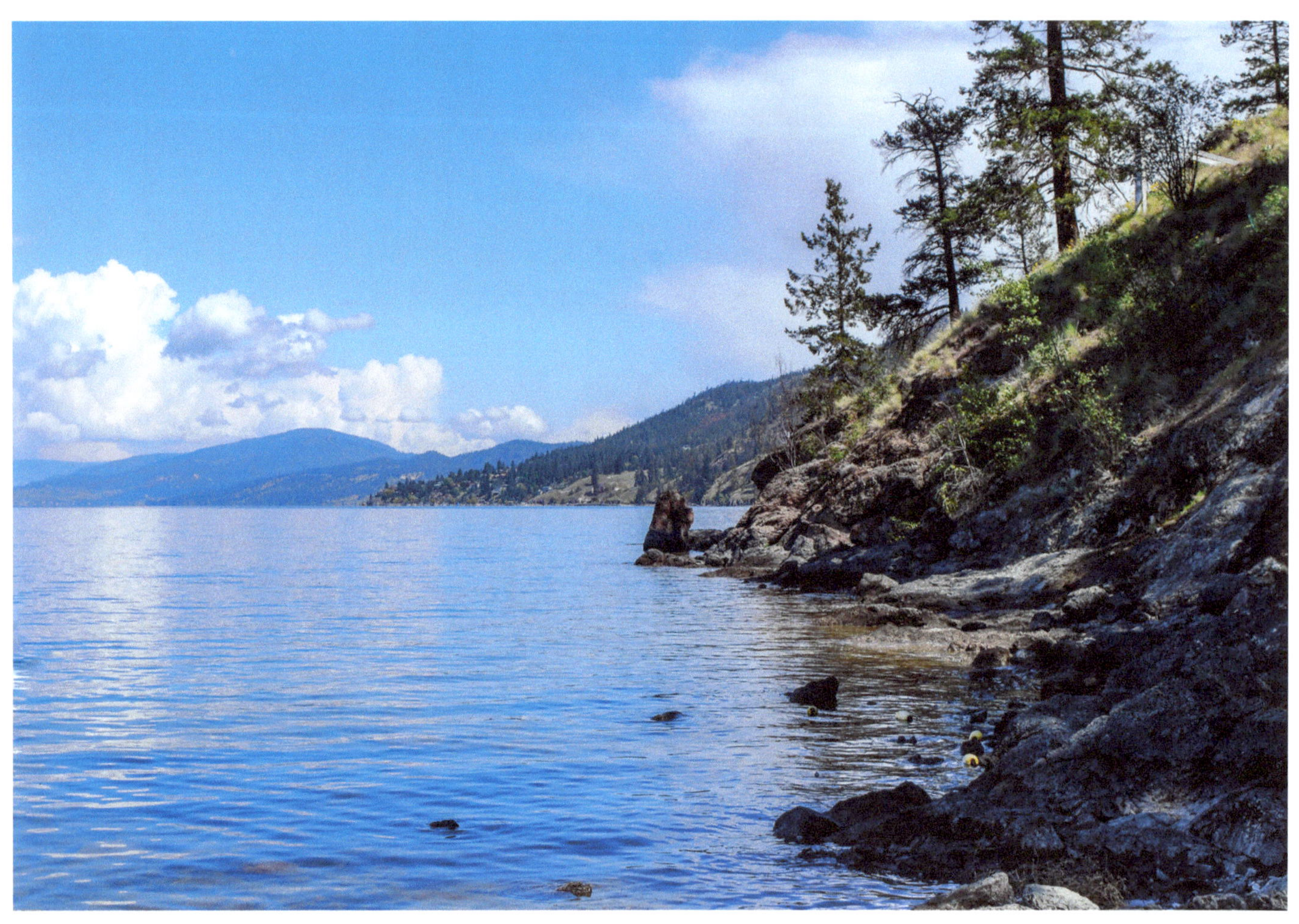

A secluded beach in a quiet cove awaits hikers. Just down a small slope beyond Paul's Tomb, it is an idyllic spot for picnics, swimming and contemplation.

# sweet reward for a hot walk

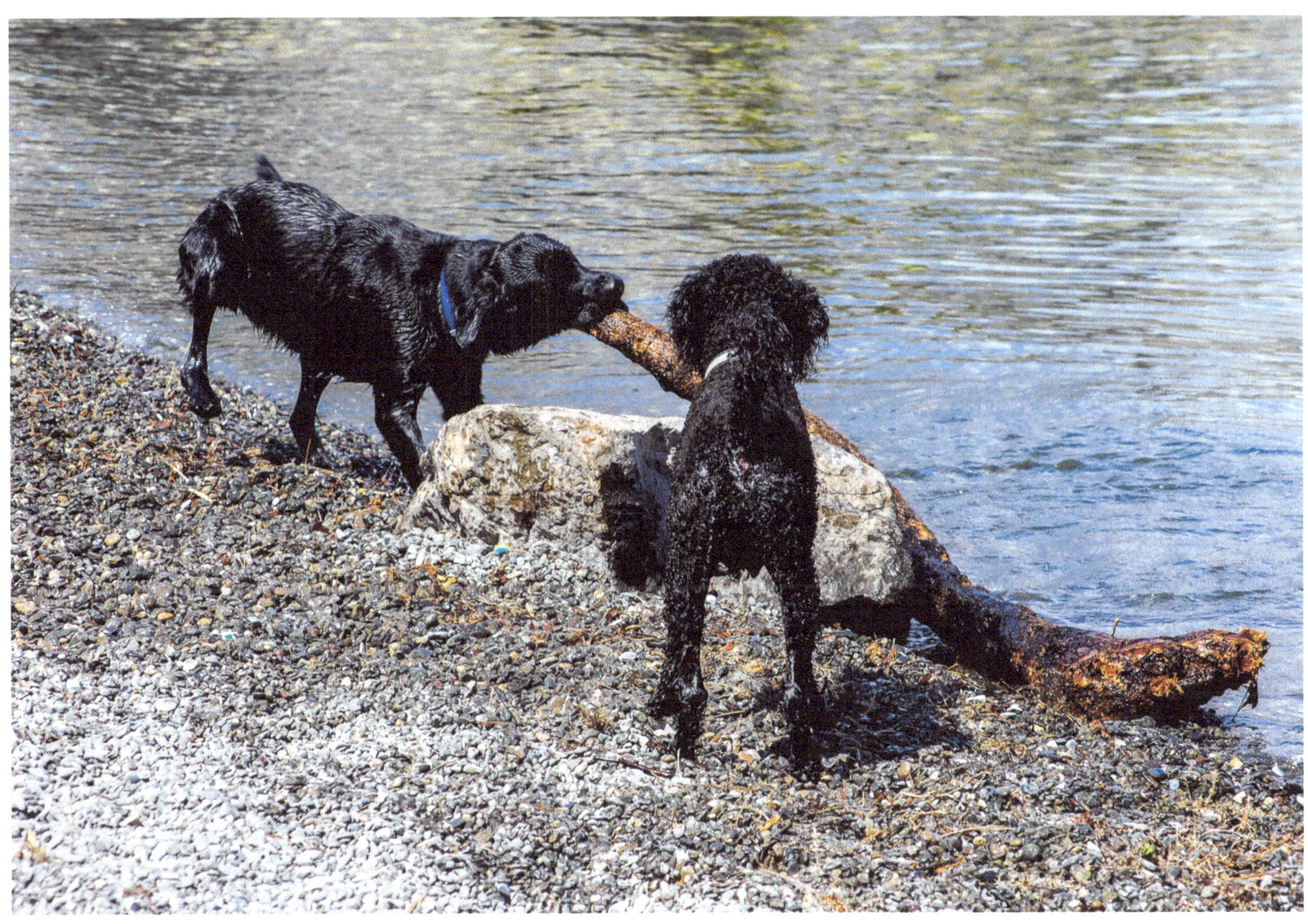

These two pals swam and played in the water just beyond Paul's Tomb. One of them did not let his people's lack of sticks to throw hamper him from playing fetch. He swam out into the lake, grabbed a log, and tugged it back to shore. His canine friend swam with him but let the other dog do all the work.

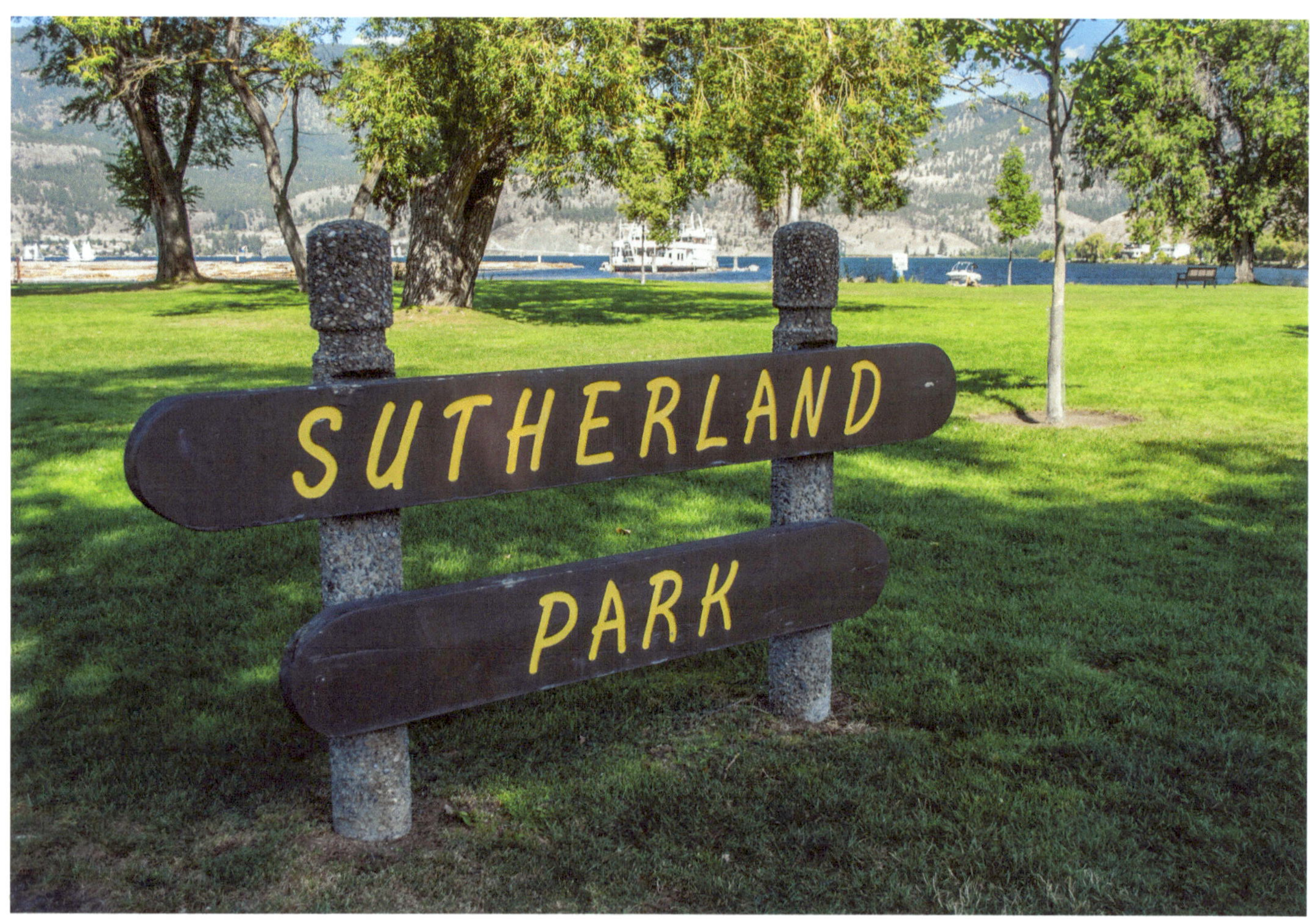



Sutherland Park serves residents of Kelowna's north end. With its small playground and large, grassy area, it is an ideal picnic spot. Yet it is rarely crowded, even on hot summer days.

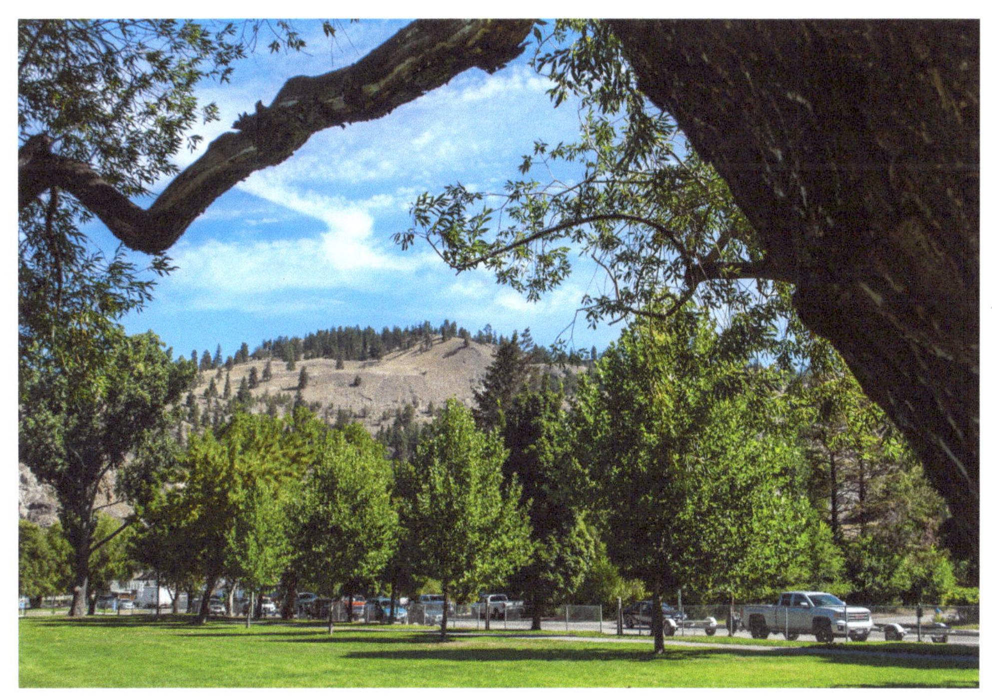

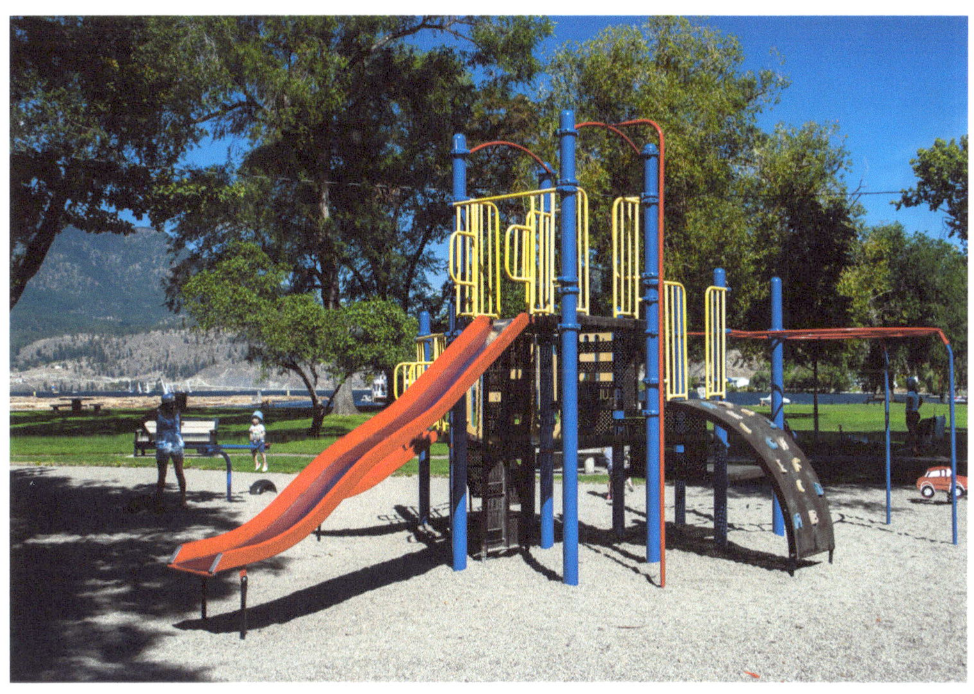

# Bertram Creek Regional Park

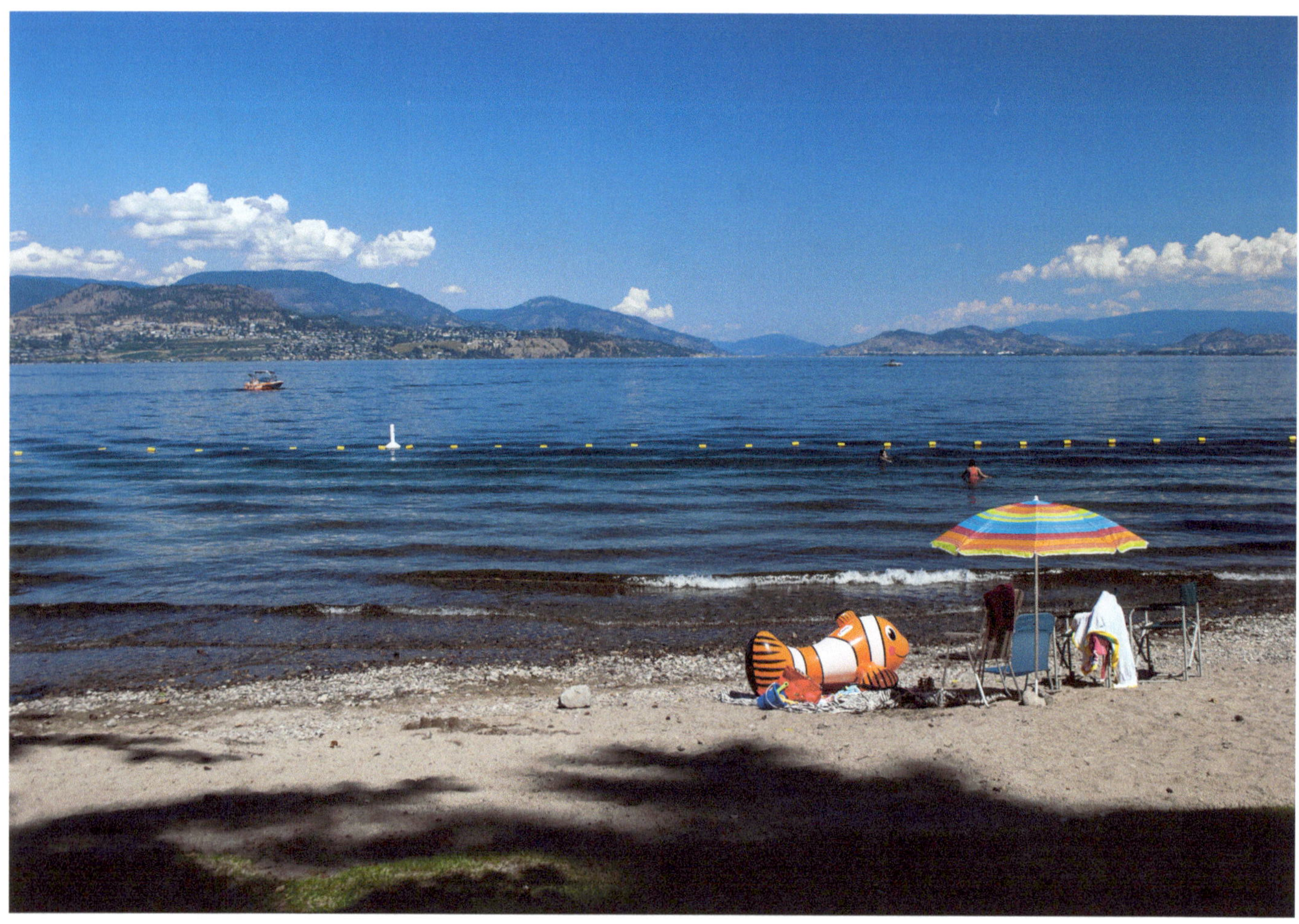

On the southeast side of Kelowna, near the end of Lakeshore Road, lies one of the Central Okanagan's jewels. Though it was also damaged in the 2003 Okanagan Mountain Provincial Park forest fire, Bertram Creek Regional Park re-opened in 2004. With beaches for swimming and boating, playground and playing fields, walking paths and even an outdoor amphitheatre, it is a destination for everything from family reunions to weddings.

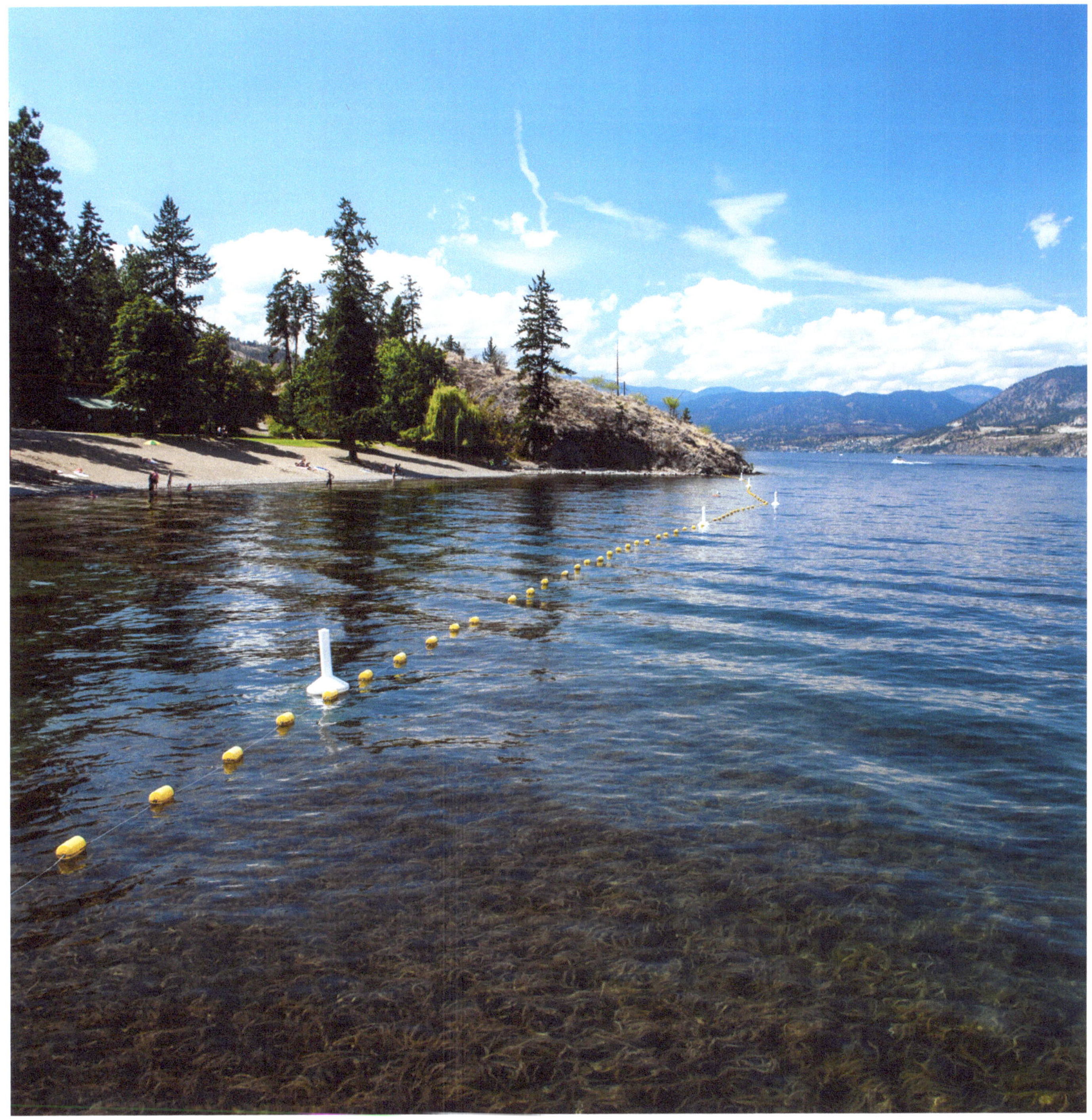

# Myra Canyon

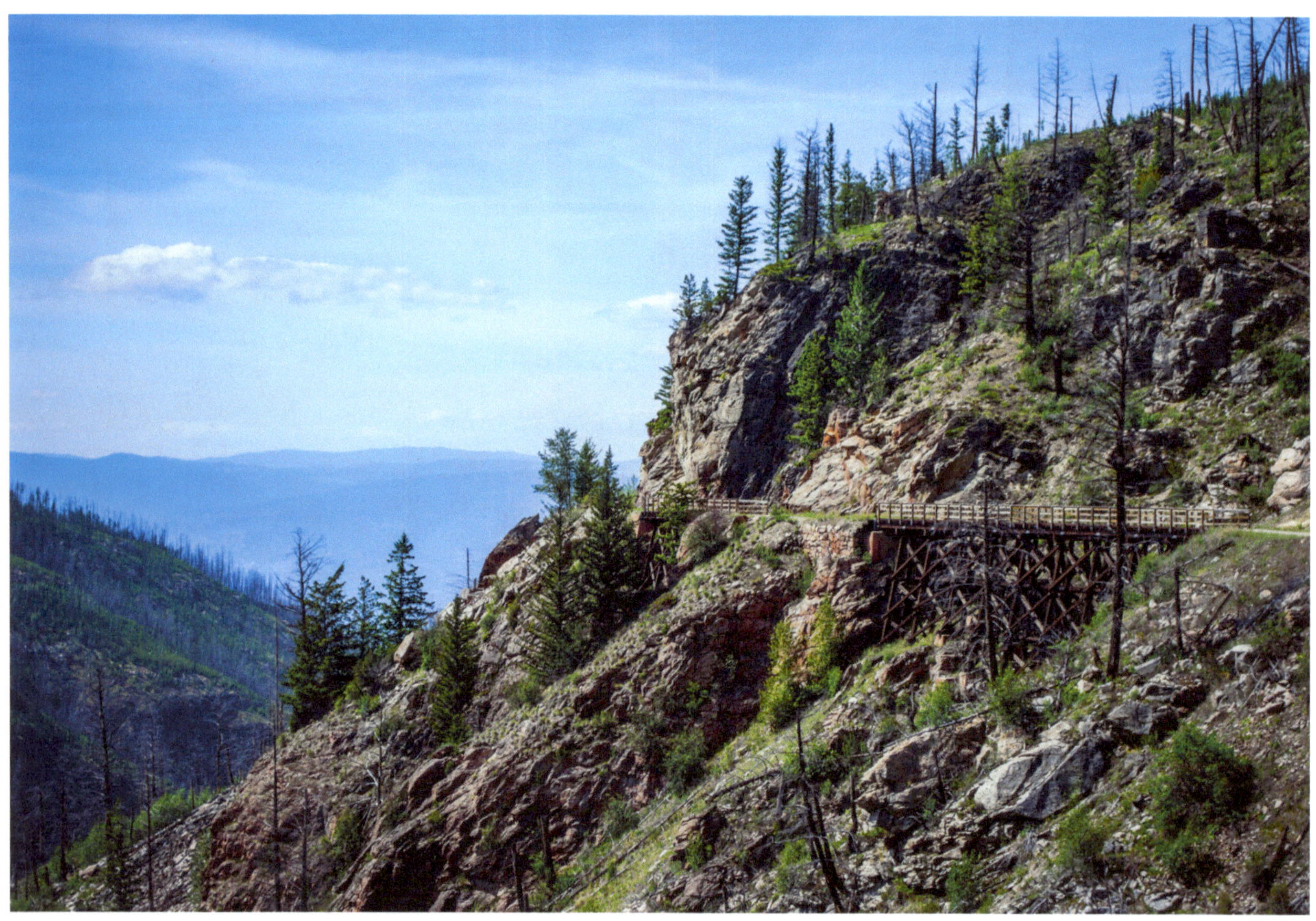

A massive forest fire swept through Myra Canyon in 2003, taking with it the trestles of the old Kettle Valley Railway. Canadian Pacific Railway had sent the last train over the tracks in 1972. Twenty years later the Myra Canyon Trestle Restoration Society began building decks and guardrails over each of the trestles. They repaired the trail, shored up the tunnels and erected signage. Their efforts attracted 30,000 annual visitors. The fire destroyed 12 of the 16 trestles, but by 2008, volunteers had restored all of them.

# volunteers worked wonders

They raised funds, solicited government support, and put in countless hours to restore the trestles and the trail. Their renewed mandate went beyond an already impressive recreational area. They committed to preserving Myra Canyon as cultural heritage, recognizing its importance to the Okanagan First Nations and its significance as a former railway corridor.

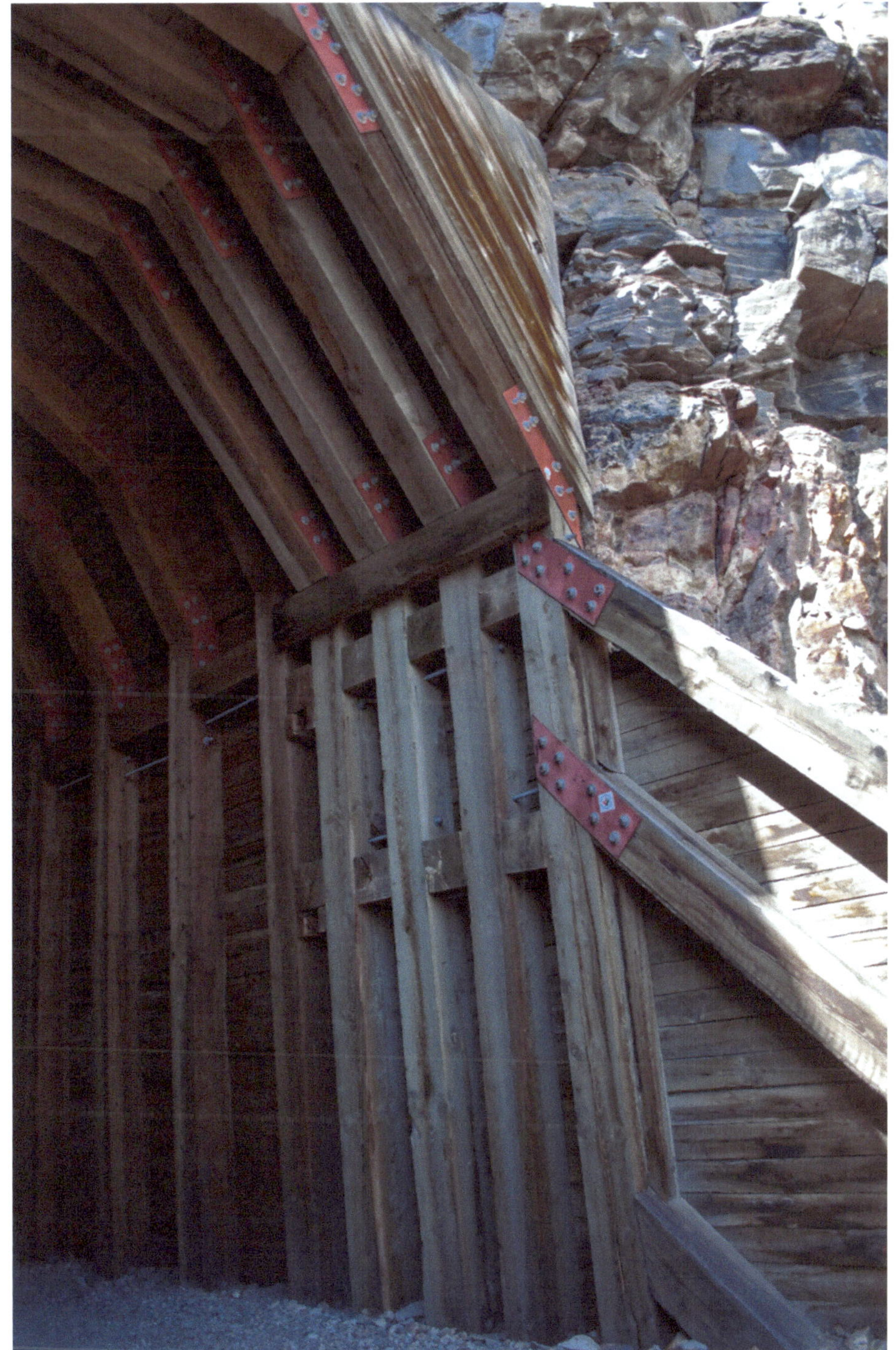

# Wildflowers flourish

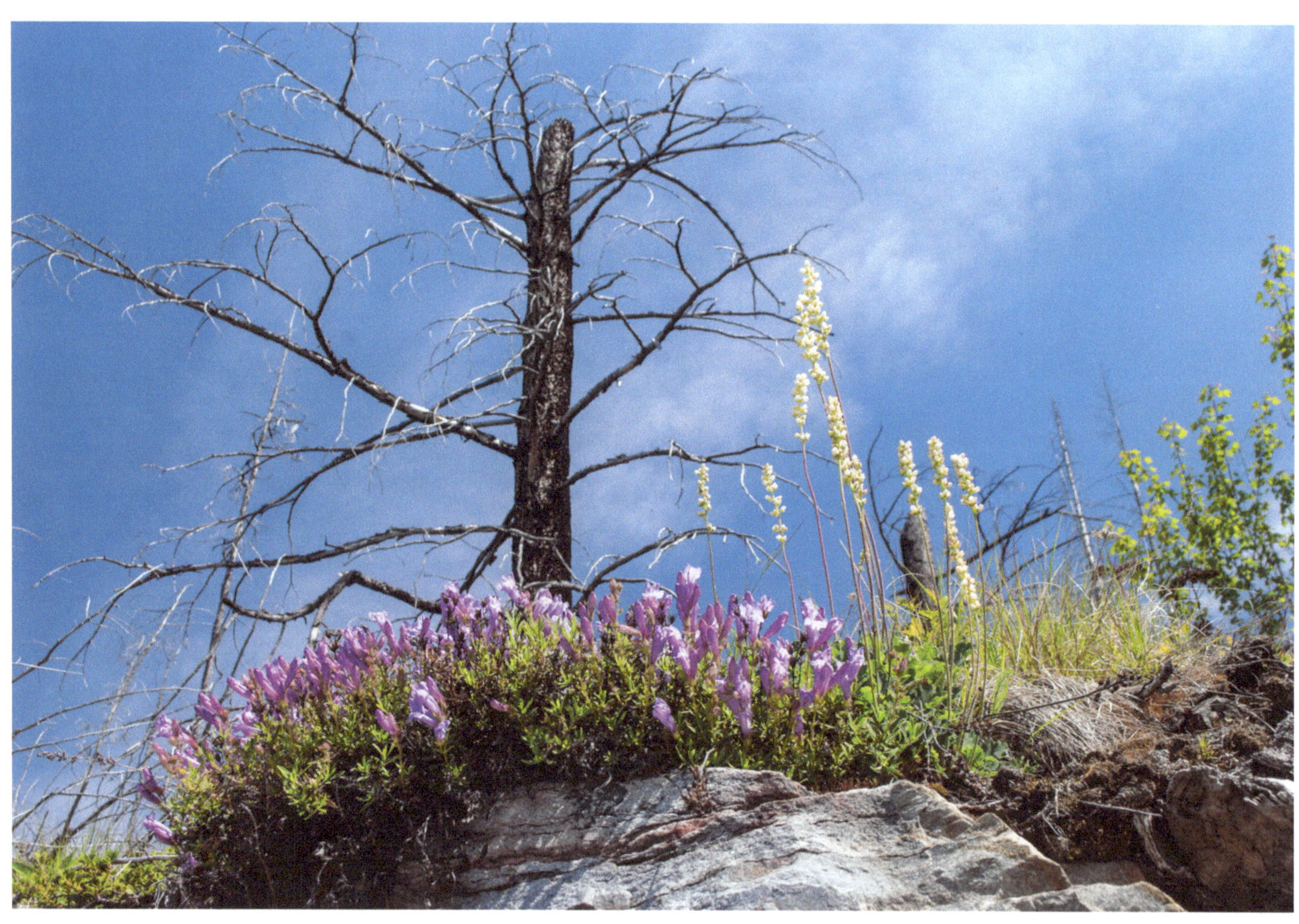

They cluster around the blackened bones of trees and tuck into crevices. They dot the hillsides with vibrant colours.

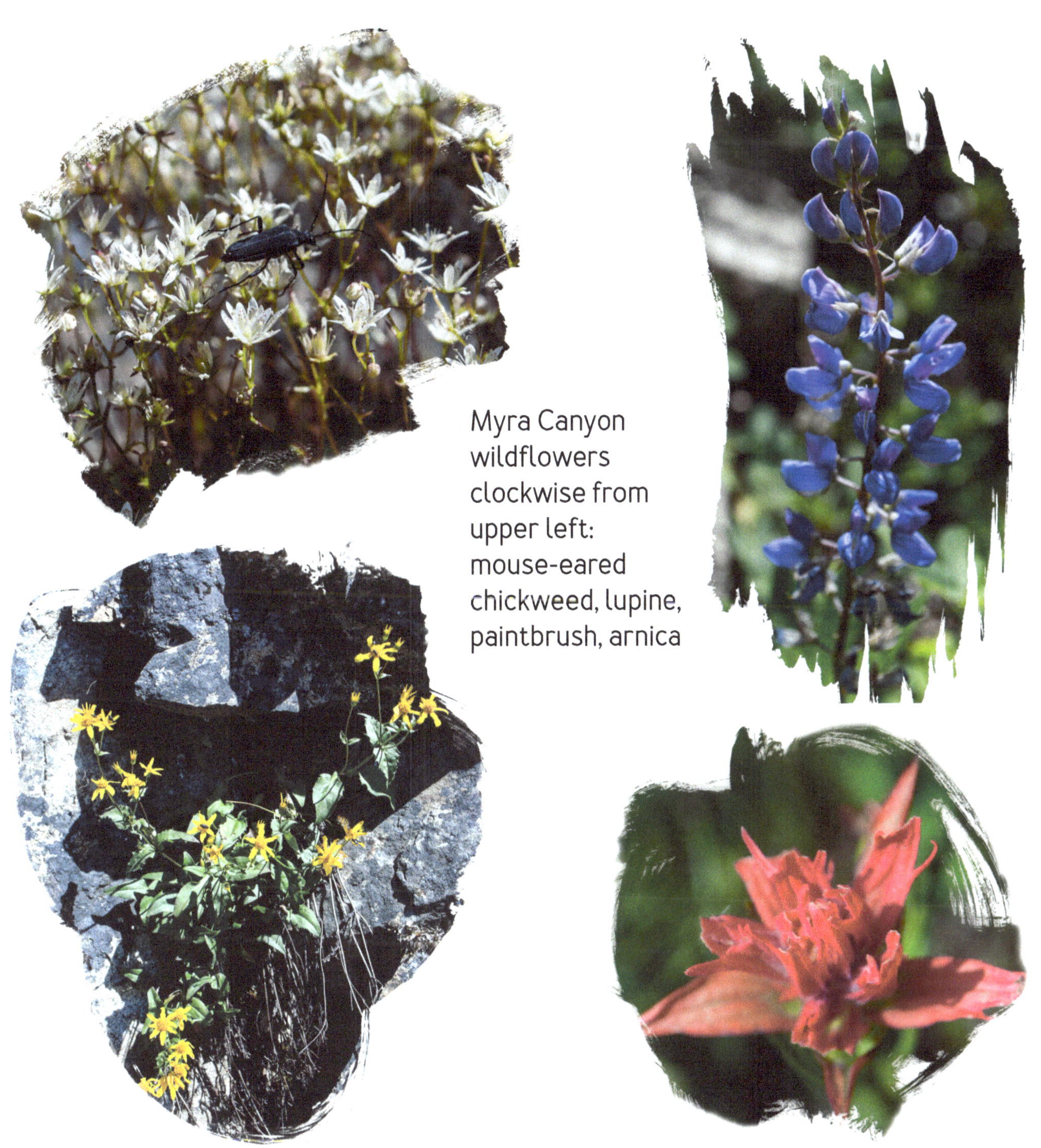

Myra Canyon
wildflowers
clockwise from
upper left:
mouse-eared
chickweed, lupine,
paintbrush, arnica

# And in the end

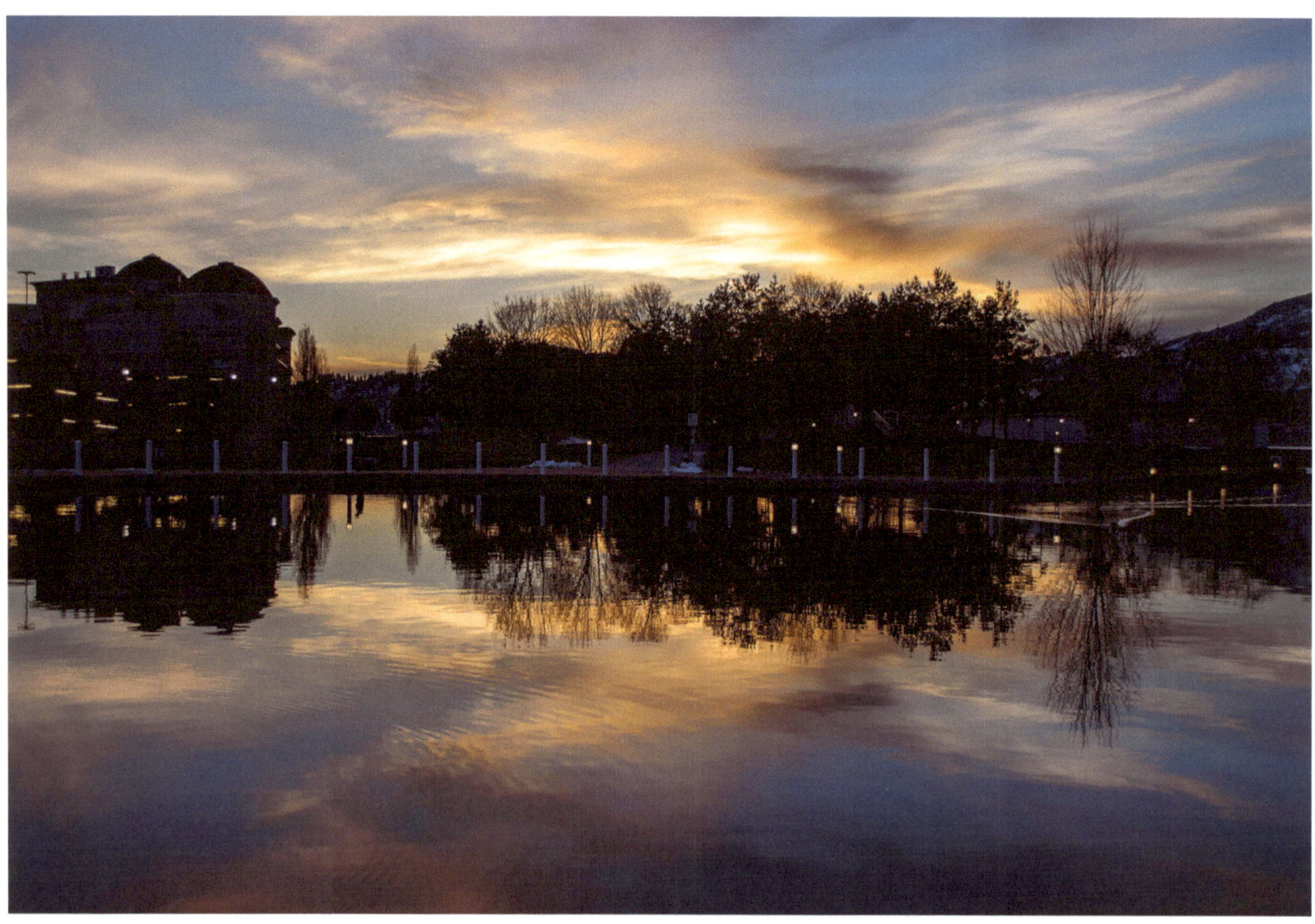

When visitors say farewell and grey clouds settle like a dark blanket over the valley, beauty remains. The sun makes enough of an appearance to give us glorious sunsets and sunrises throughout the year, like this one in January. This short visit ends with a small collection of them, with gratitude for the awe they inspire.

# March Sunset

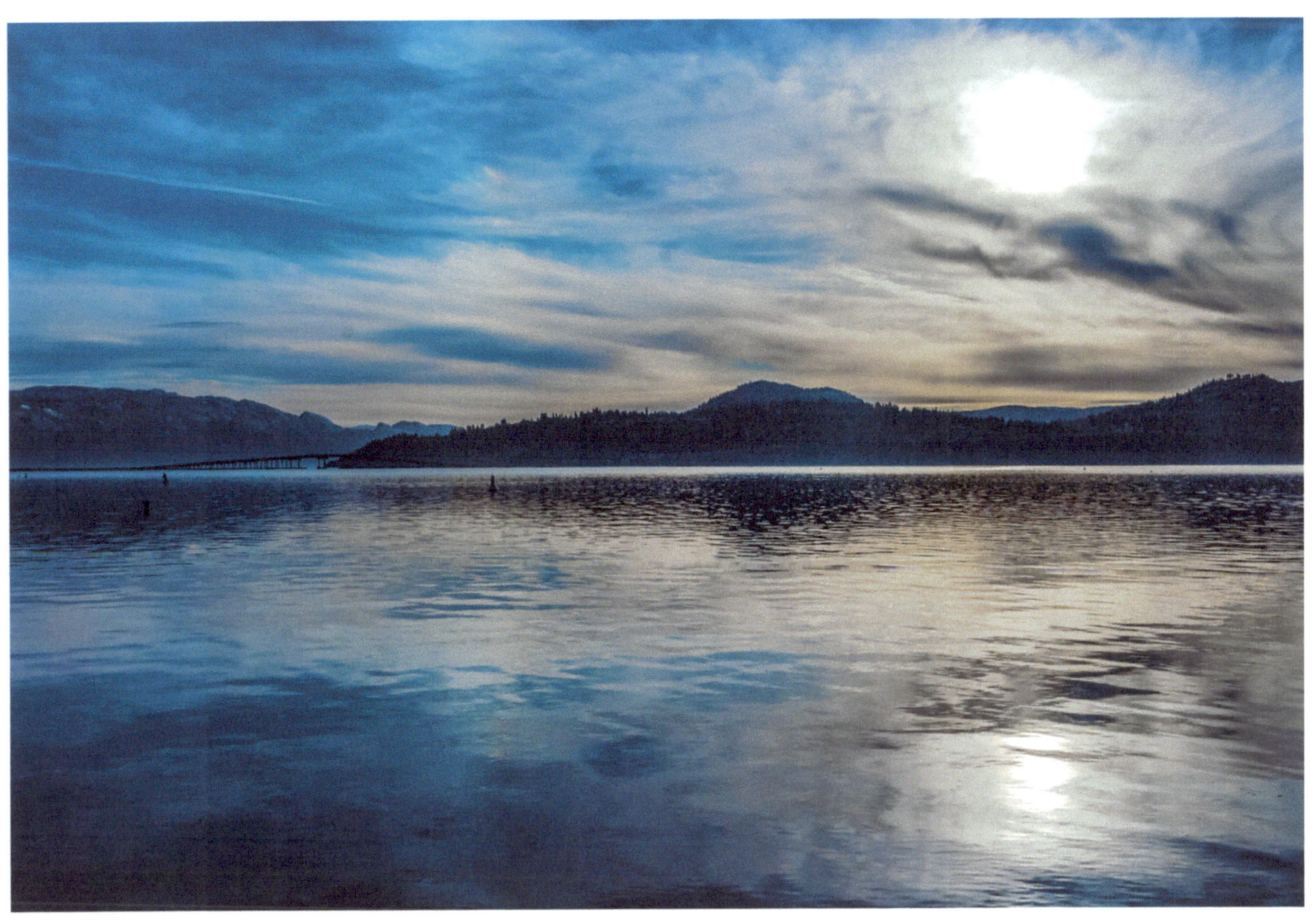

# October sunset

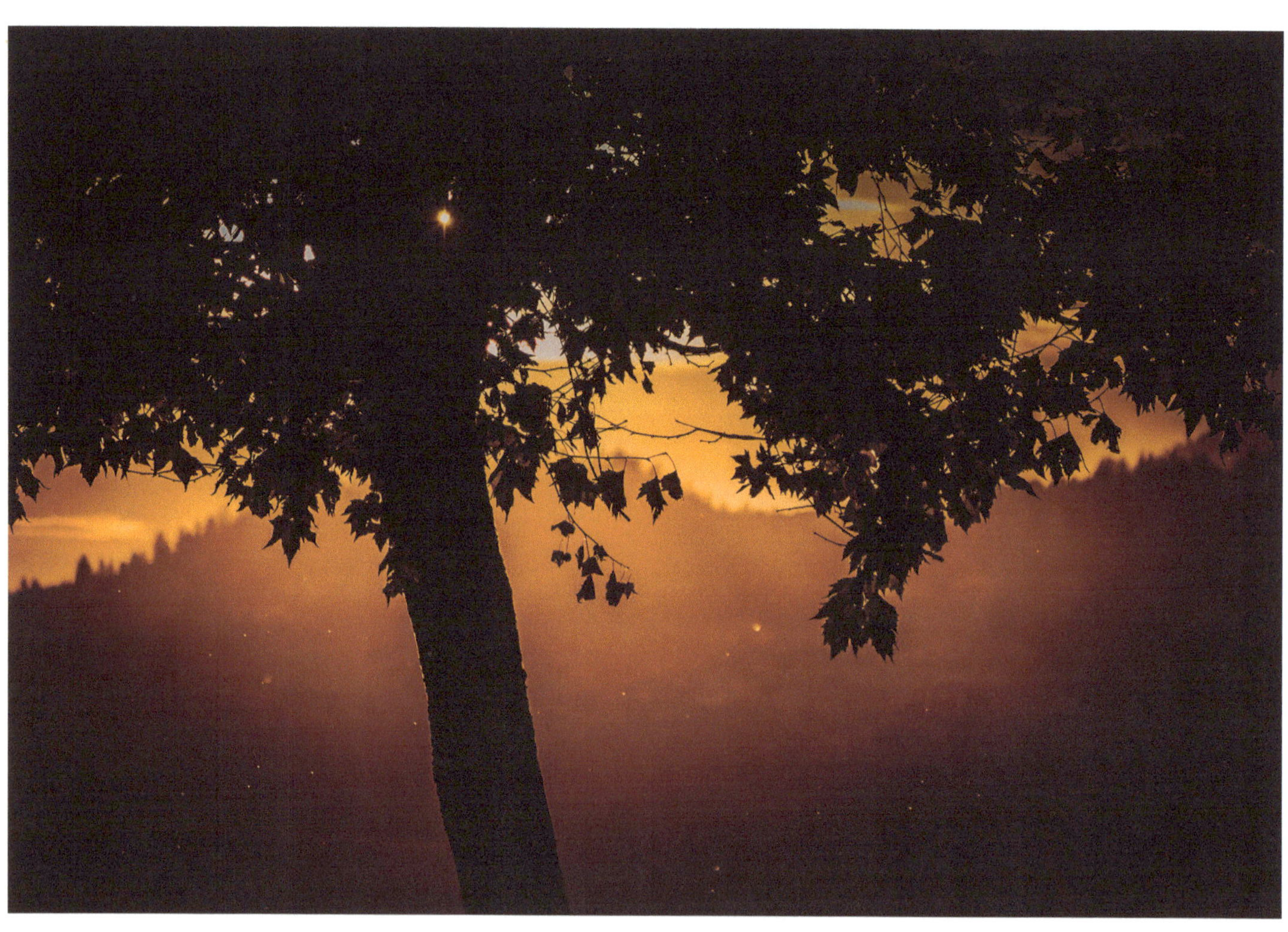

# December Sunrise

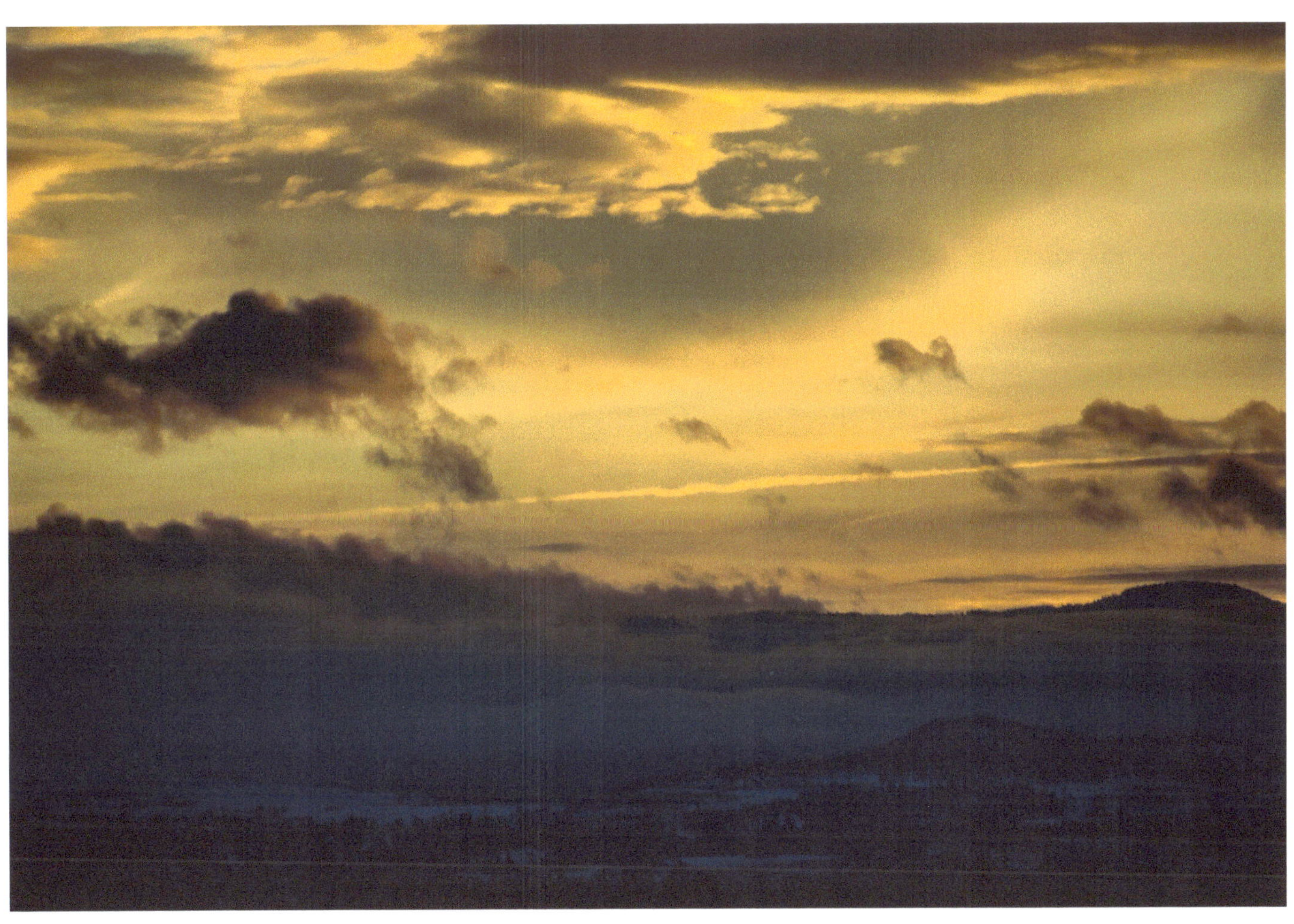

# About the Author

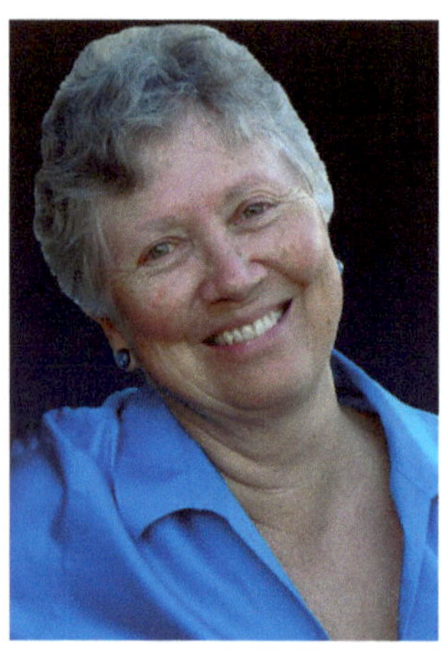

Cathryn Wellner is a writer and photographer living in Kelowna, British Columbia. She can usually be found either staring at her computer screen or taking her camera for a walk.

Recent books by Cathryn include:
*Hope Wins*
*Feisty Aging*
*Millie's Feathered Foster Family*
*Turkey Baby and the Hungry Hawk*
*Turkey Baby Finds Her Magic*
*Cloud Talk*

You can find links to these and her other books at cathrynwellner.com. Contact her at cathryn@cathrynwellner.com or 778-478-2760. Her photographs can be found on her Web site, as well as on Facebook and Instagram.

# Be a Book Review Angel

If you enjoyed this book, please tell friends to check out the Web site and find out where they can buy copies for themselves and their entire gift list. Post a review on Amazon or Goodreads. Send encouragement to the author at cathryn@cathrynwellner.com.

Authors rely on their readers to help spread the word about books they like. People who review books are special kinds of reader angels. I guarantee when you review this book, or any other book that has given you pleasure in any way, you'll feel those wings poking out your back. Look closely in the mirror, and you might even see a halo.

Designed in Adobe Photoshop CC. Cover and heading fonts: Canvas by Yellow Design Studio. Text font: Merlo by Błażej Ostoja Lniski. Masks by Ghostly Pixel and Two Lil Owls. Fonts and masks licensed through DesignCuts. Text and photographs ©Cathryn Wellner.